Legallines ®

Editorial Advisors:
Gloria A. Aluise
Attorney at Law
Jonathan Neville
Attorney at Law
Robert A. Wyler
Attorney at Law

Authors:
Gloria A. Aluise
Attorney at Law
David H. Barber
Attorney at Law
Daniel O. Bernstine
Attorney at Law
D. Steven Brewster
C.P.A.
Roy L. Brooks
Professor of Law
Frank L. Bruno
Attorney at Law
Scott M. Burbank
C.P.A.
Jonathan C. Carlson
Professor of Law
Charles N. Carnes
Professor of Law
Paul S. Dempsey
Professor of Law
Jerome A. Hoffman
Professor of Law
Mark R. Lee
Professor of Law
Jonathan Neville
Attorney at Law
Laurence C. Nolan
Professor of Law
Arpiar Saunders
Attorney at Law
Robert A. Wyler
Attorney at Law

CIVIL PROCEDURE

Adaptable to Ninth Edition*
of Friedenthal Casebook

*If your casebook is a newer edition, go to www.gilbertlaw.com
to see if a supplement is available for this title.

THOMSON
™
BAR/BRI

EDITORIAL OFFICES: 111 W. Jackson Blvd., 7th Floor, Chicago, IL 60604
REGIONAL OFFICES: Chicago, Dallas, Los Angeles, New York, Washington, D.C.

SERIES EDITOR
Linda C. Schneider, J.D.
Attorney at Law

PRODUCTION MANAGER
Elizabeth G. Duke

FIRST PRINTING—2006

Legalines®

SHORT SUMMARY OF CONTENTS

TABLE OF CONTENTS AND SHORT REVIEW OUTLINE

I. A SURVEY OF THE CIVIL ACTION

A. THE CONCERN AND CHARACTER OF CIVIL PROCEDURE

1. **Study of Civil Procedure in General.** The study of the law of civil procedure is the study of the rules of operation of those institutions and organizations that form the administrative branch of our system for resolution of civil conflicts between individuals. It is the study of the court systems of the United States, the rules of operation of those court systems, both statutory and nonstatutory, the theories behind those rules, and, perhaps most importantly, the advantages and defects of the existing system of judicial resolution as it presently exists in the United States.

2. **Purpose of Civil Procedure.** The purpose of any code of civil procedure is to facilitate the rapid, fair, and impartial administration of substantive justice between feuding parties who choose to litigate their dispute in the court system.

    a. **Underlying premise.** It is the underlying premise of most systems of civil procedure in the United States today that the rules of civil procedure governing a court system should not so arrange the organization and presentation of the civil dispute that purely procedural requirements submerge the fair litigation of controversies upon their substantive merits, without substantial justification therefor.

    b. **Example—Federal Rule of Civil Procedure 1:** "These rules govern the procedure in the United States district courts in all suits of a civil nature whether cognizable as cases at law or in equity or in admiralty . . . . They shall be construed and administered to secure the just, speedy, and inexpensive determination of every action."

3. **Function of Civil Procedure.** The function of a code of civil procedure is most easily understood when compared to a living organism. The substantive doctrines and branches of law (contract law, constitutional law, property law, and the like) form the living tissue of our legal system. It is this tissue that performs the vital functions of our legal system, the determination of legal disputes upon their respective "merits." But just as the living vertebrate organism would fall to pieces without some series of supporting bones, the administration of justice would fall to pieces without a definite, understandable, accessible system of institutions whose whole purpose is the just administration of the substantive law. In a very real sense, the court systems and their rules of operation form the skeleton upon which the legal tissue may grow, change, and find support.

4. **Courts of the United States.** Just as the governmental functions of the United States are divided between federal and state governments, and occasionally county and even city governments, so is the judicial administration of the United

States also divided into federal courts, state courts, and occasionally, county and city court systems. And just as the function of federal and state governments often duplicates and overlaps, so do the spheres of operation of the federal courts and the state courts often overlap.

a. **Federal court system.** The Constitution prescribes that the "judicial Power of the United States, shall be vested in one supreme Court, and in such inferior Courts as the Congress may from time to time ordain and establish . . . ." [U.S. Const. art. III §1] The Constitution carefully delineates the types of cases that the federal courts thus ordained may consider. As prescribed by this article of the Constitution, the federal court system of the United States is presently divided into the courts of original jurisdiction (the federal district courts), the courts of initial appeal (the circuit courts, including the D.C. Circuit and the Federal Circuit), and the court of final appeal and highest authority, the Supreme Court of the United States.

1) **Federal district courts.** There is at least one federal district court in each state (*e.g.,* the federal district court of Alaska, etc.), the District of Columbia and Puerto Rico. There are also federal district courts in the Virgin Islands and Guam, but these were established by the Organic Acts for the territories, whereas the other district courts are constituted under U.S.C., Title 28, Chapter 5. These courts handle a major part of the judicial workload that arises within the state or geographic territory in which they sit. Where large populations make a single federal district court impractical, a single state may be divided into several federal districts. For example, California, New York, and Texas are each divided into four districts.

2) **Federal circuit courts of appeal.** If an appeal is taken from a judgment in a federal district court, that appeal is generally taken to a federal circuit court of appeal. There are 13 circuit courts in the federal system, with each circuit responsible for all appeals coming out of certain enumerated district courts. For example, the Ninth Circuit Court of Appeals, which embraces all of the West Coast states, handles the appeals that come from those district courts, and no others.

3) **United States Supreme Court.** At the pinnacle of the judicial pyramid of both the federal courts and the state courts stands the United States Supreme Court, composed of nine justices, appointed by the President, who sit for life or during good behavior. It is not technically proper to classify this court as a federal court, since it also has jurisdiction over cases from the highest courts of the state court systems, and from the various special tribunals that are set up from time to time by the Congress, and even has its own special area of original jurisdiction, as prescribed by the Constitution. While the jurisdiction

of the Supreme Court is carefully prescribed in the Constitution and in the various judiciary acts of Congress under constitutional mandate, the United States Supreme Court wields a tremendous social, legal, and legislative power. Its mandates are law for the federal courts and the state courts, and even for nonjudicial institutions. Indeed, it is this tremendous power centered in the hands of the justices that often embroils the Supreme Court in controversies with every imaginable group.

b. **State courts and county courts.** Just as the federal government maintains an independent system of courts, so does each state government also maintain an independent judicial system. Usually, these judicial systems are miniature copies of the federal system. In place of the district courts of the federal system stand the county courts and the city courts of the state system. Above these courts of original jurisdiction usually stand one or two layers of appeals courts, variously denominated circuit courts of appeal, the state district courts, the state appeals court, etc. And above these appeals courts stands the highest court of each state system, the state supreme court, or, for a different nomenclature, the Court of Appeals of New York (whose first-level appeals courts are called supreme courts). Above the state supreme court stands only the United States Supreme Court, accessible to the civil litigant only after state court appeals have been exhausted. For a complex breakdown of the courts of any one state, statutes should be consulted, as each state system has its own vagaries and identifying characteristics.

c. **Special court systems.** At times, Congress ordains a special court, formally outside the federal court system, whose subject matter jurisdiction is limited to the hearing of special types of cases. Examples are the Patent Court of the United States, the Federal Tax Court, or the now-defunct Maritime Courts. These special court systems are generally mandatory courts of original jurisdiction, and provision is usually made for the taking of an appeal from the special courts either to the federal district courts or to the Supreme Court itself. Therefore, in a sense these special federal courts constitute a judicial "level" in and of themselves. Specific reference is needed to statutes vesting jurisdiction in these courts, for generalization is useless. Further, administrative agencies often set up their own intra-agency court systems, usually para-judicial bodies whose power is limited by the power vested in the administrative agency itself. The operation and description of these administrative court systems also defies generalization, so reference to specific granting statutes is usually required.

d. **Scope of our study of civil procedure.** In this outline, our study of civil procedure shall be limited to the main judicial hierarchies of the state and federal system, as governed by the various state codes of civil procedure and by the Federal Rules of Civil Procedure. No attempt shall be made in this outline to describe the rules of operation of the various special courts and para-judicial courts just described. These operations are generally covered in the study of Administrative Law, Tax Law, and Patent Law.

B. AN OUTLINE OF THE PROCEDURE IN A CIVIL ACTION

1. **Deciding to Sue.** Before initiating a legal action, a potential plaintiff must first determine whether the law furnishes relief for the harm suffered. If effective relief is available, the plaintiff must next weigh the chances of winning, *e.g.,* the existence and availability of adequate proof. Finally, recourse to the courts should be weighed against other alternatives, including settlement or arbitration. Lawsuits are expensive, time-consuming, and often attract undesirable public attention. Once the decision to sue is made, a series of steps are followed.

2. **Selecting the Proper Court.** As discussed above, there are two basic court systems in the United States. Choice of the proper court will depend largely on the jurisdiction of alternative courts. Essentially, the court selected must have jurisdiction both over the subject matter (conferred by statute) and over the persons involved. In addition, the court must have original, as opposed to appellate, jurisdiction. Finally, the court must have proper venue; *i.e.,* the court's district must include the place of residence of at least one of the parties or the property that is the subject of the action or the location where the claim arose.

   a. **State courts.** Most state court systems include both courts of *general* jurisdiction and courts of *inferior* jurisdiction. The general jurisdiction courts hear most types of cases and can grant every kind of relief, but usually have a requirement that the claim involve a minimum dollar amount. Courts of inferior jurisdiction hear minor or specialized matters, *e.g.,* municipal courts, probate courts, etc.

   b. **Federal courts.** Federal courts have subject matter jurisdiction over many cases involving federal law. Where federal law is not involved, jurisdiction lies if there is diversity of citizenship (parties are citizens of different states or countries) and the minimum amount in controversy (more than $75,000) is involved.

3. **Commencing the Action.** The plaintiff gives notice to the defendant of the action by *service of process* (a summons requiring the defendant to appear and defend under penalty of default). Service of process must take the best possible form available to assure that the defendant is notified. Generally this means personal service, but substituted service is permissible. Service by publication is permitted in certain circumstances.

4. **Pleading and Parties.** Included with the summons is the plaintiff's *complaint*, or the written statement of the plaintiff's claim. The complaint is the first of the *pleadings*, or the set of official charges and defenses which the parties present to the court. The defendant has three basic alternatives in responding to the

complaint. The defendant may file a ***motion to dismiss***, based on a challenge of the court's jurisdiction. Or the defendant could file a motion to dismiss for failure to state a claim or cause of action (demurrer), which essentially challenges the sufficiency of the complaint. If the motions are denied or not made, the defendant must file an ***answer***, in which he may also plead any ***affirmative defenses***. In addition, if the defendant has a claim against the plaintiff arising out of the same circumstances, the defendant may plead the claim as a ***counterclaim*** in the answer. The plaintiff is required to respond to any counterclaims raised by the defendant.

5. **Pretrial Discovery.** In earlier times, pleadings were an important vehicle for obtaining information from opposing parties. This function has been replaced by pretrial discovery procedures, including depositions of parties and witnesses, written interrogatories that involve more detailed or specific information, orders for the production of documents, physical examinations, etc.

6. **Summary Judgment.** If, prior to trial, one of the parties is able to show that the critical issue will be resolved in his favor at trial, a motion for ***summary judgment*** can be made, which, if granted, dispenses with the need for a trial.

7. **Setting the Case for Trial.** If the case is to proceed to trial, either party may file a ***note of issue***, after which the case will be placed on a trial calendar for eventual hearing.

8. **Jury Selection.** If the right to a jury trial applies and either party requests it, a jury will be impaneled. In order to assure impartiality, prospective jurors are questioned and, if possibly biased, may be challenged for cause and excused. In addition, each side is granted a certain number of peremptory challenges for which no reason need be given.

9. **Trial.** The trial consists of a series of arguments and introductions of evidence and testimony as follows:

   a. The plaintiff's opening statement (may be dispensed with in nonjury trial);

   b. The defendant's opening statement (optional, may be reserved until presentation of the defendant's case or dispensed with in nonjury trial);

   c. The plaintiff's presentation of case: calling of witnesses and introduction of evidence, including (i) direct examination; (ii) cross-examination; and (iii) redirect and recross examination, as needed;

   d. The defendant's presentation of case;

   e. The plaintiff's rebuttal;

   f. The defendant's rebuttal;

g. The plaintiff's final argument (often dispensed with in nonjury trials);

h. The defendant's final argument (often dispensed with in nonjury trials);

i. The plaintiff's rebuttal/closing argument (often dispensed with in nonjury trials);

j. Court's instructions to the jury (jury trial only);

k. Submission of the case to the jury (jury trial only).

10. **Submitting the Case to the Jury.** Prior to submitting the case to the jury, the judge meets with the lawyers privately to consider the content of the judge's instructions (charge) to the jury. The lawyers then make their final arguments, and the judge delivers her charge. The jury is required to analyze the evidence in accordance with the judge's instructions. The jury's verdict may take one of three forms, as determined by the judge. A *general verdict* is a statement of the jury's conclusions as to who prevails and what damages, if any, are to be awarded. A *general verdict with interrogatories* is several questions that must be answered by the jury. If these answers conflict with the general verdict, the answers control and the judge may rule accordingly. Finally, in certain cases a *special verdict* is called for; the jury resolves only the factual issues to which the judge applies the law.

11. **Post-Trial Motions.** A losing party may move for a *new trial* or may make a motion for a *judgment notwithstanding the verdict (judgment n.o.v.)*.

12. **Judgment.** The final determination of the suit is termed the judgment. If it involves damages, and the defendant is unwilling to pay, the plaintiff must seek separately a writ of execution commanding a state officer to seize the defendant's property for sale to satisfy the judgment. If the case resulted in an injunction (the judgment is then a decree), the defendant must obey or be held in contempt of court.

13. **Appeal.** Appeal procedures are somewhat complex, but basically the appellate court will review the record of the trial and consider the appellate briefs and oral arguments. Generally, only issues of law are reviewable. The appellate court may affirm or modify the original judgment, or it may reverse, either entering judgment or remanding for a new trial or other proceedings. Once all appeals and other proceedings have occurred, the judgment is final and becomes res judicata (a thing decided).

C. MOTION PRACTICE

1. **In General.** Motions are the procedural devices litigants use to formally request a court to take some action (such as a motion for summary judgment or for a new trial).

2. **Form.** Motions generally must be made in writing and conform to the format determined by local court rules. In federal court, all motions must be signed by a party or his attorney.

3. **Service.** A motion must be served upon the nonmoving party along with a notice of hearing and a brief or memorandum of law supporting the motion. Some courts also require submission of a proposed order. The adverse party may file an answer, and generally must do so within a proscribed time period.

D. REMEDIES

1. **Declarative.** A declaratory judgment merely serves to define legal relations between parties (*e.g.,* validity of a contract). This is a valuable alternative to acting under uncertainty where the risks of error are great.

2. **Specific.** Specific relief requires a defendant to act in a specified way. This includes ordering the defendant to perform a contract or to cease improper activity. This relief is generally not available where damages would be an adequate remedy.

3. **Compensatory.** This is probably the most common form of relief. Issues involving compensation (damages) primarily revolve around valuation.

E. ILLUSTRATIVE CASES

1. **Authority of the Court to Proceed with the Action.**

    a. **No federal jurisdiction--**

Capron v. Van Noorden, 6 U.S. (2 Cranch) 126 (1804).

Facts. Capron (P) sued Van Noorden (D) in federal court for trespass and damage. In his complaint, P alleged that D was "late of Pitt County" (North Carolina) but failed to allege his own citizenship. The court rendered judgment in favor of D. P appeals, claiming that the court lacked jurisdiction.

Issue. Does a federal court have diversity jurisdiction over an action in which the pleadings fail to allege that either of the parties is an alien and allege that one party is a citizen of North Carolina but fails to allege the citizenship of the other party?

Held. No. Judgment reversed.

♦   Diversity of citizenship must be shown affirmatively in the pleadings. Since there was no allegation that either party was an alien, or that P was a citizen of a state other than North Carolina, there is no diversity of citizenship.

♦   There is no federal question jurisdiction since there is no federal question involved in the litigation.

-----

b.   **Service of process procured by fraud--**

Tickle v. Barton, 95 S.E.2d 427 (W. Va. 1956).

Facts. Barton (D), knowing a suit was pending against him in West Virginia, vowed never to enter that state. Tickle's (P's) counsel, without identifying himself, telephoned D and issued an invitation to D to attend a football banquet in honor of a championship high school team in West Virginia. D, despite his vow, reentered West Virginia to attend the banquet, where he was served with process. Proof showed that there was a banquet and D's name was on the invitation list. D challenged the service. The circuit court overruled P's demurrer to D's amended plea and certified its ruling to this court on the joint application of P and D.

Issue. Is service of process valid when the defendant was induced to enter the county in which he was served by an unauthorized invitation to a banquet by the plaintiff's attorney?

Held. No. Judgment affirmed.

♦   D was induced to come into the county by the invitation to the banquet; D would not have come into the county if the plaintiff's attorney had revealed his identity and purpose in extending the invitation.

Dissent. The facts, properly alleged, do not establish fraud or wrongdoing. The attorney merely took advantage of an opportunity.

-----

2.   **Defining and Determining the Case Before Trial.**

a.   **Problems of pleading--**

Case v. State Farm Mutual Automobile Insurance Co., 294 F.2d 676 (5th Cir. 1961).

Facts. Case (P) brought this action to recover damages from State Farm (D) that he allegedly suffered when he was unlawfully terminated as local agent for three insurance companies. P's employment contract gave D the right to terminate his employment "with or without cause." The district court construed P's complaint as an action for malicious and wrongful cancellation of a written contract. The district court granted D's motion to dismiss, stating that P could not recover for alleged malicious and wrongful termination of his employment contract when D had a right to cancel with or without cause. The district court further found that P was terminated only after he refused to forgo running for the public office of county supervisor. On appeal, P argued that his case should have been considered as an action for interference with his civil rights, since he alleged that D had meddled and interfered with his efforts to obtain public office.

Issue. Did the district court improperly construe the language of P's complaint?

Held. No. Judgment affirmed.

♦ A complaint should not be dismissed for failure to state a claim unless it appears to be a legal certainty that the plaintiff is not entitled to relief under any set of facts he could prove in support of his claim.

♦ A court has no duty to create a claim that a party has not spelled out in his pleading. A court must judge a complaint by the language used in it.

♦ P's complaint merely charged that D exercised its right to terminate him under the terms of their contract. The district court correctly interpreted the "meddled and interfered" language as referring to D's intention to terminate P if he continued to run for public office. If P wanted to allege that his termination wrongfully interfered with his civil right to run for public office, he could have done so by amending his complaint. Such a claim, though, does not appear on the face of his original complaint.

Comment. Due to the prohibitive cost of modern litigation and burgeoning case loads, the courts have required a plaintiff to clearly state his theory of the case in his complaint. This allows the judge to determine the legal issues and perhaps dispose of the case before it proceeds to the costly and time-consuming pretrial discovery stage.

---

b.   **Indispensable parties--**

Temple v. Synthes Corp., 498 U.S. 5 (1990).

Facts. Temple (P), a Mississippi resident, had a device manufactured by Synthes Corp. (D), a Pennsylvania corporation, implanted in his spine by Dr. LaRocca at St. Charles General Hospital in Louisiana. The device's screw broke off in P's back. P filed suit against D in the United States District Court for the Eastern District of Louisiana, based on diversity and alleging defective design and manufacture. At the same time, P filed a state administrative proceeding against the doctor and hospital for malpractice and negligence. At the conclusion of the administrative proceeding, P filed suit in Louisiana state court. D did not file a third-party complaint in the state court action; instead, D moved to dismiss P's federal suit for failure to join necessary parties pursuant to Federal Rule of Civil Procedure 19. The federal court ordered P to join the doctor and hospital or risk dismissal. P did not join the doctor and the hospital, and the court dismissed the suit with prejudice. The court of appeals affirmed. The Supreme Court granted certiorari.

Issue. Are joint tortfeasors indispensable parties under Rule 19 such that the failure to join them must result in a dismissal of the lawsuit with prejudice?

Held. No. Judgment reversed and case remanded.

♦　　It has long been the rule that it is not necessary for all joint tortfeasors to be named as defendants in a single lawsuit. Advisory Committee Notes to Rule 19(a) state that "a tortfeasor with the usual joint and several liability is merely a permissive party to an action against another with like liability." Nothing in Louisiana tort law contradicts this.

♦　　No inquiry under Rule 19(b) is necessary because the threshold requirements of Rule 19(a) have not been satisfied.

---

c.　**Surveillance films--**

DiMichel v. South Buffalo Railway Co., 604 N.E.2d 63 (N.Y. 1992).

Facts. DiMichel (P) sued South Buffalo Railway Co. (D), alleging he sustained injuries in a fall while employed by D, charging D with violations of the Federal Employees' Liability Act and other federal statutes, and asking for $500,000 in damages. D contended that any surveillance films or videotapes it may have taken of P were not discoverable. P's motion to compel disclosure was granted but the court's order was stayed pending appeal. The appellate division modified the order, holding that only those surveillance materials D intended to use at trial had to be supplied to P. D appeals.

Issue. Is P entitled to view any surveillance material D plans to use at trial?

Held. Yes. Judgment affirmed.

♦　　Surveillance materials should be treated as material prepared in anticipation of litigation, and, as such, they are subject to a qualified privilege that can be overcome only by a pretrial showing of substantial need and undue hardship.

♦　　Because there is a very real danger of altered, deceptive tapes, adequate time for authorization so as to avoid contamination of the trial process mandates that plaintiffs view surveillance films before trial.

- To permit defendants to withhold such evidence until trial, even for the purpose of promoting vigorous cross-examination, would run counter to New York's open pretrial disclosure policy and is persuasive only if we assume that tapes are always accurate and plaintiffs are always dishonest.

- Defendants' concern that plaintiffs seek such tapes so they may tailor their trial testimony accordingly can be largely eliminated by providing that surveillance films should be turned over only after a plaintiff has been deposed.

- Plaintiffs cannot without undue hardship obtain the substantial equivalent of surveillance materials by other means. Visual evidence of this kind memorializes a particular set of conditions that can never be replicated.

---

d. Summary judgment--

Alderman v. Baltimore & Ohio Railway Co., 113 F. Supp. 881 (S.D. W.Va. 1953).

Facts. Alderman (P) was injured when the train in which she was riding derailed. The train was owned by the Baltimore & Ohio Railway Co. (D). P was traveling on a free pass, the conditions of which included an assumption of all risk of personal injury and loss. P sued D, alleging negligence, then amended the complaint charging willful or wanton conduct. D filed affidavits, not denied by P, to the effect that the derailment was caused by an unpredictable fissure, and that in fact the rail had been inspected the day before the accident. D moved for summary judgment.

Issue. Is summary judgment appropriate when the plaintiff must show willful or wanton conduct yet neither alleges facts adequate to meet that burden nor contests the defendant's affidavits showing that the defendant did not act willfully or wantonly?

Held. Yes. Summary judgment granted.

- The sole duty imposed upon D based on the facts of this case was to refrain from willfully or wantonly injuring P. P's complaint clearly states a charge of negligence but fails to state facts sufficient to substantiate a charge of willfulness. Further, D's undenied affidavits show clearly that P cannot establish these facts. Therefore, summary judgment is appropriate.

---

3. Judge and Jury.

a. **Instructing the jury.** Generally, the judge decides questions of law and the jury decides questions of fact. In order to reach a final decision as to which party is entitled to judgment, the jury must apply the law to the facts. Therefore, at the end of the trial, before the jury retires to consider its verdict, the judge instructs the jury as to the law applicable to the particular facts of the case being tried. Usually, opposing counsel will request the judge to give certain instructions to the jury. When these requests conflict, the judge must resolve the conflict and decide on the appropriate instructions for the jury.

1) Objection required when instruction erroneous--

Alexander v. Kramer Bros. Freight Lines, Inc., 273 F.2d 373 (2d Cir. 1959).

Facts. Alexander (P) sued Kramer Bros. Freight Lines, Inc. (D) for injuries resulting from a truck collision. The respective truck drivers told conflicting stories and the case was submitted to the jury. D raised the defense of contributory negligence, but the trial judge gave an erroneous charge to the jury as to the burden of proof. Although D took exception to the judge's statement of the burden of proof made during the trial, D failed to object to the charge as given. D appeals the adverse verdict.

Issue. Is D bound by a clearly erroneous charge to the jury merely because D failed to object to the charge as made?

Held. Yes. Judgment affirmed.

♦ The reason for the rule concerning objections to the judge's jury instructions is that the judge ought to have the opportunity to evaluate the objection and correct his charge if necessary. D's exception during trial was too far removed to satisfy the policy behind the objection rule.

b. Form of the verdict--

Diniero v. United States Lines Co., 288 F.2d 595 (2d Cir. 1961).

Facts. Diniero (P) sued his employer, United States Lines Co. (D), for injuries allegedly suffered from unnecessarily difficult working conditions. At the close of the evidence, the trial judge gave a charge to the jury, accompanied by a set of eight questions intended to help them in their deliberations. However, the first question, relating to the cause of P's injuries, was unclear and ambiguous. After unsuccessfully attempting to clarify the question for the jury, the judge withdrew all the questions. Subsequently, the jury reached a verdict for P. D appeals on grounds that it was improper for the judge to withdraw the question, which related to an issue that must have been decided in P's favor for him to recover.

Issue. May a judge withdraw interrogatories once submitted to the jury?

Held. Yes. Judgment affirmed.

♦ It has been held to be an abuse of discretion for a trial judge, on his own motion or pursuant to a plaintiff's request and over the defendant's objection, to withdraw material and proper interrogatories. The reason is that such a withdrawal would probably prejudice the defendant.

♦ Here, however, the question was unclear and ambiguous and could not therefore be considered material or necessary to a verdict. The withdrawal eliminated confusion caused by the question and was a proper exercise of discretion.

---

c. **Jury's deliberation--**

Texas Employers' Insurance Association v. Price, 336 S.W.2d 304 (Tex. 1960).

Facts. Price (P) sued the Texas Employers' Insurance Association (D) to set aside an award of the Industrial Accident Board. D answered by general denial and a specific pleading that P's injury was not totally or permanently incapacitating. The jury found that P's injury was total, despite P's doctor's testimony that P suffered only 20% disability. However, one of the jurors related his personal experiences in union work to persuade the jury that P was effectively totally and permanently incapacitated. D appeals the trial court's refusal to grant a new trial on grounds of jury misconduct.

Issue. Is a juror's sharing of personal experience during jury deliberations reversible error?

Held. Yes. Judgment reversed and case remanded.

♦ Despite P's doctor's testimony, there is sufficient evidence to support the verdict.

♦ The juror relating his personal union experience showed that P, even if not totally physically incapacitated, would be so in effect because of his difficulty in getting a job with a back injury. However, it was misconduct for the juror to relate to the other jurors his own personal experience as original evidence of material facts to be considered in their deliberation.

♦ The juror's misconduct, combined with the less than overwhelming evidence, probably injured D. A new trial is therefore appropriate.

---

d.   Taking the case from the jury--

Lavender v. Kurn, 327 U.S. 645 (1946).

Facts. Lavender (P), administrator of the Haney estate, sued Kurn (D) and other railroad trustees, former employers of Haney, for wrongful death resulting from D's negligence. P's evidence showed that it was conceivable that an object suspended from D's train could have struck Haney while he was working near the track at night. D's proof pointed out that such an accident was highly unlikely, and that Haney may have been murdered by a railroad tramp. No one saw the accident. Following trial, the jury returned a verdict in favor of P and awarded substantial damages. On appeal, the Supreme Court of Missouri reversed on grounds that there was no substantial evidence of negligence to support the submission of the case to the jury. The Supreme Court granted certiorari.

Issue. Where there is an evidentiary basis, albeit minimal, for more than one conclusion, may a case be taken from the jury in favor of the more probable conclusion?

Held. No. Judgment reversed.

♦   Review of the evidence indicates that it is improbable that the jury's verdict was correct. However, there is a reasonable basis in the record for the jury's inference that D's negligence resulted in Haney's death. It is an undue invasion of the jury's historic function for an appellate court to reweigh the evidence and arrive at a conclusion opposite from the jury's.

♦   Even when the jury's verdict involves speculation and conjecture, its determination may not be overturned unless there is a complete absence of probative facts to support that conclusion. Such a situation did not exist here, and the court erred in reversing the trial results.

Comment. This case vividly illustrates judicial reluctance to interfere with the right to jury trial. However, where necessary to curb abuses (as when the jury totally disregards the evidence and/or the law), the trial judge has full authority to take the case from the jury.

4.   **Review on Appeal.** Appellate courts generally do not consider further evidence, will not weigh the evidence in the trial court's record, and will reverse a trial court only for errors of law. However, an appellate court will not reverse a trial court for harmless errors (errors not impairing the parties' rights to a fair trial). The appellate court will reverse a trial court for prejudicial error, such as the admission of improper and persuasive evidence on a material issue.

a.   **Incorrect application of legal standard to uncontroverted evidence--**

Hicks v. United States, 368 F.2d 626 (4th Cir. 1966).

Facts. Hicks (P), administrator of the Greitens estate, sued the United States (D) for death due to the negligence of the military doctor to whom Greitens was taken for examination. The doctor performed a brief examination. The symptoms indicated two possible maladies: gastroenteritis (not serious) and an intestinal obstruction (lethal). The doctor diagnosed gastroenteritis without making further inquiries, which probably would have revealed the obstruction that caused Greitens's death. The expert testimony was essentially uncontested and indicated a failure to exercise due care, but D's expert testified that the doctor exercised "average judgment." Sitting without a jury, the district judge dismissed the complaint; P appeals.

Issue. When the trial court sits without a jury and the evidence is essentially uncontradicted, may the appellate court overturn the trial judge's findings?

Held. Yes. Judgment reversed.

♦ The standard of care applicable here is that if the doctor uses ordinary care in reaching his diagnosis and acts upon it, even if the diagnosis is mistaken, the doctor incurs no liability. Here it is apparent that the doctor failed to make the further investigation expected under the generally accepted standard. Therefore, the doctor was negligent and D is liable.

♦ The trial judge apparently relied excessively on D's witness's purely conclusory opinion. It has often been held that when the trial court's conclusions are based on undisputed facts, they are not entitled to the finality customarily accorded basic factual findings. Although in most cases appellate courts are limited to review of the law, the determination of negligence involves application of the legal standard to the evidence. The appellate court is entitled to make such a determination, and, having done so, may overrule the trial judge.

5. Conclusiveness of Judgments--

Des Moines Navigation & Railroad Co. v. Iowa Homestead Co., 123 U.S. 552 (1887).

Facts. The Iowa Homestead Co. (P) sued the Des Moines Navigation & Railroad Co. (D) to recover taxes that had been involved in an earlier suit. The earlier suit resulted in a decree favorable to D; D claims the decree bars the present action. P alleges that the earlier suit was tried in a federal court that lacked proper jurisdiction. P failed to challenge the court's jurisdiction in the earlier case. The state courts held for P; D appeals.

Issue. Is a judgment void if rendered by a court not having proper jurisdiction but where the jurisdiction was not challenged by the parties?

Held. No. Judgment reversed.

♦ Early decisions recognized that judgments and decrees made by courts with improper but unchallenged jurisdiction were not nullities, but were binding until reversed or otherwise set aside. The earlier case involving these parties and the subject matter reached the United States Supreme Court, and therefore will be binding.

II. SELECTING THE PROPER COURT

A. JURISDICTION OVER THE PARTIES TO THE ACTION

1. Traditional Bases of Jurisdiction—Natural Persons and Unincorporated Associations.

a. Requirements of due process--

Pennoyer v. Neff, 95 U.S. (5 Otto) 714 (1877).

Facts. Neff (P) brought suit in federal court to recover possession of a parcel of land purchased at a sheriff's sale by Pennoyer (D). The sheriff's sale was made in execution of a default judgment rendered against P in an earlier case. The judgment was based on in personam jurisdiction; however, P was a nonresident and was not personally served with process. Constructive service by publication in Oregon newspapers was deemed adequate by the court in the original suit. P sued here to recover his land, claiming that the court in the original suit did not have jurisdiction to render a judgment. The federal circuit court upheld P's claim; D appeals.

Issue. Is constructive notice (by publication) upon a nonresident adequate as a basis for in personam jurisdiction in a state court?

Held. No. Judgment affirmed.

♦ The Due Process Clause of the Fourteenth Amendment requires that a defendant be given a just chance to defend himself in an action filed against him. This requirement is satisfied if the defendant is "properly and seasonably notified" of the action pending against him.

♦ To gain in personam jurisdiction over a defendant and the concurrent power to adjudicate the full dispute between the parties and award full judgment as called for, the court must see that the defendant is personally served with process while actually present in the state.

♦ To gain in rem or quasi in rem jurisdiction over the property of a defendant, the court must see that the defendant owns property in the state, and that this property is legally attached *before* the instigation of suit or very shortly thereafter. Attachment of the defendant's land serves as constructive notice that there is a legal action pending and vests the state court with the power to dispose of the attached land in favor of the plaintiff in case the plaintiff prevails upon the merits.

♦ Neff, as the defendant in the original suit, had not been served with process while in the state, nor had his land been attached at the outset of the suit. Therefore, the court had no jurisdiction over him (neither in personam, in rem, nor quasi in rem), and could not have rendered a judgment against him. Any execution of such an invalid judgment is unauthorized and void.

♦ Even if the Oregon court had properly attached Neff's land at the outset of the suit, it exceeded this in rem jurisdiction by returning a full judgment against him not limited by the value of the attached land. The court confused the jurisdictional power of in rem jurisdiction with that of in personam jurisdiction. Only the latter allows a court to fully adjudicate and compensate upon the merits of the action. The recovery of the former is limited absolutely to the value of the land attached.

---

b. **The *Pennoyer* rules.** *Pennoyer* established the rule that for a court to obtain valid in personam jurisdiction over a defendant, it was absolutely necessary that the defendant be served with process within the state in which the court was sitting. *Pennoyer* further established that such personal service within the state was always sufficient, without anything else, to vest that court with in personam jurisdiction over the defendant.

c. ***Pennoyer*: traditional modifications and extensions.** *Pennoyer's* requirement of in-state service of process before vesting of in personam jurisdiction over a defendant proved more and more confining and impractical as interstate travel and communications improved. Therefore, that aspect of the *Pennoyer* rule that required service of process within the territorial jurisdiction of the court has long since been "excepted into oblivion." The most important of these traditional exceptions to the *Pennoyer* rules are:

1) Domicile, residency, and nationality in a jurisdiction now are sufficient to confer in personam jurisdiction even though the service of process is made outside the jurisdiction [*See* Blackmer v. United States, (*infra*); Milliken v. Meyer, (*infra*)];

2) Appearance to defend upon the merits confers in personam jurisdiction upon the court, whether or not the court originally had in personam jurisdiction;

3) Prior consent, whether express or implied, to confer in personam jurisdiction over a chosen court is sufficient to vest that court with jurisdiction [*See, e.g.,* Adam v. Saenger, (*infra*)];

4) Nonresident motorist statutes, equating use of a state's highways with consent to appear in its courts, have been found constitutional [*See* Kane v. New Jersey, 242 U.S. 160 (1916)];

5) The concept of "continuing jurisdiction" has done away with the necessity of repeated service of process in long suits subject to reopening;

6) The conduct of state regulated business in a state has been declared the constitutional equivalent of consent to submit to jurisdiction;

7) Ownership of real property in a state, out of which arises the cause of action sued upon, has been held sufficient to vest in personam jurisdiction in the state court over the nonresident property owner;

8) "Long arm" statutes, basing in personam jurisdiction upon the doing of a specified single act within the state (such as the commission of a tort in the state), have been held constitutional;

9) And finally, the Supreme Court has declared that it would probably not defeat any exercise of in personam jurisdiction over a nonresident that was "fair, just, and reasonable," whether or not the exercise in such jurisdiction falls within one of the traditional exceptions enumerated above. [International Shoe Co. v. Washington, 326 U.S. 310 (1945)]

d. **Nationality.** United States citizenship is probably sufficient contact with the United States to subject citizens abroad to the in personam jurisdiction of American courts without violating due process. It is not clear, however, whether such foreign service would be upheld unless specifically authorized by federal statute.

1) In *Blackmer v. United States*, 284 U.S. 421 (1932), Blackmer, a United States citizen living in France, refused to comply with a subpoena issued by a federal district court, and was convicted in absentia for contempt. Service upon American citizens abroad was specifically authorized by federal statute, which Blackmer challenged as violative of due process. The Court held that the statute was constitutional. "The jurisdiction of the United States over its absent citizens is an in personam jurisdiction . . . and the absent citizen is bound to take notice of all domestic laws that apply to him and obey them . . . ."

e. **Domicile.** Domicile is, loosely, the legal state citizenship of an individual or an unincorporated association. It is almost universally recognized today that the state courts have in personam jurisdiction over all domiciliaries of the state, wherever they are residing and wherever they are served with process.

1) In *Milliken v. Meyer*, 311 U.S. 457 (1940), Milliken sued Meyer, a domiciliary of Wyoming, in the Wyoming state courts. Milliken served Meyer in Colorado, where Meyer was vacationing. Meyer

objected to the exercise of in personam jurisdiction over him by the Wyoming courts, citing *Pennoyer's* requirement of in-state service for vesting of in personam jurisdiction in any court. The Supreme Court held that the Wyoming courts properly exercised in personam jurisdiction. It is now the rule that domicile in a state is per se sufficient contact with that state to confer in personam jurisdiction on the state courts, whether or not service is made within the state.

f. **Residence.** Residence must be carefully distinguished from domicile. Domicile is equivalent to legal citizenship in a state. Residence is more equivalent to long-term presence, with or without establishment of citizenship. While the Supreme Court has not passed upon whether mere residence in a state is sufficient contact with that state to vest in personam jurisdiction in its courts wherever service of process is made, it is probable that such an exercise of jurisdiction would be upheld whenever it is not "unreasonable" that the defendant be required to defend in the state of his residence.

g. **Consent by bringing suit.** In *Adam v. Saenger*, 303 U.S. 59 (1938), Beaumont Export Co., a Texas corporation, originally brought suit in California state court against Montes, who in turn counterclaimed and eventually won a default judgment. Montes then assigned his judgment to Adam. Adam sought to enforce the judgment against Beaumont's successor in interest, Saenger, in a Texas court. The Texas court refused to give full faith and credit to the counterclaim judgment, accepting Saenger's argument that Beaumont had not been sufficiently present in California to justify California's exercise of in personam jurisdiction. The Supreme Court held that the California court properly exercised in personam jurisdiction over Saenger's predecessor in interest, who had impliedly consented to such an exercise of jurisdiction by filing an action in the California court. "The defendant, by itself originally appealing to the California court for justice, impliedly submitted itself to the in personam jurisdiction of the court for purposes of any counterclaims or cross-claim which might arise . . ." The Court determined that "[o]nce a party has voluntarily submitted himself to the judicial processes of the state, there is nothing inequitable in treating him as if he is there for purposes of counterclaim as well as for purposes of his own complaint . . ."

2. Expanding the Bases of Personal Jurisdiction--

Hess v. Pawloski, 274 U.S. 352 (1927).

Facts. A state statute dictated that any nonresident motorist using the state's highways impliedly appointed the secretary of state as his agent for service in any action arising out of the motorist's use of the highways. The statute further required the secretary of state, upon receipt of service of process against such a motorist, to make a diligent effort to locate the residence of the motorist and, by registered mail, to inform the motorist of the suit pending against him. Hess was served under such a statute, and in this action attacked the statute as unconstitutional as a deprivation of due process and in conflict with *Pennoyer*.

Issue. Does a state statute that deems nonresident motorists to have appointed a state official as their agent for service of process in cases arising out of in-state accidents involving them violate their due process rights?

Held. No. Judgment affirmed.

♦ The statute is constitutional. Because of the rapid change in interstate traffic patterns, the *Pennoyer* requirement of personal service within the forum state is no longer practicable.

♦ Exercises of in personam jurisdiction, prescribed by statute, based upon constructive in-state service upon an agent of the defendant, coupled with registered mailing of service out-of-state, gave the defendant ample notice of the suit pending against him. Therefore, there was no deprivation of due process.

Comment. It is now commonly agreed, contrary to *Pennoyer*, that a nonresident motorist involved in an accident in the forum state need not be personally served with process within the state but may be served constructively by registered mail. This constructive service confers in personam jurisdiction upon the state courts just as if the defendant had been personally served within the state.

---

3. **Personal Jurisdiction Over Nonresident Corporations.**

a. **In general.** Originally, it was thought that incorporation in the state was the exclusive basis for the exercise of in personam adjudicatory power over a corporation. This belief mandated the conclusion that a corporation could not be sued in personam outside the state of its incorporation. The first major change occurred when courts recognized that, since a state could preclude a foreign corporation from engaging in local, as distinguished from interstate, business, a state could also permit the foreign corporation to engage in local business on the condition that the corporation consent to being sued within the state. Consent so given created in personam jurisdiction over the foreign corporation to the fullest extent. When corporations failed in fact to give their consent by filing the appropriate form with the secretary of state or some other local official, the courts held that, by engaging in business within the state, a foreign corporation gave its "implied consent" to be sued there. However, the reasoning of implied consent broke down when applied to corporations engaged in interstate business, since they could not be excluded from the state. To deal adequately with the need to exercise adjudicatory authority over foreign corporations engaged in interstate business, states began to rely upon the doctrine of "presence" to enforce a personal liability in the absence of consent if the corporation did business within the state in such a manner and to such an extent as to warrant the inference that it was present there.

b. Minimum contacts test.

1) Solicitation of orders--

International Shoe Co. v. Washington, 326 U.S. 310 (1945).

Facts. International Shoe Co. (D) was incorporated in Delaware and had its principal place of business in Missouri. It employed several salespersons in Washington state to solicit orders there, but the salespersons had no authority to enter into any contracts, and the contracts were formally consummated in Missouri. D had no office in Washington, it made no contracts in Washington, and it maintained no stock of merchandise there. The state of Washington (P) sued D in state court to force it to contribute to the workers' compensation fund of the state. Service of process was delivered to one of the salespersons, with copy sent by registered mail to the Missouri office. In a special appearance, D challenged the jurisdiction of the court, alleging that there was no in personam jurisdiction since D was not "doing business" in the state.

Issue. Does mere solicitation of orders for the purchase of goods within a state, to be accepted without the state and filled by shipment of the purchased goods interstate, render a corporation-seller amenable to suit within the state?

Held. Yes.

♦ The state court had in personam jurisdiction over D. Whether an exercise of jurisdiction over a nonresident entity is to be validated depends upon the circumstances of each individual case, whether that entity is an individual or a corporation. Hard and fast rules are totally inadequate. Due process requires only that the defendant have some "minimum contact" with the forum state, and that the exercise of jurisdiction not violate "traditional notions of fair play and substantial justice."

Concurrence (Black, J.). States have power to regulate or tax a business carried on within their boundaries. This is a right preserved by the Tenth Amendment and the Court's due process approach is an unwise limitation on that right.

---

      2) Balancing of interests. The minimum contacts doctrine of *International Shoe* could be restated as a balance of interests test. A corporation is amenable to suit in a foreign jurisdiction if, and only if, its corporate contacts are of such a quantity or quality that it is reasonably justifiable, both economically and socially, that it be required to defend in the state. The economic burden of defending in the foreign state must be weighed against the extent of corporate contact before any decision concerning the propriety of an exercise of long arm jurisdiction can be reached. Thus, for example, in *Fisher Governor Co. v. Superior Court*, 347 P.2d 1 (Cal. 1959), the court upheld California's refusal to exercise jurisdiction over an injury that occurred in another state based on a balance of competing considerations.

4. **Specific Jurisdiction and State Long Arm Statutes.**

   a. **Development of the long arm statutes.**

      1) **Growth.** In order to protect their citizens from harms inflicted by nonresidents, states have expanded jurisdiction over nonresidents through "long arm" statutes. Most such statutes list various acts on which jurisdiction can be based; a defendant's activity would have to fall both within the terms of the statute and measure up to the constitutional "minimum contacts" standard. Some states (*e.g.,* California) provide that their courts may exercise jurisdiction whenever the constitutional minimum standard is met. The general justification for long arm jurisdiction is that modern means of transportation, communication, and conducting business have reduced earlier obstacles to defending suits brought in other states.

      2) **The "single contact" jurisdictional rule.** In *McGee v. International Life Insurance Co.*, 355 U.S. 220 (1957), the Court upheld California's exercise of in personam jurisdiction over an out-of-state insurance company in a suit by a California resident to collect the proceeds of an insurance policy the company issued to a California resident. The only contact between the company and the forum state in *McGee* was the mailing of premiums by a California resident to the office of the company in Texas. This case should be compared to *Hanson v. Denckla, infra.*

      3) **Injury as only contact--**

Gray v. American Radiator & Standard Sanitary Corp., 176 N.E.2d 761 (Ill. 1961).

Facts. Gray (P) sued American (D) to recover damages for personal injury. D, a manufacturer of safety valves for hot water heaters and an Ohio corporation, was found subject to the state long arm jurisdiction of the Illinois courts in an action arising out of an explosion of a hot water heater, allegedly due to a faulty safety valve. D resisted the exercise of jurisdiction on grounds that it had not purposefully shipped its valves into Illinois (since they had arrived there only as a part of a larger unit manufactured by another corporation) and that its economic contacts with the forum state were too small and too tenuous to reasonably justify an exercise of jurisdiction. P appeals the trial court dismissal of the action.

Issue. Can a state exercise in personam jurisdiction over a nonresident whose only contact with that state occurred when its manufactured product shipped into the state by a third party allegedly caused an injury to one of the state's residents?

Held. Yes. Judgment reversed and case remanded with directions.

♦ It is reasonable to infer that commercial transaction of D's products results in substantial and continuous use in this state, that it derives a substantial profit thereby, and that it thereby engages in contact that may be said to have invoked the protection of this forum's laws. It should not matter, therefore, that the ultimate purchase was made from a middleman, or that someone other than D actually made the final shipment into the state.

Comment. When a nonresident engages in activities that it should reasonably expect to directly or indirectly affect the residents of another state, and to the extent the nonresident benefits directly or indirectly from the laws of another state, such other state is justified in exercising in personam jurisdiction over such nonresident.

---

4) **Tort-based long arm statutes.** Commission of a single tort within a state usually justifies in personam jurisdiction over the tortfeasor, but the wording of the statute conferring jurisdiction may be critical. Typically, these statutes are worded either in terms of "commissions of a tort in whole or in part" in the forum state, or in terms of "commissions of a tortious act" within the state.

    a) **"Tortious acts" statutes.** A long arm statute worded in terms of a tortious act or omission within the forum state favors the nonresident defendant. To fall within the operation of such a statute, the defendant must actually have committed some positive negligent act within the forum state. It is not enough that the consequences of his negligent act are felt there.

    b) **"Tort in whole or in part" statutes.** Long arm statutes that allow the state court to exercise nonresident in personam jurisdiction over tortfeasors committing a tort in whole or in part in the forum state favor the injured plaintiff. Under such a statute, if any result of the tortious act of the defendant is felt in the forum state, there is enough contact to justify an exercise of jurisdiction wherever the actual negligent act was performed.

(1) In *Hoagland v. Springer*, 183 A.2d 678 (N.J. App. 1962), New Jersey courts affirmed an exercise of in personam jurisdiction over a nonresident repairman under a long arm statute that provided for such jurisdiction whenever a tort was committed "in whole or in part" in New Jersey. The plaintiff was injured when a tank truck, repaired outside the state by the defendant, exploded upon return to the owner in New Jersey. The state courts ruled that since the explosion occurred in New Jersey, the tort was partially committed there.

(2) But in *Feathers v. McLucas*, 209 N.E.2d 68 (N.Y. 1965), under a long arm statute worded in terms of a "tortious act" committed within the state, New York refused to exercise in personam long arm jurisdiction over a Kansas repairman in an action arising out of the explosion of a tank-truck repaired in Kansas and delivered to the plaintiffs in New York. The court reasoned that "the place of a tortious act is not necessarily the place of the tort. The tort per se occurred in New York with the explosion of the truck. But the tortious act causing the tort occurred in Kansas, during repair of the truck." The statute did not, the court reasoned, reach tortious acts committed outside the state, even if the consequences were felt within the state.

b. **Due process constraints on the exercise of long arm statutes.**

1) **In general.** The "fair play" test of *International Shoe* provides the modern base for almost all exercises of in personam jurisdiction over nonresident individuals and corporations. It can be stated with some confidence that a defendant with any substantial contacts with a forum state is amenable to suit there unless a strong argument against such exercise of jurisdiction can be presented. However, *International Shoe* does not provide for unlimited exercise of national jurisdiction—the defendant must have some "minimum contact" with the forum jurisdiction.

2) **Involuntary contacts.** In *Hanson v. Denckla*, 357 U.S. 235 (1958), the Supreme Court held that a Florida court did not have personal jurisdiction over a nonresident trustee whose only contact with the forum state was mailing trust earning reports to the settlor who lived there. The trustee had no office in Florida and did not transact or solicit business there. The fact that the will was probated in Florida and that most of the beneficiaries lived there was not sufficient to confer jurisdiction. The dissent argued that Florida had sufficient interest in the case to justify its exercise of sovereign authority over the dispute because Florida was the domiciliary of the settlor and the principal parties to the lawsuit.

a) This case can be distinguished from *McGee, supra*, on two grounds. First, the trustee in *Hanson* received orders but no benefits from the forum state, whereas the insurance company in *McGee* received benefits from the forum state. Second, the forum state in *Hanson* had no special interest in litigating the lawsuit, whereas the forum state in *McGee* had a special interest in litigating the lawsuit—namely, providing a convenient forum for its citizen injured by a nonresident "engaged in activity that the State treats as exceptional and subjects to special legislation."

3) Foreseeability alone is not a minimum contact--

World-Wide Volkswagen Corp. v. Woodson, 444 U.S. 286 (1980).

Facts. The Robinsons (Ps) bought an Audi in New York from Seaway, a retail dealer. The next year Ps moved to Arizona. On the way, they had a collision in Oklahoma that resulted in severe burn injuries to three family members. Ps brought suit in an Oklahoma state court against the car's manufacturer, its importer, the retailer dealer (Seaway), and World-Wide Volkswagen Corp. (D) (the regional distributor). D claimed that exercise of jurisdiction over it offended the Due Process Clause. Woodson, the trial judge, rejected D's claim and D sought a writ of prohibition in the state supreme court against exercise of jurisdiction. That court upheld jurisdiction and the Supreme Court granted certiorari.

Issue. Is foreseeability that a product could cause an injury in a particular state a sufficient contact to justify that state's exercise of jurisdiction over the product manufacturer?

Held. No. Judgment reversed.

♦   The Due Process Clause prevents state courts from rendering a valid personal judgment against a nonresident defendant over whom it has no personal jurisdiction. To exercise such personal jurisdiction, the state must have a minimum contact with the defendant. This protects defendants from unfairly inconvenient litigation and ensures that states do not exceed the limits of their status as coequal sovereigns in a federal system.

♦   Although modern business conditions have justified relaxation of the due process limits on state jurisdiction, state lines retain relevance for jurisdictional purposes. Each state's sovereignty depends in part on the limited sovereignty of the other states.

♦   In this case, there are no contacts between D (a regional distributor in New York, New Jersey, and Connecticut) and Oklahoma. Although a car is mobile and it could foreseeably cause injury in any state, a foreseeability test would be impractical. It would make the chattel the seller's agent for service of process wherever the chattel goes. This is analogous to the principle of *Harris v. Balk* (*infra*), which has been rejected. The only relevant foreseeability is that of a defendant whose conduct and connection with the forum would justify an anticipation of jurisdiction.

Dissent (Brennan, J.). By purposefully becoming part of a nationwide system for marketing and servicing cars, D is subject to personal jurisdiction in whatever state in which its cars cause an injury. D receives economic advantage from the nationwide system and should anticipate being subject to court action wherever its products cause an injury.

Comment. In *Kulko v. Superior Court*, 436 U.S. 84 (1978), an ex-wife moved from New York to California and then sued her New Yorker ex-husband in California to modify child custody arrangements. The Court held that the ex-husband's act of buying the couple's daughter a plane ticket to move to California, at the daughter's request, was not sufficient to support California jurisdiction, even though the ex-husband could have foreseen effects there. The Court reasoned that the ex-husband did not purposefully derive any benefits from activities related to California, and he had no other relevant contact with California. Thus, he could not reasonably anticipate being haled into court there.

4) Franchise contracts--

Burger King Corp. v. Rudzewicz, 471 U.S. 462 (1985).

Facts. Rudzewicz (D), a Michigan resident, entered into a 20-year franchise contract with Burger King Corp. (P), a Florida corporation, to operate a restaurant in Michigan. D fell behind in his monthly payments and P brought a diversity action in federal district court in Florida, alleging that D had breached his franchise obligations and requesting damages and injunctive relief. D challenged the district court's jurisdiction, arguing that he had no contacts with Florida that would justify forcing him to defend a suit there. The district court found that it had jurisdiction pursuant to Florida's long arm statute, which extends jurisdiction to persons who breach contracts in Florida by failing to perform acts required by the contract. The court of appeals disagreed, holding that "jurisdiction under these circumstances would offend fundamental fairness, which is the touchstone of due process." The Supreme Court granted certiorari.

Issue. Do franchise contracts subject the nonresident franchisee, who has purposefully directed his activities at the forum, to the personal jurisdiction of the forum court?

Held. Yes. Judgment reversed.

♦ The Due Process Clause mandates that a defendant have "fair warning" that his activities may subject him to a court's jurisdiction. This requirement is satisfied when a nonresident defendant purposefully directs his activities toward the forum state.

♦ An individual's contract with a forum resident is insufficient by itself to establish minimum contacts with the forum state. Rather, all the exigent circumstances surrounding the contract, including but not limited to prior negotiations, contemplated future actions, the terms of the contract and the parties' actual course of dealing, must be examined to determine whether the defendant purposefully established minimum contacts with the forum.

♦ Here, D deliberately entered into a franchise contract that has substantial connections with the forum state, Florida. The contract provided that all relevant notices and payments had to be sent to Florida, all agreements were to be made and enforced there, and all disputes were to be governed by Florida law. D thus knew that he was affiliating himself with an enterprise based primarily in Florida and consequently could foresee that his refusal to make the required payments would cause injury in Florida. Consequently, the district court's exercise of jurisdiction pursuant to Florida's long arm statute did not violate the Due Process Clause of the Fourteenth Amendment.

Dissent (Stevens, White, JJ.). It is fundamentally unfair for D to have to defend a suit based on the franchise contract in Florida. He maintained no place of business there, had no employees there, and was not licensed to do business there. The court of appeals correctly found that nothing in the course of negotiations gave D sufficient reason to expect to defend a franchise suit outside of Michigan. Jurisdiction under these circumstances would offend fundamental fairness, which is the touchstone of due process.

Comment. The majority emphasized that when a question of personal jurisdiction arises out of a business relationship, underlying realities of the relationship should be examined to determine whether jurisdiction exists. The defendant must then demonstrate that by defending the action he is subjecting himself to unreasonable burdens that cannot be relieved by other means.

---

5) Jurisdiction unreasonable despite minimum contacts--

Asahi Metal Industry Co. v. Superior Court, 480 U.S. 102 (1987).

Facts. Gary Zurcher was severely injured and his wife killed in a motorcycle accident in California, allegedly caused by the explosion of the cycle's defective rear tire. There he sued, among others, Cheng Shin, the Taiwanese manufacturer of the tube. Cheng Shin (P) impleaded Asahi (D), the Japanese manufacturer of the tube's valve assembly. The main claims were settled, leaving only P's indemnity claim against D. D moved to quash service. Significantly, D made its valves in Japan and sold some of them to P in Taiwan, where P made its tubes using valves made by D or other suppliers and then sold them throughout the world, with P selling a fair number in California. D apparently had no other contacts with California. The supreme court of California ultimately upheld personal jurisdiction as being within the state's long arm statute and consistent with due process. D appeals.

Issue. Is California's exercise of personal jurisdiction consistent with constitutional due process?

Held. No. Judgment reversed (plurality opinion).

♦ California exercise of jurisdiction would be unreasonable and unfair, considering the severe burdens on D of defending in a foreign legal system, the slight interests of P and California in the exercise of jurisdiction, and the international interests in not subjecting this alien corporation to an indemnification offshoot of a product liability action in an American court.

Comment. Justice O'Connor delivered the plurality opinion. Also, joined by Chief Justice Rehnquist and Justices Powell and Scalia, Justice O'Connor asserted that "a finding of minimum contacts must come about by an action of the defendant purposefully directed toward the forum." She maintained that Asahi did not purposefully avail itself by the California market. On the other hank, in Justice Brennan's concurrence, he was joined by Justices White, Marshall, and Blackmun in contending that minimum contacts existed because Asahi placed its product into the stream of commerce and was aware that its product was regularly sold in the forum state. Justice Stevens was joined by Justices White and Blackmun in his concurrence, in which he asserted that a determination of minimum contacts was not necessary to conclude that California's exercise over Asahi would be unreasonable and unfair.

---

5. **General Jurisdiction and State Long Arm Statutes.**

   a. **"Continuous and systematic" contacts required where cause of action arises elsewhere--**

Helicopteros Nacionales de Colombia, S.A. v. Hall, 466 U.S. 408 (1984).

Facts. Four United States citizens were among those who lost their lives in a helicopter crash in Peru. The survivors and representatives of the United States decedents (Ps) brought these wrongful death actions in Texas state court against Helicol, the owner of the helicopter (D); Consorcio/WSH, a Peruvian consortium with headquarters in Houston, Texas, which employed decedents to work on construction of a pipeline in Peru; and Bell Helicopter Company, which sold and provided maintenance and instruction for D's helicopters out of its Fort Worth, Texas, office. Ps are not residents of Texas. D is a Colombian corporation that does not have a place of business in Texas and has never been licensed to do business in the state. D's only contacts with Texas consisted of its chief executive officer going to Houston for a contract-negotiating session; accepting into its New York bank account checks drawn on a Houston bank; purchasing helicopters, equipment, and training services from Bell Helicopter for substantial sums of money; and sending personnel to Bell's Fort Worth facilities for training. Significantly, all parties agree that Ps' wrongful death action did not "arise out of" and is not related to D's Texas activities. The Texas trial court, over D's special appearance, ruled that it had personal jurisdiction, and a jury returned a verdict in favor of Ps. The higher Texas courts affirmed and D appeals.

Issue. Do D's Texas activities constitute "continuous and systematic" contacts with Texas so that a Texas court may exercise in personam jurisdiction with respect to a cause of action that does not arise out of or relate to D's activities within Texas (*i.e.,* "general in personam jurisdiction")?

Held. No. Judgment reversed.

♦ A court may exercise what has been called "limited" or "specific" in personam jurisdiction "[w]hen a controversy is related to or 'arises out of' a defendant's contacts with the forum . . . ." [International Shoe Co. v. Washington, *supra*]

♦ "Even when the cause of action does not arise out of or relate to the foreign corporation's activities in the forum state," a court may exercise in personam jurisdiction if defendant corporation's in-state activities are conducted on a continuous and systematic basis, not occasionally or irregularly. [Perkins v. Benguet Consolidated Mining Co., 342 U.S. 437 (1952)]

♦ Purchases and related trips ("even if occurring at regular intervals"), standing alone, are not a sufficient basis for in personam jurisdiction. [Rosenberg Bros. & Co. v. Curtis Brown Co., 260 U.S. 516 (1923)]

♦ Applying these rules to the present case, it cannot be said that D's Texas activities were conducted on a continuous and systematic basis. Even if it could be said that they constituted continuous and systematic activity, they amounted to mere purchases and related trips, which is not enough to warrant the exercise of in personam jurisdiction.

Dissent (Brennan, J.). By relying on *Rosenberg Bros.'s* narrow view of in personam jurisdiction, which does not comport with *International Shoe's* subsequent expansion of personal jurisdiction or with "the fundamental transformation of our national economy" that has taken place since 1923, and by refusing to consider any distinction between controversies that "relate to" a defendant's contacts with the forum state and causes of action that "arise out of" such contacts, the Court may be placing severe limitations on the type and amount of contacts that will satisfy the constitutional minimum.

B. NEW BASES OF JURISDICTION—TECHNOLOGICAL CONTACTS

1. Use of the Internet and Technological Advances—Purposeful Availment Through Electronic Means--

Bellino v. Simon, 1999 WL 1059753 (E.D. La. 1999).

Facts. Forensic Document Services (P), a sole proprietorship with a principal place of business in California, Simon (D1), and Spence (D2), were all engaged in the business of selling, buying, and authenticating sports memorabilia. P filed suit in Louisiana against both defendants alleging defamation, fraud, and deceptive trade practices. Specifically, P alleged that D1 made defamatory statements about P to the New York City Department of Consumer Affairs, which caused P to be suspended from doing business on eBay, and that both D1 and D2 made defamatory statements about P to Aubert, a Louisiana customer, causing him to return two baseballs he had purchased from P for $25,000. D1 is a resident of New York and the president of a New York Corporation. D2 is a Pennsylvania resident and the managing member of a limited liability company formed in Pennsylvania. P argued that the Louisiana court had general jurisdiction over D1 because of his extensive Internet website solicitations, and over D2 because he also maintained a website and had advertised his business in a national trade magazine. P further argued that the court had specific jurisdiction over Ds because the defamatory remarks were made in a series of e-mails and telephone calls between Aubert and D1, and that D2 participated in one of those phone calls. Thus, P argued, Ds had reached out to Louisiana. Ds asserted that these activities did not establish minimum contacts with Louisiana and moved to dismiss the action due to lack of personal jurisdiction.

Issue. Do allegedly defamatory phone calls and e-mails constitute minimum contacts such that the nonresident defendants purposefully availed themselves of the privileges and benefits of the foreign state?

Held. Yes. However, there must be more than one contact. Motion to dismiss granted with respect to D2, and denied with respect to D1.

♦ One unsolicited and defamatory phone call from the forum state to a nonresident defendant does not establish contacts sufficient to support personal jurisdiction. Aubert, the Louisiana customer, initiated this phone call, and it was the only contact between Aubert and D2. Further, D2's website and magazine advertisements are related to his limited liability company, not to D2 individually. Thus, this court does not have personal jurisdiction over this defendant.

♦ Aubert submitted a visitor form on D1's website, which invited users to contact D1 personally. Several e-mail communications between D1 and Aubert followed. Although Aubert initiated the first phone call to D1, he did so in response to an e-mail invitation from D1. In a broad sense, D1's use of the visitor form on his website solicited the contact between himself and Aubert.

♦ In making allegedly defamatory remarks through use of the telephone and Internet, D1 "purposefully established minimum contacts with Louisiana such that he could reasonably anticipate being haled into court here."

2. **The Internet and Personal Jurisdiction.**

    a. **Application.** Applying existing concepts of personal jurisdiction to businesses operating over the Internet has proven extremely difficult. Most Internet business solicitations do not target specific geographic markets, but instead are directed at any Internet user, which makes traditional purposeful availment analysis problematic. The Supreme Court has yet to address the issue and lower courts have reached different conclusions.

    b. **First cases.** In one of the first decisions addressing Internet commerce, the Connecticut district court found that a nonresident's operation of a website advertisement *alone* was sufficient to establish personal jurisdiction under the purposeful availment test. [Inset Systems, Inc. v. Instruction Set, Inc., 937 F. Supp. 161 (D. Conn. 1996)] Subsequently, most courts have required "something more" than just maintenance of a website. [*See* Cybersell, Inc. v. Cybersell, Inc., 130 F.3d 414 (9th Cir. 1997)]

    c. **"Sliding scale" test.** Many commentators believe that the best approach is the "sliding scale" test adopted in *Zippo Manufacturing Co. v. Zippo Dot Com, Inc.*, 952 F. Supp. 1119 (W.D. Pa 1997). Under that test, "the likelihood that personal jurisdiction can be constitutionally exercised is directly proportionate to the nature and quality of commercial activity that an entity conducts over the Internet." The court indicated that at one end of the spectrum are "active" websites, which are those that actually conduct business over the Internet. At the other end of the spectrum are "passive" websites, which merely make information available to anyone who visits the site. Jurisdiction is almost always proper in cases involving "active" websites, and improper in cases involving "passive" websites. But in cases involving so-called "interactive" websites, which allow the user to exchange information with a host computer, courts continue to reach inconsistent conclusions.

C. JURISDICTION BASED UPON POWER OVER PROPERTY

1. **In Rem and Quasi In Rem Jurisdiction.**

    a. **Jurisdiction in rem.** Jurisdiction "in rem" means that a state through its courts may render a valid judgment affecting the interests of all persons *in a thing* where it has jurisdiction over the thing, even though it may not have jurisdiction over the persons whose interests in the thing are affected. Examples include a court of admiralty affecting the interests of all persons in a vessel subject to the jurisdiction of the state; a statutory proceeding brought to register title to certain land and that is designed to affect the interests of all persons in the land; and a statutory proceeding for the forfeiture to the government of (and extinguishment of all the interests of all parties in) a thing used in violation of the revenue (or other) laws.

b. **Jurisdiction quasi in rem.** Quasi in rem jurisdiction means that the state may render, through its courts, a valid judgment affecting the interests of a particular person in a thing when it has jurisdiction over the thing even though it may not have personal jurisdiction over the person whose interests are affected. Two types of quasi in rem proceedings exist:

1) **Preexisting interest.** The plaintiff may seek to establish a preexisting interest in the thing and to extinguish or to establish the nonexistence of interests of other particular persons in the thing, such as actions to quiet title to land, and actions to foreclose mortgages.

2) **Enforcement of a personal claim.** The plaintiff may seek to enforce a personal claim against the defendant by applying the thing owned by the defendant to the satisfaction of the claim (such as by attachment, garnishment, or creditor's bill) in actions to recover damages for breach of contract or for tort. In all of the above situations, the state need have no jurisdiction over the person of the defendant as long as it has jurisdiction over the thing belonging to the defendant, or over a person who is in possession of a thing belonging to the defendant or is indebted or under a duty to the defendant.

2. **Nature of an In Rem Proceeding.** In *Tyler v. Judges of the Court of Registration*, 55 N.E. 812 (Mass. 1900), a procedure for clearing title was challenged. Chief Justice Holmes, in dismissing the claim, wrote that "a proceeding in rem, dealing with a tangible res, may be instituted and carried to judgment without personal service upon claimants within the state, or notice by name to those outside of it. . . . Jurisdiction is secured by the power of the court over the res . . . . All proceedings, like all rights, are really against persons. Whether they are proceedings or rights in rem depends on the number of persons affected."

3. **Nature of a Quasi In Rem Proceeding.** In *Pennington v. Fourth National Bank*, 243 U.S. 269 (1917), the Court stated, "garnishment or foreign attachment is a proceeding quasi in rem. . . . The only essentials to the exercise of the state's power are presence of the res within its borders, its seizure at the commencement of proceedings, and the opportunity of the owner to be heard."

4. **Debt Situs and the Nature of the Foreign Debtor's State Contacts.** In *Harris v. Balk*, 198 U.S. 215 (1905), Harris, a resident of North Carolina, owed Balk, also a resident of North Carolina. Balk owed a sum to Epstein, a resident of Maryland. While Harris was in Maryland, Epstein attached the debt Harris owed to Balk. Judgment was entered against Harris, and he duly paid the sum to Epstein. Later, Balk brought suit against Harris to collect the debt Harris owed to Balk, and Harris pleaded in bar of recovery the Maryland judgment and his payment thereof, and that it was conclusive against Balk. The trial court and state supreme court ruled that the Maryland judgment was not a bar to recovery, because the Maryland court had no personal jurisdiction over Harris, since he was only in Maryland temporarily and the situs of the debt (the

thing) was in North Carolina and not subject to the jurisdiction of Maryland's courts. The Supreme Court held that the obligation of the debtor to pay his debt clings to and accompanies him wherever he goes. He is as much bound to pay his debt in a foreign state when therein sued upon his obligation by his creditor as he was in the state where the debt was contracted. A creditor (A) has a right to sue in the state where the debtor (B) may be found, even if but temporarily there. Upon that right is built the further right of another creditor (C) to attach a debt owing by the garnishee (B) to his creditor (A). Although a garnishee has the duty to give his creditor notice, so that the creditor may have an opportunity to protect himself, the defendant here had notice of the attachment and a year and a day in which to recover his debt. Harris's claim was therefore barred.

5. **Reconciliation.**

a. **In general.** The classification of jurisdiction as in personam, in rem, and quasi in rem has been criticized as impractical, especially since *International Shoe*. The law remains somewhat tangled in traditional notions, but some attempts have been made toward clarification.

b. **Modern interpretation of minimum contacts--**

Shaffer v. Heitner, 433 U.S. 186 (1977).

Facts. Heitner (P), owner of one share of stock in Greyhound Corporation, a Delaware corporation with its principal place of business in Phoenix, Arizona, filed a shareholder's derivative suit against Greyhound and 28 officers and directors (Ds). P sued in Delaware although not a Delaware resident. The substantive transactions involved occurred in Oregon. Pursuant to a Delaware statute that allows a state court to take jurisdiction of a lawsuit by sequestering any property of D that happens to be in the state, P filed a motion for an order of sequestration, which was granted. Based on the "statutory presence" of all stock in Delaware corporations, shares of several Ds were seized by placing "stop transfer" orders on the books of Greyhound. Ds challenged the Delaware courts' jurisdiction, but the Delaware Supreme Court upheld the lower court. Ds appeal.

Issue. Does a "minimum contacts" standard apply to the exercise of in rem jurisdiction by a state?

Held. Yes. Judgment reversed.

♦ The concept of in personam jurisdiction has been greatly expanded since *Pennoyer*. Although in rem jurisdiction principles have not changed so dramatically, this Court has recognized that an adverse judgment in rem directly affects the property owner by divesting him of his rights in the property before the court. *Pennoyer* failed to recognize this and is no longer a secure foundation.

♦ The term "in rem jurisdiction" is merely a customary way to refer to jurisdiction over the interests of persons in a thing. The basis for such jurisdiction therefore ought to be sufficient to justify jurisdiction over the interests of persons in a thing. Such basis is to be measured by the *International Shoe* minimum contacts standard.

♦ Requiring existence of minimum contacts before a state may exercise jurisdiction will not affect most of the traditional in rem cases, since, if the subject matter of the case is the property itself, the standard is met. However, it will affect cases such as this one and *Harris v. Balk (supra)*. Although adoption of this standard might complicate some litigation, simplicity is not to be preferred to "fair play and substantial justice."

♦ The sole basis for Delaware's jurisdiction here is the statutory presence of Ds' stock in the state. The stock is totally unrelated to the cause of action. Since P has failed to allege any of the types of contacts required by constitutional minimum contacts standards, Delaware cannot exercise jurisdiction over the case.

Concurrence (Powell, J.). The concept of quasi in rem jurisdiction without minimum contacts might still be appropriate in the case of real property.

Concurrence (Stevens, J.). The Delaware statute is unconstitutional on its face.

Concurrence and dissent (Brennan, J.). While the minimum contacts standard is appropriate to state jurisdiction cases, the Court goes too far in deciding that there were insufficient contacts here. The Court in effect has issued an advisory opinion. It should be left up to the state to determine whether it wished to base jurisdiction on Ds' voluntary association with the state through its corporation laws.

———————————

c. **Attachment of insurance policies.** Prior to *Shaffer*, some courts had exercised jurisdiction over a defendant by attaching the defendant's insurance policy, in effect "seizing" the insurance company's obligation to defend the defendant policyholder. In *Seider v. Roth*, 216 N.E.2d 312 (N.Y. 1966), which involved an auto accident, the court upheld the attachment of the defendant's insurer's contractual obligation. The insurer and the defendant were Canadian, but the insurer did business in New York, where the attachment papers were served. The attachment was upheld on the grounds that the contractual obligation constituted an attachable debt. The Supreme Court rejected this type of quasi in rem jurisdiction in *Rush v. Savchuk*, 444 U.S. 320 (1980), for lack of minimum contacts.

d. **Seizure of property related to the claim: in rem jurisdiction.** *Shaffer* makes it clear that in rem jurisdiction, in which the plaintiff and the defendant claim an *interest* in the property that is brought before the court by attachment, is largely unaffected by the minimum contacts rule. Thus, typical in rem actions (*e.g.*, actions to clear title, foreclose liens, or recover possession) are still permissible. The reason is that, as the Court in *Shaffer* stated, "[i]n such cases the defendant's claim to property located in the state would normally indicate that he expected to benefit from the state's protection of his interest." This reasoning has clear relevancy to tangible property (whether real or personal) because the situs of such property can be fixed within the forum state with a degree of certainty. On the other hand, it is more difficult to fix the situs of intangible property (*e.g.,* a debt) in a way that could clearly indicate that the defendant is receiving benefits and protections from the forum state. The rule that "a debt follows the debtor" may be too abstract to establish the requisite nexus between the defendant and the forum in every case. Thus, the plaintiff may have to establish more direct ties or contacts between the defendant and the forum state in cases involving intangible property. It might, therefore, be correct to conclude that while the minimum contacts rule has not affected in rem actions involving tangible property, it might affect in rem actions involving intangible property.

e. **Divorce jurisdiction.** Courts classify a divorce proceeding as in rem, the marital relationship being the property and the property being located wherever the husband or wife may be domiciled. An action to dissolve a marriage, therefore, can be brought in either the husband's or wife's state. However, issues of spousal and child support are classified as in personam and, hence, must be litigated in a state in which a court can exercise in personam jurisdiction over the defendant. This is the principle of divisible divorce. Because of this principle, it is best for the plaintiff to sue where personal jurisdiction over the defendant can be established if spousal or child support is an issue in the divorce proceeding.

D. PHYSICAL PRESENCE AS BASIS FOR JURISDICTION

–1. Transient Jurisdiction--

Burnham v. Superior Court, 495 U.S. 604 (1990).

Facts. Francie Burnham (P) brought suit for divorce in California state court against her husband, Dennis Burnham (D), from whom she had been separated for 18 months. D, a resident of New Jersey, was served with process at P's home in California. At the time of service, D was visiting southern California on business and had traveled to northern California to visit his children. He took his older child to San Francisco for the weekend and was served with process upon returning the child to P's home. D returned to New Jersey, but later made a special appearance in a California trial court to file a motion to quash service. The motion was denied, and the California appellate courts affirmed. D appeals.

Issue. Is it consistent with constitutional due process for California to exercise personal jurisdiction over a nonresident who was personally served with process for a claim that was unrelated to his in-state activities while temporarily in California? In other words, is transient jurisdiction constitutional?

Held. Yes. Judgment affirmed (plurality opinion).

♦ Personal jurisdiction based on service on a nonresident defendant while the defendant is in the state comports with traditional notions of fair play and substantial justice.

Conncurrence. (White, J.). Transient jurisdiction is so widely accepted that I could not possibly find that it denies due process.

Concurrence. (Brennan, Marshall, Blackmun, O'Connor, JJ.). Minimum contacts are established because a transient defendant actually avails himself of significant benefits provided by the state. His health and safety are guaranteed by the state's police, fire, and emergency services. Thus, the transient rule is consistent with reasonable expectations and is entitled to a strong presumption that it comports with due process. In addition, the exercise of transient jurisdiction is reasonable because modern transportation and communications have made it much less burdensome for a party sued to defend himself. And any burdens that do arise can be ameliorated by a variety of procedural devices.

Concurrence. (Stevens, J.). Justices Scalia and Brennan's opinions are unnecessarily broad. For me, it is sufficient to note that the historical evidence and consensus identified by Justice Scalia, the considerations of fairness identified by Justice Brennan, and the common sense displayed by Justice White, all combine to demonstrate that this is, indeed, a very easy case.

Comment. While the decision upholding transient jurisdiction was unanimous, the reasoning was not. Justice Scalia, who announced the judgement of the Court, was joined by Chief Justice Rehnquist and Justices Kennedy and White in asserting that jurisdiction based on physical presence alone constitutes due process because it is one of the continuing traditions of our legal system that defines the due process standard of "traditional notions of fair play and substantial justice." These four Justices believed that transient jurisdiction comports with traditional notions of fair play and substantial justice simply because it has been consistently upheld since the 19th century and has been supported by the consensus of state court judges. On the other hand, Justices Brennan, Marshall, Blackmun, and O'Connor believed that transient jurisdiction passes the fairness test because it satisfies both the minimum contacts and reasonableness subtests.

E. OTHER BASES OF JURISDICTION: CONSENT AND NECESSITY

1. Consent.

a. Party agreements concerning jurisdiction.

1) **Consent in advance of litigation.** Since *Pennoyer v. Neff*, it has always been permissible for a plaintiff and a defendant to consent to

jurisdiction in a particular forum state in advance of litigation, provided that there is no "overweening" on the part of the stronger party. [*See* M/S Bremen v. Zapata Off-Shore Co., 407 U.S. 1 (1972)]

b. **Involuntary waiver.** When the defendant agrees in writing to submit to a court's in personam jurisdiction, she in effect gives up the right to insist that minimum contacts be established before a court can render a valid judgment against her. In addition to such a voluntary waiver of minimum contacts, there are circumstances under which a defendant may involuntarily waive this constitutional right. One such circumstance involves the defendant's failure to comply with a court's discovery order designed to ascertain whether the court has personal jurisdiction.

1) **Preliminary note on discovery.** Discovery, discussed in Chapter XI., *infra*, basically refers to a number of procedural devices (*e.g.,* interrogatories and depositions) designed to uncover, or "discover," the facts of a lawsuit. Although discovery is normally used to ascertain facts relating to the substantive aspect of the lawsuit, it is sometimes used to unearth facts about a jurisdictional issue as well. Sometimes the court has to rely upon discovery to obtain facts on which to determine the existence of minimum contacts.

2) **Discovery sanctions.** If a party disobeys a court's discovery order, the Federal Rules allow the court to impose sanctions against that party. One severe sanction is provided in Rule 37(b), which basically says that the facts that were the subject matter of an attempted discovery will be presumed to be contrary to the interests of the party who disobeyed the discovery order. Rule 37(b) raises the question of whether a "court can say to the party disobeying a discovery order (on the ground that there is no authority for the order, because minimum contacts is lacking) that minimum contacts will be presumed."

3) **Rule 37 and waiver.** In *Insurance Corp. of Ireland v. Compagnie des Bauxites de Guinee*, 456 U.S. 694 (1982), a group of foreign insurance companies contested the exercise of personal jurisdiction over them by a Pennsylvania federal district court. The companies refused to comply with court-backed discovery requests designed to ascertain jurisdictional facts on the ground that the requests were too burdensome. The district court entered an order finding personal jurisdiction because the companies failed to comply with its order after fair warning. The companies appealed. The Supreme Court held the sanction imposed by the district court pursuant to Rule 37(b) was not an abuse of discretion under the facts of this case. The Court reasoned a theoretical distinction exists between subject matter and personal jurisdiction. Unlike subject matter jurisdiction, the requirement of personal jurisdiction may be intentionally waived or the defendant may, for various reasons, be estopped from raising it as an issue. This is because personal jurisdiction does not implicate "the

sovereign power of the court," a constitutional power that cannot be conferred upon a court by consent, waiver, or estoppel. In other words, personal jurisdiction, unlike subject matter jurisdiction, does not flow from "Article III, but from the Due Process Clause" (which "itself makes no mention of federalism concerns") and, hence, "represents a restriction on judicial power not as a matter of sovereignty, but as a matter of individual liberty."

2. **Necessity.** In some instances, the needs of society have been found to prevail over the requirements of the "minimum contacts" standard, *e.g.*, actions to quiet title where some of the potential claim holders are unknown or lack the requisite minimum contacts with the forum. Similarly, situations in which no one forum is capable of exercising jurisdiction over all interested litigants may give rise to a necessity jurisdiction. [*See* Mullane v. Central Hanover Bank & Trust Co., *infra*]

F. LONG ARM JURISDICTION IN THE FEDERAL COURTS

1. **In General.** A number of restrictions are imposed by federal law or rules of civil procedure on the exercise of personal jurisdiction by federal courts. [*See, e.g.*, Fed. R. Civ. P. 4(f)] Note, however, that Congress has, in particular statutes and regulations, authorized nationwide (or even worldwide) service of process. [*See, e.g.*, Clayton Act, 15 U.S.C. §22; Securities Exchange Act of 1934, 15 U.S.C. §78aa]

   a. **Federal act.** *Omni Capital International v. Rudolf Wolff & Co.*, 484 U.S. 97 (1987), involved an action brought under the Commodity Exchange Act, a federal act which is silent on service of process. The Supreme Court held that a federal court does not have authorization under Rule 4 of the Federal Rules of Civil Procedure to serve process on and exercise personal jurisdiction over a foreign defendant where the requirements of the state long arm statute have not been met. The Court held that a nationwide service provision was not implicit in the Act, and therefore, the federal act could not be used as a basis for personal jurisdiction when the requirements of the state's long arm statute had not been met.

   b. **Federal Rule of Civil Procedure 4(k)(2).** Rule 4(k)(2) was promulgated partially in response to the Supreme Court's decision in *Omni, supra*. The rule allows federal courts to exercise jurisdiction in situations where federal claims are asserted against a defendant, but the defendant is not subject to the jurisdiction of any single state, as long as the United States Constitution would permit jurisdiction. The Rule thus operates as a limited federal long arm provision.

G. CHALLENGING THE JURISDICTION OF A COURT

1. **In General.** It is commonly said that the jurisdictional requirements of a court over the person of the defendant and over the subject matter of the suit are

mandatory, in the sense that any action taken by a court without proper jurisdiction is totally void when subjected to collateral attack. While this generalization remains true for many state courts, it is not exactly accurate when applied to the federal court system.

a. **State courts.** Under most state codes, lack of jurisdiction may be raised at any time in the course of an action—there is no "waiver" of an objection to personal jurisdiction, and neither is there ever a "waiver" of an objection to subject matter jurisdiction of the court. In many states, jurisdictional defects may even be raised for the first time on appeal, and such a tactic is effective in wearing down the financial resources of an unwary plaintiff.

b. **Federal Rules.** Under the Federal Rules of Civil Procedure (and corresponding state rules), an objection to the jurisdiction of the court over the defendant (lack of personal jurisdiction) is deemed waived if it is not timely raised prior to trial, in the interests of substantive justice. However, even under the Rules, lack of subject matter jurisdiction is never waived and may at any time be brought to the attention of the court.

2. **Effect of Judgment Erroneously Entered.** If a trial court lacking jurisdiction erroneously enters a judgment, and it is erroneously affirmed upon appeal, whether the judgment entered thereafter legally binds the defendant to the exclusion of collateral attack upon the judgment depends on whether the defendant has contested the jurisdiction, or whether he has appeared in the action to defend upon the merits.

a. **Default judgments.** When the defendant has appeared neither to contest the jurisdiction of the court nor to defend upon the merits without contesting jurisdiction (where he has taken a default against himself), he is allowed to attack the jurisdiction of the judgment court collaterally, that is, in another, separate proceeding, and the lack of jurisdiction is recognized as a sufficient defense to attempted enforcement of the judgment.

b. **Judgments on the merits.** When the defendant has appeared in the action, however, either to contest the jurisdiction of the court or to defend upon the merits, and the judgment has been finalized by appeal, the lack of original jurisdiction of the trial court is not subject to collateral attack by the defendant. The judgment entered is entitled to full faith and credit in all other state courts. This remains true even if, in defending on the merits, the defendant does not actually litigate the jurisdictional objection, as long as he had sufficient opportunity to so litigate. It is said that each defendant is afforded one, and only one, appearance to contest jurisdiction—once litigated, appealed, and finalized, a decision about the jurisdiction of the court becomes binding to the exclusion of further attack, whether objectively erroneous or not.

3. **Special Appearance Problem.** A general appearance is an appearance in court to defend on the merits. A special appearance is an appearance in court only to protest the jurisdiction of the court to hear a pending case. Most states do not equate a special appearance with a general appearance—it is considered good policy to allow defendants to protest jurisdiction without exposing themselves to the full in personam jurisdiction of the court. However, it is not unconstitutional for a statute to equate a special appearance and a general appearance—to provide that any appearance at all constitutes consent to defend upon the merits.

4. **Collateral Attack on Personal Jurisdiction.** Generally, if the defendant makes a special appearance contesting the jurisdiction of the first forum and he loses, he may not later contest the same issue in a later suit. [*See, e.g.,* Baldwin v. Iowa State Traveling Men's Association, 283 U.S. 522 (1931)]

III. PROVIDING NOTICE AND AN OPPORTUNITY TO BE HEARD

A. REQUIREMENT OF REASONABLE NOTICE

1. **In General.** The rigid and prescriptive notification requirements of earlier eras have been replaced by the due process requirement that in every suit, a "reasonable method of notification given the individual circumstances" must be supplied. The black letter definition of a "reasonable method" of notification is "that method which, given the circumstances, resources, and nature of the court and the pending suit, is most likely to reach the defendant, or insure that his side of the case does not go unpresented . . . ."

2. **Constitutional Standards--**

Mullane v. Central Hanover Bank & Trust Co., 339 U.S. 306 (1950).

Facts. Central Hanover Bank was trustee of a common trust fund with 113 participating trusts. Pursuant to New York Banking Law, it petitioned the court for settlement of its first account as common trustee. The court appointed Mullane (P) as special guardian and attorney for all persons known or unknown not otherwise appearing who had or might thereafter have any interest in the income of the common trust fund. In an attempt to discharge its obligations to notify the beneficiaries of the pendency of the petition for settlement, Central Hanover complied with the New York law and published notice by newspaper, setting forth merely the name and address of the trust company, the name and date of establishment of the common trust fund and a list of all participating estates, trusts, and funds. P objected to the settlement petition on the ground that the notice given by Central Hanover was inadequate to afford due process under the Fourteenth Amendment, thus rendering the court without jurisdiction to render the final decree, which would otherwise bind both the appearing and nonappearing beneficiaries. The state court held that service was proper and P appeals.

Issue. Is notice by publication a violation of due process when the out-of-state parties so served are known and have known addresses?

Held. Yes. Judgment reversed. The objections of P insofar as they relate to known beneficiaries with a known place of residence are sustained.

♦ A fundamental requirement of due process in any proceeding that is to be accorded finality is notice reasonably calculated, under all circumstances, to reach the interested parties and afford them an opportunity to be heard.

♦ The method of publication was insufficient with respect to the known beneficiaries, whose names were not mentioned, and many of whom lived outside of the town where the newspaper was published.

♦ However, we disagree with P's objections to the published notice insofar as it applied to beneficiaries whose addresses were unknown to the trustee and not reasonably discoverable by due diligence. Notice by publication is sufficient in such a case.

Comment. The notice must be reasonable under the factual circumstances and consideration must be given to feasible alternatives. In some cases, compliance with a state statute may not be sufficient. In *Greene v. Lindsey*, 456 U.S. 444 (1982), the Court held that compliance with a Kentucky statute requiring that the summons in a forcible entry and detainer action be posted on the door of a tenant's apartment resulted in a failure of actual notice and was held insufficient to satisfy due process. The case involved tenants in a public housing project who claimed never to have received the notices. The tenants testified that postings in the building were frequently removed by children and other tenants before they could be seen by the intended recipient. The Court held that under these facts, other supplemental means, such as mailing, should have been employed.

B. THE MECHANICS OF GIVING NOTICE

1. **Introduction.** There are three prerequisites for a judgment to be valid. The parties must have had adequate notice; the court must have had territorial jurisdiction over the parties; and the court must have had subject matter jurisdiction over the action. Thus, adequate notice is more than a technical legal requirement. Notice is provided by service of process.

2. **Service of Process.** A summons orders the defendant to appear at the risk of losing a default judgment. The summons must be accompanied by a copy of the complaint under most state rules and under the Federal Rules. [Fed. R. Civ. P. 4]

    a. **Issuance and service.** The court clerk issues a summons over his signature. Some states have the sheriff serve the summons; others allow any nonparty over 18 years of age to do so. In federal court, the United States Marshal serves process, or the court may designate another person to do so.

    b. **Methods of service.** Notice must actually reach the defendant or be given through a procedure reasonably probable to reach the defendant.

        1) **Personal delivery.** The individual (or an authorized agent) may be served personally.

        2) **Substituted service.**

            a) **Federal Rules.** The Federal Rules provide that a copy of the summons and complaint may be left at the defendant's usual place of abode with a person of suitable age and discretion residing there. Any other means authorized by the law of the state in which the federal court is located is also permitted. Rule 4 also provides that any means of service in the state in which the defendant is served is also permitted, unless the defendant is a minor or incompetent.

b) **State law.** State law varies. Normally, the best available means must be used. Methods such as mailing with acknowledgment of receipt and publication are available.

c. **Content.** Most jurisdictions require that the summons describe the proceeding and the court and warn that a judgment will be entered.

3. **Application of the Service Provisions.**

a. **Waiver of service--**

Maryland State Firemen's Association v. Chaves, 166 F.R.D. 353 (D. Md. 1996).

Facts. The Maryland State Firemen's Association (P) sued Chaves (D), who was president of the Firefighters Association of America, for allegedly soliciting charitable contributions that were rightfully P's. P served D with the summons and complaint via first class mail sent to the address on D's letterhead. P's attorney received several phone calls from an individual who claimed to be speaking on D's behalf, and who indicated the case was being referred to an attorney in New York. When D failed to file an answer, P filed a motion for judgment by default for failure to plead.

Issue. Was service by first class mail alone effective under the Federal Rules of Civil Procedure?

Held. No. Motion for default judgment denied.

♦ Federal Rule of Civil Procedure 4(d) allows a plaintiff to mail a defendant notice of the action and a request for waiver of service. While the defendant has a duty to avoid unnecessary costs of service, if he does not consent to waiver, his failure to waive does not provide the basis for a default judgment.

♦ When no waiver was received from D, Rule 4(d) required P to effect service on D by other means. Costs of service will be imposed upon D unless there was good cause for the failure to waive service.

Comment. Even though it was obvious in this case that D *had* actual knowledge of the suit, service was nonetheless held invalid due to P's failure to strictly comply with Rule 4(d).

---

b. **Service at defendant's dwelling house or usual place of abode.** Federal Rule of Civil Procedure 4(e)(2) allows service to be made upon an individual by leaving a copy of the summons and complaint at the individual's "dwelling house or usual place of abode with some person of suitable age and discretion then residing therein." [Fed. R. Civ. P. 4(e)(2)]

c. **Technique of service--**

National Equipment Rental, Ltd. v. Szukhent, 375 U.S. 311 (1964).

Facts. National (P) and Szukhent (D) entered into a written contract for lease of certain farm implements. Contained in the contract, unknown to D, was a "boilerplate" clause stating that D appointed Florence Weinberg as in-state agent for service of process in any action arising out of the contract. D did not know Florence Weinberg, nor was he aware of the agency until service of process was made upon her as his agent. D protested the exercise of jurisdiction over him on the basis of the agency, on the grounds that: (i) the contract did not require the agent to actually notify him of the service of process; (ii) he was unaware of the agency, and therefore it was invalid; (iii) the agent was also an agent for P, so that there was a conflict of interest. The district court quashed service, and the court of appeals affirmed. The Supreme Court granted certiorari.

Issue. Is a person an agent by appointment who was designated in the litigants' private contract as agent to receive service of process, even though she is not personally known to the litigants and is not expressly required by the contract's terms to transmit notice to the parties?

Held. Yes. Judgment reversed and case remanded.

♦ The agency was valid. In *Wuchter v. Pizzutti*, 276 U.S. 13 (1928), we found a state nonresident-motorist statute to be invalid because it did not expressly require the secretary of state to communicate notice of the action to the defendant. When an agent is appointed by act of law rather than by contract, the law must require notification of the defendant by the agent. However, *Wuchter* is inapplicable here because Florence Weinberg was appointed by private contract rather than by operation of law.

♦ The fact that D did not know personally of Florence Weinberg does not invalidate the agency, since the agent actually performed her task quite well, and informed D of the suit immediately upon service upon her. Therefore, D had no reason to complain.

Dissent (Black, J.). D's consent is nullified by overreaching on the part of P. P's big city lawyers drafted the contract, and the agency provision was written in small print. P was definitely the stronger party and took unfair advantage of D. Hence, D's consent was not entirely voluntary.

Dissent (Brennan, J., Warren, C.J., Goldberg, J.). Federal standards must define who is "an agent authorized by appointment" within the meaning of Rule 4(d)(1).

Comments.

◆ Appointment by contract of a special agent for acceptance of service of process in place of the defendant is valid, both under the Federal Rules of Civil Procedure and under most state rules. Such a contractual appointment is valid even if the contract contains no provision that the agent must actually notify the defendant of the service of process, and even if the defendant does not personally know or give overt approval of the agent so appointed.

◆ In *Overmyer Co. v. Frick Co.*, 405 U.S. 174 (1972), the Court, faced with a cognovit provision that waived service and authorized confession of judgment, held that due process rights to notice and hearing prior to entry of a civil judgment are subject to waiver, provided the ***waiver is voluntary, knowing, and intelligently made*** and not part of an adhesion contract.

---

d. **Service on artificial entities.** Under Federal Rule 4(h), service may be made on corporations, partnerships, and unincorporated associations. Typically, such service is made by delivery of process to an officer, managing agent, or general agent of the entity. In *Insurance Company of North America v. S/S "Hellenic Challenger,"* 88 F.R.D. 545 (S.D.N.Y. 1980), however, a court disregarded these labels when it held that leaving a summons and complaint with a claims adjuster at the defendant's office was sufficient even though the adjuster was not expressly authorized by the defendant to accept process. The court reasoned that the adjuster was well-integrated into the organization, was familiar with the formalities of service, and had accepted service on the defendant's behalf on prior occasions in connection with his duties.

e. **Service on foreign individuals.** Rule 4(f) provides that service may be effected on individuals outside the United States by "any internationally agreed means reasonably calculated to give notice," as directed by foreign authority or law, or upon the individual in person or by mail unless prohibited by law.

f. **Effect of a defective summons.** A defective summons is a summons that does not conform to the statutory form prescribed by the state. Not all defective summonses invalidate service of process, but those summonses that are so vague, confusing, or uninformative as to fail to give reasonable notice of time, place, and manner of hearings are fatally defective.

4. **Return of Service.** In most jurisdictions, the return of service is considered strong evidence of the facts stated, but is not conclusive and may be controverted by proof that the return is inaccurate. In *Miedreich v. Lauenstein,* 232 U.S. 236

(1914), the plaintiff sought to vacate a mortgage foreclosure judgment, claiming that the sheriff had made a false return of summons. The plaintiff was not a resident of the county where the action was brought, was not served with process, and had no knowledge of the earlier proceeding. The Court found that the original party in the foreclosure proceeding did all that the law required and that the plaintiff's remedy was against the sheriff upon his bond. The purchaser at the sheriff's sale, the Court stated, had a right to rely upon the record.

5. **When Suit "Commences."** In a federal court case based on federal law, a suit commences for purposes of a statute of limitations when a copy of the complaint is filed with the district court. In state court or in federal court actions based on state law, state law governs when an action is commenced for limitations purposes. Some states require service of process on the defendant before an action is deemed commenced.

C. IMMUNITY FROM PROCESS AND ETIQUETTE OF SERVICE

1. **Immunity from Service of Process.** For reasons of public policy, judicial convenience, and general fairness, certain persons are immune from service of process while in the forum state. This immunity extends to witnesses at other litigation, counsel for the parties at other litigation, the parties to another litigation, and certain persons acting in some official capacity within the forum state, *e.g.,* as marshals, officers of the court, government officials, or investigators for the government.

    a. **No immunity from process--**

State *ex rel.* Sivnksty v. Duffield, 71 S.E.2d 113 (W. Va. 1952).

Facts. While he was vacationing in West Virginia, Sivnksty's (P's) automobile hit and injured two children. P was arrested and charged with reckless driving and, unable to post bond, was incarcerated until his trial. P was served with process in a tort action while awaiting trial. P was found guilty of the criminal charge and his appeals from the conviction were unsuccessful. P made a special appearance in the civil action and filed a plea of abatement, claiming lack of jurisdiction because he was a nonresident at time of service and a prisoner. The court sustained a plea of demurrer. P petitions the supreme court for a writ of prohibition.

Issue. Is a nonresident immune from process who voluntarily enters a county with the intent of remaining for a few days, but is then incarcerated in the county jail and is served with process in a civil action while he is incarcerated?

Held. No. Writ denied.

♦   The underlying public policy of the privilege of immunity from civil process of a nonresident charged with a crime is not to deter the appearance of the nonresident before the courts by the threat of civil or other process. Thus, because of the immunity, one charged with a crime will be encouraged to return to the county or state in which he is charged to respond to the criminal process.

♦ Here, P did not enter the county in response to criminal process; he was voluntarily in the jurisdiction at the time of arrest and confinement.

Dissent. A person has a right to be tried by a jury in the vicinity in which he resides. This ruling provides potential for widespread abuse of judicial process.

Comment. It is not clear whether immunity from service of process is of right or only of judicial discretion in the furtherance of justice. In *Sivnksty*, above, the court spoke of the immunity as one of right, even though it disallowed the challenge to service on separate grounds.

---

2. **Etiquette of Service.**

    a. **Fraud, force, involuntary entry into the forum.** Service of process upon the defendant will usually be quashed if the defendant was induced to enter the jurisdiction of the court by fraud, or was compelled or forced by the plaintiff or the plaintiff's agent to enter the jurisdiction of the court, or was involuntarily brought into the jurisdiction of the court against his knowledge or will. But if the defendant has somehow voluntarily entered the forum without fraud by the plaintiff, then the perpetration of a deception by the plaintiff in order to compel the defendant to come out of hiding will usually not invalidate the service.

    b. **Service by fraud--**

Wyman v. Newhouse, 93 F.2d 313 (2d Cir. 1937), *cert. denied,* 303 U.S. 664 (1938).

Facts. Wyman (P) sued Newhouse (D) to recover money loaned, money advanced, and damages for seduction under promise of marriage. D was induced to enter the jurisdiction of the court by a letter from P, to the effect that P's mother was dying in Ireland, that P was dropping all charges against D, and that P could not bear to leave the United States without once more seeing D. When D, acting in reliance upon this false information, stepped off the plane in the forum state, he was met by a marshal with process. D did not appear in court and P obtained judgment against D by default. The federal district court in New York granted D's motion to dismiss P's attempt to enforce the judgment against D in New York. P appeals.

Issue. Will a sister state's courts enforce a judgment procured in another state by fraudulent service of process?

Held. No. Judgment affirmed.

◆ We refuse to allow service of process in this manner. We will not have the good name of the court soiled by allowing a suit based upon fraudulent misrepresentation to the defendant. This court will not be a party to a fraud.

Comment. Note that the outcome of the above case would have been different had the defendant entered the forum without inducement from the plaintiff, and then the plaintiff had mailed the letter to the defendant to induce the defendant to come out of hiding. Courts balk at the idea of fraudulent inducement to enter their jurisdiction, but do not have reservations, in most cases, about the method of service when the defendant is already within the jurisdiction of the court but is hiding from suit.

D. OPPORTUNITY TO BE HEARD

1. **Introduction.** In addition to establishing a constitutionally sufficient basis for jurisdiction over the persons or property involved (*supra*), and showing that the court in which the action is filed has subject matter jurisdiction (*infra*), it must also appear that "reasonable steps" were taken to give each defendant notice of the proceedings (*supra*) and an ***opportunity to be heard and to defend***. This is a fundamental requirement of constitutional due process.

2. **Leading Case--**

Fuentes v. Shevin, 407 U.S. 67 (1972).

Facts. This case is a review of two district court decisions upholding the constitutionality of Florida and Pennsylvania laws authorizing the summary seizure of goods or chattels in a person's possession under a writ of replevin. Under the Florida law, Mrs. Fuentes's stove and stereo were seized by the sheriff when she defaulted after paying $400 on a $600 installment contract. The Florida statute allowed any person whose goods are wrongfully detained by any other person to obtain a writ of replevin to recover them. To get the writ, a party had to file a complaint, initiating a court action for repossession and reciting that he was lawfully entitled to possession of that property, and file a security bond for double the value of the property replevied. The officer who seized the property was required to hold it for three days, during which time the debtor could recover it by posting bond for double its value. However, the debtor was provided no prior notice and allowed no opportunity whatever to challenge the issuance of the writ. Unlike the Florida statute, the Pennsylvania law did not require the creditor to initiate a court action; thus, no court hearing was ever ***required*** under this law. The experience of the plaintiffs under Pennsylvania law had been similar to that of Mrs. Fuentes (except Rosa Washington, whose ex-husband was a local deputy sheriff who used the writ of replevin to gain possession of their son's clothes, furniture, and toys).

Issue. Are state statutes that fail to provide for a hearing before a creditor can replevy goods from a defaulting debtor unconstitutional?

Held. Yes. Judgments vacated and cases remanded.

- Due process requires an opportunity for a hearing before a deprivation of property can take place. The constitutional right to be heard is a basic aspect of the duty of government to follow a fair process of decisionmaking when it is acting to deprive a person of his possessions. The right to notice and an opportunity to be heard must be granted at a meaningful time and in a meaningful manner.

- Wholly unfounded applications for a writ are deterred by the requirements that a party seeking a writ post bond, allege that he is entitled to specific goods, and open himself to possible liability in damages if he is wrong. These requirements, however, are hardly a substitute for prior hearing, for they test no more than the strength of the applicant's belief in his rights.

- Although the debtors lacked full legal title to the goods, they were deprived of possessory interests that were within the protection of the Fourteenth Amendment. And it is well settled that a temporary nonfinal deprivation of property is nonetheless a deprivation in terms of the Fourteenth Amendment. Moreover, there is no rule that the goods seized must be "necessities."

- Although there are extraordinary situations that justify postponing notice and opportunity for hearing, in order to so qualify (i) the seizure must be directly necessary to secure an important governmental or general public interest, (ii) there must be a special need for prompt action, and (iii) the state must keep strict control over its monopoly of legitimate force. These statutes fail to qualify under these standards.

- Although the debtors here signed contracts providing that the seller could repossess the property in the event of a default, they did not thereby waive their due process rights. The conditional sales contracts simply provide for repossession without indicating how or through what process the seller could retake the goods.

- Our holding is a narrow one. We do not question the power of a state to seize goods before a final judgment in order to protect the security interests of creditors as long as those creditors have tested their claim to the goods through the process of a fair, prior hearing. The hearing must provide a real test.

Dissent (White, J., Burger, C.J., and Blackmun, J.).

- The issue here is whether it comports with due process to permit the seller, pending final judgment, to take possession of property through replevin served by the sheriff without affording the buyer opportunity to insist that the seller establish at a hearing that there is a reasonable basis for his claim of default. Since the interests of buyer and seller are antagonistic during this interim period, these state statutes are reasonable in that, for all intents and purposes, the property is immobilized during this time. The buyer loses use of the property temporarily but is protected against loss; the seller is protected against deterioration of the property but must undertake by bond to make the buyer whole in the event the latter prevails. The Court ignores the creditor's interest in preventing further use and deterioration of the property in which he has a substantial interest. Under the Court's own definition, the creditor has a property interest as deserving of protection as that of the debtor.

♦ In the end analysis, the result the Court reaches will have little impact, since creditors could withstand attack under this case simply by making clear in the controlling credit instruments that they may retake possession without a hearing.

Comment. In *Mitchell v. W.T. Grant Co.*, 416 U.S. 600 (1974), the Court upheld a Louisiana sequestration procedure that provided for dissolution of the writ upon the debtor's request, unless the creditor could prove his grounds and post a bond.

Comment. In *North Georgia Finishing, Inc. v. Di-Chem, Inc.*, 419 U.S. 601 (1975), a Georgia garnishment procedure was struck down because there was no hearing, no notice, and the debtor could recover his property only by posting a bond for the debt amount.

---

3. Prejudgment Attachment Without Notice or Opportunity to Be Heard--

Connecticut v. Doehr, 501 U.S. 1 (1991).

Facts. DiGiovanni (D) obtained in the Connecticut Superior Court an attachment on the home of Doehr (P), whom D was suing for an assault and battery unrelated to the property. A Connecticut statute permitted this type of attachment without notice to the property owner or a preattachment hearing as long as the plaintiff provided an affidavit that there was probable cause to sustain his claim, among other requirements. There was no requirement that the plaintiff post a bond. P filed suit against D in federal district court, claiming that the statute was unconstitutional under the Due Process Clause. The federal district court upheld the statute and granted summary judgment in favor of D; the Second Circuit Court of Appeals reversed. The Supreme Court granted certiorari.

Issue. Does a state statute that authorizes prejudgment attachment of real estate without prior notice or hearing and without a showing of extraordinary circumstances violate the Due Process Clause?

Held. Yes. Judgment affirmed.

♦ We must consider the factors of *Mathews v. Eldridge,* 424 U.S. 319 (1976), in determining what process is due when a defendant is deprived of property. The

Mathews factors are: (i) the private interest that will be affected by the prejudgment attachment; (ii) the risk of erroneous deprivation through the procedure under attack and the probable value of additional or alternative safeguards; and (iii) the interest of the party seeking the prejudgment remedy, giving due regard to burdens on the government in providing the additional procedure.

♦ Because the property interests that attachment affects are significant, even temporary or partial impairments to property rights that liens, attachments, and similar encumbrances entail are sufficient to merit due process protection.

♦ We do not need to resolve the various interpretations of probable cause advanced by the state or by D, since the statute presents too great a risk of erroneous deprivation under any of them. The issue, unlike determining the existence of a debt or delinquent payments, does not concern "ordinarily uncomplicated matters that lend themselves to documentary proof."

♦ Further, the risks are not reduced by the statute's safeguards: (i) post-attachment hearing; (ii) notice of such a hearing; (iii) judicial review of an adverse decision; and (iv) double damages if the original suit is commenced without probable cause.

♦ D had no existing interest in P's real estate when he sought the attachment, and there was no allegation that P was about to take any available action during the pendency of the action that would render his real estate unavailable to satisfy a judgment. Absent such allegation, there is no exigent circumstance that permits postponing any notice or hearing until after the attachment is procured.

♦ (Part IV, below, adopted only by White, Marshall, Stevens, O'Connor, JJ.)

Due process requires the posting of a bond or other security in addition to requiring a hearing or the showing of some exigency. The mere existence of a claim is inadequate to allow the subjection of an opponent to prejudgment proceedings that carry a significant risk of erroneous deprivation.

A bond does not render unnecessary the safeguards of pre-attachment and post-attachment hearings. A wrongful attachment can inflict injury that will not fully be redressed by recovery on the bond after a prompt post-attachment hearing determines that the attachment was invalid.

Concurrence (Rehnquist, C.J., Blackmun, J.). The Court's opinion here breaks new ground. In previous cases, such as *Fuentes, Mitchell,* and *Di-Chem, supra,* the debtor was deprived of the use and possession of property. Here, the statute does not deprive P of the use or possession of property. However, the deprivation here is significant.

Comment. The opinion implies that proof of exigent circumstances may be constitutionally necessary to allow seizure not only without notice, but even after notice. The Court suggests that less rigorous standards may apply where the plaintiff's interest in the property antedates the suit. The difficulty inherent in evaluating an assault claim on the basis of plaintiff's filings implies that seizure without notice may be available only where there is reliable documentary proof on which a court may base its evaluation.

———————

IV. JURISDICTION OVER THE SUBJECT MATTER OF THE ACTION— THE COURT'S COMPETENCY

A. BASIC PRINCIPLES

The American system of law distributes the judicial workload among several types of courts, and assigns to each type of court the responsibility for hearing cases of a certain nature, involving a certain subject. This subject matter jurisdiction of each type of court is entirely statutorial and varies radically from state to state: division is sometimes made on a basis of the amount in controversy, sometimes on the type of legal question involved in the suit, sometimes by the identity of the litigating parties. We shall be concerned, in this outline, primarily with the subject matter jurisdiction of the federal court system. An examination of the theories and operation of the limited competence of the federal system will provide general insights into the workings of all the state systems.

B. SUBJECT MATTER JURISDICTION IN STATE COURTS

1. Distinguish Lack of Power to Reach Merits--

Lacks v. Lacks, 359 N.E.2d 384 (N.Y. 1976).

Facts. Husband Lacks (P) and wife Lacks (D) were married in New York in 1938. On August 10, 1965, P sued for a separation; however, later he added a prayer for a judgment of divorce, which was granted on March 16, 1970. The judgment was affirmed by the Appellate Division on October 26, 1972. Leave to appeal to the Court of Appeals was denied. Nearly two years later, D moved to vacate the judgment, contending that the court had been without subject matter jurisdiction to entertain the divorce action because section 230 of the Domestic Relations Law provides that an action for divorce may be maintained only when the residence requirements have been met. P had not been a resident of New York for a full year preceding the commencement of the original action. Thus D argued that the court had erroneously granted a divorce judgment in violation of section 230. The Supreme Court, Special Term, New York County, granted the motion, but the Supreme Court, Appellate Division, modified the order by denying the motion and reinstating the final judgment of divorce. D appealed.

Issue. Did the court lack subject matter jurisdiction over this divorce action?

Held. No. Order of Appellate Division is affirmed.

- A statement that a court lacks jurisdiction to decide a case may mean that elements of a cause of action are absent. Likewise, questions of mootness and standing may be characterized as raising questions of subject matter jurisdiction. But these are not the kind of judicial defects that N.Y. Civ. Prac. L & R 5015 addresses. N.Y. Civ. Prac. L & R 5015 is designed to preserve objections so fundamental to a court's adjudicatory powers that they survive even a final judgment or order. Accordingly, N.Y. Civ. Prac. L & R 5015 was not meant to include the question of P's residency status or to vacate a final judgment after all direct appeals have been exhausted.

- A judgment rendered without subject matter jurisdiction is void, and the defect may be raised at any time and may not be waived. The principle that lack of subject matter jurisdiction makes a final judgment absolutely void is not applicable to cases that do not involve jurisdiction, but merely substantive elements of a cause for relief. To do so would be to undermine significantly the doctrine of res judicata, and to eliminate the certainty and finality in the law and in litigation that the doctrine is designed to protect. Thus, whereas absence of competence to entertain an action deprives the court of "subject matter jurisdiction," absence of power to reach the merits does not.

- Here, the order of the Appellate Division must be affirmed. The durational residency requirements of section 230 apply only to the substance of the divorce action, not to the competence of the court to adjudicate the cause. Hence, a divorce judgment granted in the absence of one of the specified connections with the state, even if erroneously determined as a matter of law or fact, is not subject to vacatur under N.Y. Civ. Prac. L & R 5015. Consequently, even if P did not fulfill the statutory residency requirements of section 230, any alleged error by the court did not involve jurisdiction, but merely substantive elements of a cause for relief. Since D allowed this litigation to proceed to a final judgment without objecting to this alleged error and failed to raise this issue on appeal, this matter is at an end.

---

2. **Full Faith and Credit Clause.** In *Hughes v. Fetter*, 341 U.S. 609 (1951), the Supreme Court held that the Full Faith and Credit Clause precluded Wisconsin from closing its courts to a suit under the Illinois wrongful death act in the absence of substantial justification for doing so. Thus, a state court of general jurisdiction may be under a constitutional duty to entertain a cause of action arising under the laws of another state.

3. **Cases Arising Under Federal Law.** In *Howlett v. Rose*, 496 U.S. 356 (1990), the Court held that a state court could not decline to hear a case arising under federal law on sovereign immunity grounds when it would not allow that defense to bar a similar state law claim.

C. SUBJECT MATTER JURISDICTION OF THE FEDERAL COURTS—DIVERSITY OF CITIZENSHIP

1. **In General.** The federal judicial power also includes controversies between citizens of different states when the amount in controversy exceeds $75,000. Determination of citizenship depends upon who the party is as follows:

   a. Corporations are treated as citizens of the state of incorporation and of the state in which they have their principal place of business.

   b. Citizenship of individuals is determined by the same criteria used to establish domicile. Additionally, there must be complete diversity between the parties. For example, if there is one plaintiff and two defendants, there is no diversity jurisdiction if one defendant is a citizen of the same state as the plaintiff.

2. **Determining Citizenship.**

   a. **Domicile not changed by marriage alone--**

Mas v. Perry, 489 F.2d 1396 (5th Cir. 1974), *cert. denied,* 419 U.S. 842 (1975).

Facts. Jean Mas, a citizen of France, and Judy Mas (Ps) were married at Judy's home in Mississippi. After the wedding they returned to Louisiana State University to resume their studies, with no intention of returning to Mississippi. Ps brought a diversity action against their Louisiana landlord (D), alleging that D had watched them through two-way mirrors installed in their bedroom and bathroom. A jury awarded $5,000 to Jean Mas and $15,000 to Judy Mas. D appealed, contending that Ps failed to prove diversity of citizenship among the parties, thus depriving the court of subject matter jurisdiction.

Issue. For purposes of federal diversity jurisdiction, does a woman's domicile change solely because of her marriage to an alien?

Held. No. Judgment of the district court is affirmed.

♦ Federal diversity jurisdiction under 28 U.S.C. section 1332 provides for original jurisdiction in federal district court of all court actions that are between citizens of different states or citizens of a state and citizens of a foreign state and in which the amount in controversy is more than $10,000. For a court to exercise diversity jurisdiction, there must be complete diversity among the parties; that is, no party on one side may be a citizen of the same state as any party on the other side.

♦ The question of citizenship for diversity jurisdiction purposes is a matter of federal, not state, law. The requisite diverse relationship must exist at the time the complaint is filed and is unaffected by subsequent changes in the citizenship of the parties. The party invoking diversity jurisdiction has the burden of pleading the diverse relationship and, if properly challenged, also bears the burden of proof.

♦ To be a citizen of a state within section 1332, a natural person must be both a citizen of the United States and a domiciliary of that state. For diversity purposes, "citizenship" means domicile; mere residence in a state is not enough. Further, a person's domicile is the place of his true, fixed, and permanent home and principal establishment, to which he has the intention of returning whenever he is absent therefrom.

♦ A change of domicile may be effected only by (i) taking up residence at the new domicile and (ii) intending to remain there at least for the time being. Neither physical presence nor the intention to remain is alone sufficient.

♦ Here, the district court had jurisdiction over Jean Mas's claim against D (a citizen of Louisiana) pursuant to section 1332(a)(2). The district court also had jurisdiction under section 1332(a)(1) over Judy Mas's claim against D. The general rule, that domicile of a wife for purposes of diversity jurisdiction is that of her husband, is not applicable where the husband is a citizen of a foreign country. Since a woman does not lose her United States citizenship solely by reason of her marriage to an alien, an American woman does not have her domicile or state citizenship changed because of such a marriage. Thus, despite her marriage to a French citizen, Judy Mas remained a domiciliary of Mississippi. Also, although she had no intention of returning to Mississippi, she never changed her domicile because she was only a student and lacked the requisite intention to remain in Louisiana. Finally, because Jean and Judy Mas's claims arise from the same operative facts, sound judicial administration militates in favor of federal jurisdiction of Judy Mas's claim.

---

b. **Business associations.** Unlike a person, a corporation can be a citizen of more than one state (*see supra*). Generally, unincorporated associations are not treated as citizens; instead, the court considers the citizenship of each of its members.

3. **Subject Matter Jurisdiction of the Federal Courts—Amount in Controversy.**

a. **Introduction.** The jurisdiction of the federal district courts is limited in diversity of citizenship cases to those in which the amount in controversy, exclusive of costs, exceeds $75,000. (The amount in controversy requirement in federal question cases was eliminated in 1980.) In most cases, the prayer for relief in the complaint, if made without obvious bad faith, is conclusive of the amount in controversy for purposes of jurisdiction, even if the eventual recovery is $75,000 or less. While only a positive showing of bad faith is usually enough to defeat federal jurisdiction when the complaint is well pleaded, the filing of "inflated" complaints is somewhat discouraged by the practice in federal courts (in some cases) of assessing costs to the plaintiff if his eventual recovery is less than the jurisdictional amount.

b.   Jurisdictional amount in question--

A.F.A. Tours, Inc., v. Whitchurch, 937 F.2d 82 (2d Cir. 1991).

Facts. A.F.A. Tours (P) brought a diversity action against Whitchurch (D) for misappropriation of trade secrets. D had been employed by P in P's deluxe travel and tour business and when D resigned, P alleges D misappropriated a confidential customer list, marketing information, and tour information. D contacted 100 to 200 former A.F.A. tour participants for a tour D planned and received responses from two A.F.A. customers. D admitted he remained interested in conducting tours in the future that would compete with A.F.A. tours. D moved for summary judgment on the grounds that P's information was not confidential. At the hearing on the motion, the court raised the question of whether the value of P's claims exceeded $50,000, the jurisdictional minimum for a diversity action. In addition to damages for the two A.F.A. customers D already took on tour, P sought recovery of damages P might suffer in light of D's continued interest in the tour business, noting that D had escorted approximately 1500 clients while employed by P. P stated that a 10-customer tour would generate more than $50,000. Further, P asked for punitive damages in the amount of $250,000. The court granted D's motion and dismissed the case. P appeals.

Issue. Was the court's dismissal for lack of jurisdiction improper because the court failed to:

(i)   Give P an appropriate opportunity to show that it satisfied the jurisdictional amount?

(ii)   Apply the proper standard to P's requests for damages and injunctive relief?

Held. (i) Yes. (ii) Yes. Judgment vacated and case remanded.

♦   In determining the jurisdictional amount, the sum claimed by the plaintiff controls if the claim is made in good faith. To support a dismissal, it must appear to a legal certainty that a claim is actually for less than the jurisdictional amount.

♦   In a misappropriation of trade secrets case, damages may be measured by a plaintiff's losses or by a defendant's unjust profits. Where punitive damages are allowed, they are included in the calculation of damages. Where an injunction is sought, the value of the claim is determined by referring to the right for which protection is sought and measuring the impairment the injunction will prevent; past and future potential harm may be considered by the court.

- Here, P was not afforded an appropriate and reasonable opportunity to show good faith in his belief that a recovery in excess of the jurisdictional amount was possible. On the present record, the court could not determine to a legal certainty that P's claims did not exceed the minimum required.

- In addition, injunctive relief would address not only customer solicitation but any other use of the information, such as D's sale of P's client list.

---

c. **Injunctive relief.** In *McCarty v. Amoco Pipeline Co.*, 595 F.2d 389 (7th Cir. 1979), Amoco Pipeline Co. sued in state court in Indiana to condemn an easement for a pipeline across land owned by McCarty. McCarty filed no objections, and the court entered an order condemning the easement and appointing appraisers to assess the property. The appraisers valued the property at $1,625, and this sum was deposited with the court. McCarty filed exceptions to the appraisals, which entitled him to a jury trial on the value question. Subsequently, McCarty moved that the state court reconsider its original order of condemnation, arguing that Amoco was not taking the property for a public use. The state court overruled the motion, and McCarty took no appeal. Instead, McCarty brought a new action in state court, based on the same theory that the taking was not for a public use, and asking that Amoco be enjoined from using the land for its pipeline. Amoco removed the action to federal court, and McCarty's motion to remand, on the ground that the required amount in controversy was not present, was denied. McCarty contended that, because the value to him of the matter in controversy did not exceed $10,000, the jurisdictional minimum amount required by 28 U.S.C. section 1332 was not present. The district court sustained its jurisdiction over the case by evaluating the matter in controversy from Amoco's viewpoint. The court held that a federal court may view the jurisdictional amount from the perspective of either party. The court reasoned that although it may be true that the "plaintiff viewpoint" rule results in some degree of certainty and simplicity of application, the interests of equity and fairness as well as the purposes behind the removal statute would be well served by allowing McCarty's claim to be evaluated for jurisdictional purposes by applying the "either viewpoint" rule. Here, Amoco showed by an unchallenged affidavit that the pecuniary result to Amoco that the judgment prayed for would exceed the jurisdictional amount. Thus, removal was proper and the district court had jurisdiction.

D. SUBJECT MATTER JURISDICTION OF THE FEDERAL COURTS—FEDERAL QUESTIONS

1. **Title 28, United States Code, Section 1331(a):** "The district courts shall have original jurisdiction of all civil actions arising under the Constitution, laws, or treaties of the United States. . . ."

2. Federal Question Arising from Anticipated Defense--

Louisville & Nashville Railroad Co. v. Mottley, 211 U.S. 149 (1908).

Facts. Mottley (P) sued the Railroad (D) for breach of contract in the cancellation of a "free ride for lifetime" ticket held by P as a settlement in a prior tort action by P against D. In order to gain federal jurisdiction, P asserted in his complaint that D would assert as a defense a law just passed by Congress outlawing certain types of lifetime tickets. D filed a demurrer to P's complaint for failing to state a cause of action. Ignoring the issue raised by the litigants, the United States Supreme Court, on appeal on their own motion, raised the issue of whether the federal court had jurisdiction to entertain the case.

Issue. May a plaintiff obtain federal jurisdiction by alleging in his complaint that the defendant in his answer will raise a federal question that would give the federal court federal question jurisdiction?

Held. No. Judgment reversed and case remanded with orders to dismiss for lack of federal jurisdiction.

♦ P's complaint must allege and show that an essential element of P's breach of contract suit against D arises under a law or treaty of the United States.

♦ Federal jurisdiction cannot be granted here on the basis of the anticipated federal defense. The complaint did not show that an essential element of P's breach of contract suit against D arose under a law or treaty of the United States—only that there is some chance that a federal question might, at some future time, have to be litigated in the course of this suit.

Comment. Federal jurisdiction must be determined from the complaint alone, and jurisdiction that is invoked by the plaintiff's bringing in a federal issue not necessarily a part of his immediate cause of action does not suffice. To invoke the federal question jurisdiction of the federal courts, a plaintiff must assert that a right explicitly protected by the Constitution, laws, or treaties of the United States has been violated.

3. Actions "Arising Under" Copyright Act--

T.B. Harms Co. v. Eliscu, 339 F.2d 823 (2d Cir. 1964), *cert. denied,* 381 U.S. 915 (1965).

Facts. Harms (P) brought this action in federal court for equitable and declaratory relief against Eliscu (D). Jurisdiction was predicated on 28 U.S.C. section 1338, which grants federal courts exclusive jurisdiction of any civil action "arising under" the copyright laws of the United States. P had acquired a composer's publication rights to the music and lyrics of four copyrighted songs. D, a lyricist employed to write lyrics for the songs in question, allegedly assigned his rights to the existing and renewal copyrights of the songs to P in return for certain royalties on June 30, 1933. When the copyrights were about to expire, the composer's children assigned their rights in the renewal copyrights to P. But D, by an instrument dated February 19, 1962, and recorded in the Copyright Office, assigned his rights to another. D also filed an action in a state court for a declaration that he owned a one-third interest in the renewal copyrights and for an accounting. In the federal action, D moved to dismiss P's complaint for failure to state a claim on which relief can be granted and for lack of federal jurisdiction. The district court dismissed the complaint for lack of federal jurisdiction, since there was no evidence to support a claim of actual or threatened infringement. P appeals.

Issue. Did the district court have jurisdiction over this cause of action?

Held. No. Judgment affirmed.

- In *Osborn v. Bank of the United States*, 22 U.S. (9 Wheat) 738 (1824), Chief Justice Marshall construed the language "arising under" in the context of Article III of the Constitution broadly. He indicated that it granted federal courts jurisdiction in every case in which federal law furnished a necessary ingredient to the claim even though antecedent and uncontested. The Supreme Court, though, has long given a narrower definition to the "arising under" language in statutes defining the jurisdiction of lower federal courts.

- In explaining which suits arise under the copyright and patent laws, Justice Holmes stated that "a suit arises under the law that creates the cause of action." As the Holmes creation test explains, the federal courts have authority for hearing copyright infringement actions, since such actions are clearly authorized by the Copyright Act and, thus, unquestionably within the scope of section 1338.

- Here, P's claim is not within Holmes's definition. The copyright statute and regulations create no explicit right of action to enforce or rescind assignments of copyrights, nor do they specify a cause of action to determine ownership. It is true that federal civil claims have been "inferred" from federal statutes labeling behavior criminal or otherwise regulating it. Such statutes usually impose a federal duty or create some express remedy as well. Notwithstanding, the relevant copyright statute provision, 17 U.S.C. section 28, merely authorizes an assignment by written instrument and thus no cause of action can be inferred.

- Finally, even though a claim is created by state law, a case may "arise under" a law of the United States if the complaint discloses a need to determine the application or meaning of such a law. P's claim does not meet this test.

Comment. Federal courts may exercise jurisdiction over a case within Article III of the Constitution only when a federal statute grants jurisdiction. Thus, there must be a statutory basis, express or implied, for jurisdiction.

---

4. "Arising Under" Test--

Merrell Dow Pharmaceuticals Inc. v. Thompson, 478 U.S. 804 (1986).

Facts. The Thompsons (Ps) sued Merrell Dow Pharmaceuticals (D) in state court alleging that their child was born with deformities resulting from the mother's ingestion of Bendectin during pregnancy. Five counts alleged negligence, breach of warranty, strict liability, fraud, and gross negligence and one count alleged that D violated the federal Food, Drug, and Cosmetic Act ("FDCA") and that the violation constituted a rebuttable presumption of negligence. D filed for removal to federal district court on the ground that the action was founded in part on a claim "arising under" the laws of the United States. After removal, Ps moved to remand to state court on the ground that the federal court lacked subject matter jurisdiction. The federal district court denied Ps' motion to remand but granted Ps' motion to dismiss on forum non conveniens grounds. The court of appeals reversed, holding that the FDCA does not create a private cause of action and that Ps' right to relief did not depend necessarily on a substantial question of federal law; *i.e.,* the jury could find that D was negligent without finding a violation of the FDCA. The Supreme Court granted certiorari.

Issue. Does the incorporation of a federal standard in a state law private action, when Congress has intended that there not be a federal private action for violations of that federal standard, make the action one arising under federal law for purposes of federal jurisdiction?

Held. No. Judgment affirmed.

♦ Most cases brought under the federal question jurisdiction of the federal courts are those in which federal law creates the cause of action. A case may also arise where the vindication of a right under state law necessarily turns on the construction of a federal law—the presence of a federal issue in a state-created cause of action. Although the parties agree that there is no federal cause of action for FDCA violations, Ps argue that the presence of a federal issue should confer federal question jurisdiction.

♦ However, the mere presence of a federal issue in a state cause of action does not automatically confer federal question jurisdiction.

♦ Some combination of the following factors that incorporate the settled framework for evaluating whether a federal cause of action lies is present: (i) Ps are not part of the class for whose benefit the statute was passed; (ii) legislative intent reveals no congressional purpose for a private cause of action; (iii) a federal cause of action would not advance the underlying purposes of the legislative scheme; (iv) Ps' cause of action is a subject traditionally relegated to state law.

♦ To provide a federal remedy for the violation of the federal statute would flout congressional intent. Because a violation of a federal statute is said to be a rebuttable presumption or a proximate cause under state law, to conclude that the federal courts might nevertheless exercise federal question jurisdiction would similarly undermine congressional intent.

♦ Ps argue that there is a strong federal interest in uniformity of interpretation of federal statutes. However, this interest is safeguarded by this Court's power to review the decision of a federal issue in a state cause of action.

Dissent (Brennan, White, Marshall, Blackmun, JJ.). There may be federal question jurisdiction even when the right asserted and the remedy sought by the plaintiff are state-created. Ps asserted as their only basis for finding D negligent that negligence per se was established by D's labeling of the drug in violation of the FDCA. As pleaded, Ps' right to relief depended on the construction or application of United States law. The fact that Congress did not create a private federal remedy should not affect jurisdiction unless the reasons for withholding the remedy are also reasons for withholding jurisdiction. The majority did not examine this. Congress recognized the importance of uniformity and of applying federal law correctly to make it more likely that federal laws would shape behavior in the way Congress intended. Thus, a case like this "arises under" federal law within the meaning of section 1331. Given that Congress structured the FDCA so that all express remedies are provided by the federal courts, it seems rather strange to conclude that it either flouts or undermines congressional intent for the federal courts to adjudicate a private state law remedy that is based upon a violation of the FDCA.

E. SUBJECT MATTER JURISDICTION OF THE FEDERAL COURTS— SUPPLEMENTAL CLAIMS AND PARTIES

1. **In General.** In addition to the limited subject matter jurisdiction conferred upon the federal courts by 28 U.S.C. sections 1331 and 1332, the federal courts have declared themselves, by judicial fiat arising out of necessity, competent forums for the consideration of nonfederal, nondiversity legal questions when the determination of such questions is necessary to the complete adjudication of a suit legitimately before the federal courts. Formerly known as the doctrines of pendent and ancillary jurisdiction, in 1990, these doctrines were collectively named "supplemental jurisdiction."

2. **Pendent Jurisdiction.** The concept of pendent federal jurisdiction is based upon the logical notion that often the consideration of nonfederal questions in a case will be necessary and desirable to disposition of a federal claim before the federal courts. Federal jurisdiction is said to extend to the whole litigation, not just isolated federal parts of it.

3. **Ancillary Jurisdiction.** The basic idea behind ancillary jurisdiction of the federal courts is that the court acquires jurisdiction of a case in its entirety, and hence may, as an incident to the plaintiff's claim, possess jurisdiction over matters such as counterclaims, cross-claims, or third-party claims of which it would otherwise not have cognizance if they were presented independently.

4. **Supplemental Jurisdiction.** In 1990, Congress combined the doctrines of ancillary and supplemental jurisdiction under the name "supplemental jurisdiction." The statute grants supplemental jurisdiction over all claims that "form part of the same case or controversy under Article III," and explicitly authorizes supplemental jurisdiction over "claims that involve the joinder or intervention of additional parties." [28 U.S.C. §1367]

5. **Common Nucleus of Operative Fact--**

United Mine Workers of America v. Gibbs, 383 U.S. 715 (1966).

Facts. Gibbs (P) sued the United Mine Workers of America (D) in federal court for interference with both his employment contract and a separate haulage contract, both contracts relating to a union that was a rival of D. P's claims were based on both federal and state law. After a jury verdict for P under both legal theories, the trial court set aside the damages under the haulage contract and held that the damages based on the employment contract were sustainable only on the state law claim. D appealed, claiming that the district court improperly entertained jurisdiction of the state law claim, but the court of appeals affirmed. The Supreme Court granted certiorari.

Issue. May federal courts hear state claims when they are derived from a common nucleus of operative fact that gives rise to a substantial federal claim?

Held. Yes. Judgment reversed, however, on other grounds.

♦ Federal court power over state claims, termed "pendent jurisdiction," exists wherever the relationship between a federal and state claim justifies a conclusion that the entire action before the court is one constitutional "case"; *i.e.,* the claims must derive from a common nucleus of operative fact.

♦ Pendent jurisdiction is a doctrine of discretion, not one of right, and is governed by consideration of judicial economy, convenience, and fairness to litigants. Thus, although P's federal claims ultimately failed and the district court could have dismissed the state claim, it was not an abuse of discretion for it to fail to do so.

Comment. Statutory law as well as the Constitution may limit a federal court's jurisdiction over nonfederal pendent party claims. In *Owen Equipment & Erection Co. v. Kroger,* 437 U.S. 365 (1978), the Court held that the requirement of complete diversity of citizenship cannot be circumvented by the exercise of pendent party jurisdiction. In *Aldinger v. Howard,* 427 U.S. 1 (1976), the Court held that pendent party jurisdiction cannot be exercised if Congress has expressly or by implication negated its existence. In *Finley v. United States,* 490 U.S. 545 (1989), however, the Court held that in cases arising under federal law, federal courts cannot exercise jurisdiction over parties sued under state law absent express statutory authorization. Congress effectively overruled *Finley* by enacting the Supplemental Jurisdiction Act, which provides the express statutory authorization found lacking by the Court in *Finley.*

Executive Software of North America, Inc. v. United States District Court for the Central District of California, 24 F.3d 1545 (9th Cir. 1994).

Facts. Page (P), a black female, filed a complaint in California state court alleging racial and religious discrimination by her previous employer, Executive Software of North America, Inc. (D). P alleged two federal causes of action and three causes of action under California state law. D removed to federal court based on the federal claims. Citing *United Mine Workers of America v. Gibbs, supra*, the district court subsequently remanded the state law claims. D petitioned the Ninth Circuit Court of Appeals for a writ of mandamus to compel the district court to retain jurisdiction over the supplemental state law claims.

Issue. Did the district court err in remanding the state law claims?

Held. Yes. Writ of mandamus granted and remand order vacated.

♦   Supplemental jurisdiction over pendent state law claims is conferred upon federal courts under 28 U.S.C. section 1367(a). Section 1367(c) provides the exclusive means by which supplemental jurisdiction can be declined. Therefore, a court may only decline to exercise supplemental jurisdiction if it finds that one of the four instances listed in section 1367(c) applies.

♦   Section 1367(c) permits remand when (i) the claim raises a novel or complex issue of state law, (ii) the state law claim "substantially predominates," (iii) the federal claims are dismissed, or (iv) "in exceptional circumstances, there are other compelling reasons for declining jurisdiction."

♦   The district court did not provide statutory reasons for its remand in this case, but instead simply cited *Gibbs*. It is clear that the state claims did not meet any of the listed exceptions in section 1367(c). The court did not indicate any exceptional circumstances or compelling reasons for declining jurisdiction under section 1367(c)(4), or engage in any analysis of *Gibbs* values. Therefore, remand was inappropriate.

Dissent. The district court committed no error unless it relied on an unauthorized ground in exercising its discretion to remand. The record does not tell us which ground the court relied upon.

F.   SUBJECT MATTER JURISDICTION OF THE FEDERAL COURTS—REMOVAL

1.   **In General.** Federal jurisdiction is exclusive only in rare cases. Most cases that possess all the necessary attributes for federal jurisdiction may be brought in a

state court by the plaintiff. If this occurs, the defendant has the option of remaining in state court or removing the case to federal court.

2. **Removal of Federal Question Cases.** Generally, when the plaintiff's state cause of action is based upon a substantial federal question, the defendant may remove the action to the federal district court without regard to the citizenship of the parties, as long as the requisite jurisdictional amount is in controversy. "Any civil action of which the district courts have original jurisdiction founded on a claim or right arising under the Constitution, treaties or laws of the United States shall be removable without regard to the citizenship or residence of the parties. . . ." [28 U.S.C. §1441(b)]

3. **Removal of Diversity Cases.** Diversity cases brought by the plaintiff in a state court are removable to the corresponding federal district court only if none of the parties in interest properly joined and served as defendants is a citizen of the state in which the plaintiff has brought his action. [28 U.S.C. §1441(b)] Since the only justification in theory for diversity jurisdiction of the federal courts is a desire to avoid state court prejudice against out-of-state citizens, if the plaintiff has chosen a state court in a state of which the defendant is a citizen, there is no remaining justification for federal court intervention. Therefore, the defendant may not remove in such a case. Note that a case can be removed only if the required amount in controversy in diversity cases is also met.

4. **Derivative Nature of Removal Jurisdiction.** It is often repeated that "removal jurisdiction is strictly a derivative jurisdiction." This means that only those actions that are properly filed in the state court are removable—if the plaintiff mistakenly files his action in an improper state court, the defendant may *not* remove to the corresponding federal court, even if such is a proper court. It is said that there is no proper state jurisdiction from which the federal jurisdiction can "derive." The state court must dismiss the action, and the plaintiff must thereafter commence a proper action if the defendant is to have the option of removing to the federal courts.

5. **Separate and Independent Claims--**

Borough of West Mifflin v. Lancaster, 45 F.3d 780 (3d Cir. 1995).

Facts. Two shopping mall patrons (Ps) alleged that they had been "harassed, threatened, and assaulted" by mall security guards and by a Borough of West Mifflin police officer who arrested them. Ps filed suit against the borough, the police officer, the security guards, and the mall owners for assault, wrongful arrest, malicious prosecution, and negligence. Along with the state law claims, Ps alleged violation of 42 U.S.C. section 1983, arguing that the municipal defendants (the borough and the police officer) and the mall owners and security officers had conspired to deprive Ps of their civil rights. The municipal defendants (Ds) removed the case to federal court on the basis of the section 1983 claim.

The district court found that state law issues predominated, and remanded the entire case, including the section 1983 claim, under 28 U.S.C. section 1441(c). Ds petitioned for a writ of mandamus arguing, that the remand order was improper.

Issue. Was remand proper under section 1441(c)?

Held. No. Petition granted.

♦ Under section 1441(c), a federal claim must be *separate and independent* from the state law claim to allow removal or remand. If the claims are not separate and independent, the court's discretion to remand under section 1441(c) pertains to only those state law claims that the court could decline to hear under section 1367, and the district court must retain the federal claim.

♦ Under *Gibbs*, supplemental state claims that "derive from a common nucleus of operative fact" are not separate and independent, and thus not within the scope of section 1441(c). In this case, the state law claims and the section 1983 claim arose from the identical series of events. The remedy sought based on the state claims is the same as that based on the federal claim—damages for the same set of alleged injuries. The state and federal claims here are not separate and independent. Judicial economy would not be served by two separate trials on identical facts.

♦ Nor can the state claims be said to "substantially predominate" allowing the court to remand them under section 1367(c)(2). Although the number of state law claims here is greater than the number of federal claims, the "substantially predominate" standard is not met by a simple numerical analysis.

Comment. For a claim to qualify for removal under section 1441(c), the federal claim must be "separate and independent" from the state claim. To qualify for supplemental jurisdiction under section 1367, a claim must "form part of the same case or controversy." This case indicates that a claim cannot meet both of these standards at the same time.

G. CHALLENGING THE SUBJECT MATTER JURISDICTION OF THE COURT

1. **Direct Attack.** Lack of subject matter jurisdiction may be asserted at any time by an interested party in federal court. The challenge to subject matter jurisdiction may be made in the answer, by notice to the court prior to final judgment, or on appeal.

2. **Collateral Attack.** Collateral attack results when a challenge is made in a subsequent trial-level action to the jurisdictional basis of the prior action. Collateral attack is more successful against a prior default judgment than a prior contested action.

V. VENUE, LOCAL AND TRANSITORY ACTIONS, AND FORUM NON CONVENIENS

A. VENUE

1. **The Concept of Venue.** Venue does not refer to jurisdiction at all. Questions of venue, as a matter of procedure, do not arise until the standard jurisdictional questions have all been answered affirmatively. Jurisdiction of the court means the inherent power to decide a case, whereas venue designates the particular district, county, or city court among a set of courts with jurisdiction that may hear and decide a case. The doctrine of venue is that set of rules that allows counsel to isolate one particular court, out of the entire set of courts with jurisdiction, in which to bring the action.

2. **Comparative Considerations for Some Venue Statutes.** Venue is purely statutory within a court system. Modern venue statutes usually try to incorporate and balance one or several of the considerations that follow.

    a. **Local action rule.** Many statutes try to preserve the idea that "local actions" should be tried locally, where particular environmental considerations will be known to the court. There is, however, considerable difference of opinion as to which types of actions are "local." Almost all courts agree that actions in which legal title to a tract of real property is in question are local actions. Beyond this, there is rarely agreement.

    b. **Convenience of witnesses.** Many venue statutes try to accommodate the witnesses to the litigation. These statutes prescribe as proper venue for such actions the place of the accrual of the cause of action, which is where most witnesses will probably reside.

    c. **Protection of the defendant.** To avoid vexatious suits costing innocent defendants great sums of money, some venue statutes prescribe as proper venue the place where one or more of the defendants reside. Such statutes are designed to deter fraudulent causes of action where the plaintiffs must undertake the expense of traveling to the defendant's residence. Similar statutes also prescribe as the proper venue for an action the defendant's "place of doing business," or the place of the defendant's incorporation.

3. **Local and Transitory Actions--**

Reasor-Hill Corp. v. Harrison, 249 S.W.2d 994 (Ark. 1952).

Facts. Planter's Flying Service (P) sued Barton in Arkansas for payment for spraying Barton's cotton crop in Missouri. Barton answered, alleging that Planter's damaged his crop by using an adulterated insecticide. Barton also filed a cross-complaint against Reasor-Hill (D), the manufacturer of the insecticide, for damages to the crop, alleging negligence on the part of D for placing on the market a chemical unsuited for spraying cotton. D brought a writ of prohibition in this action to prevent Harrison, the judge of the circuit court in Arkansas, from taking jurisdiction of Barton's cross-complaint. If the cross-complaint were not allowed in the Arkansas court, then Barton would have no remedy against D since it is an Arkansas corporation, is not authorized to do and does not do business in Missouri, and therefore cannot be sued there.

Issue. May a state court entertain a suit for damage to real property situated in another state?

Held. Yes. Writ denied.

◆   If the local action rule, which is the majority position and was first formulated in 1811 in *Livingston v. Jefferson*, were followed, Barton would be deprived of any compensation at all. D was not amenable to constructive service of process in Missouri, and would not venture into the jurisdiction of the Missouri state court until the statute of limitations had passed. Therefore, the Arkansas court properly exercised jurisdiction. The purpose of venue rules is not to deprive a plaintiff of his day in court. It is only to make sure that that day in court does not work an undue procedural hardship upon any party.

Dissent. Actions for damages to real property are, according to the majority rule, local actions that must be tried, if at all, in local courts.

Comment. In personam actions are usually "transitory," meaning that they can be maintained wherever the necessary personal jurisdiction over the defendant can be established. The one major exception to this rule is that actions for trespass to land, which are in personam in nature, are still considered by most courts to be "local" actions. This exception results from the historical tradition that only local courts should decide disputes involving local land. As *Reasor-Hill* illustrates, venue rules are not rigid; the courts will recognize venue in order to do substantial justice.

---

4.   **Venue in the Federal Courts.** Although venue in federal courts is determined by federal law, the federal court will apply the law of the state in which it is sitting to determine whether the action is "local" or "transitory" for venue purposes.

   a.   **Venue in local actions.** In "local" actions, venue is proper only in the district where the property that is the subject of the action is located. If the property is located in more than one district of the same state, the action may be brought in any such district.

1) **"Do not forward" or be subject to personal jurisdiction--**

Bates v. C & S Adjusters, Inc., 980 F.2d 865 (2d Cir. 1992).

Facts. Bates (P) received a collection notice from C & S Adjusters (D) in New York and P filed suit against D there for violations of the Fair Debt Collection Practices Act ("FDCPA"). P incurred the debt at issue while he resided in Pennsylvania. The creditor, a corporation with its principal place of business in that district, referred the debt to D, which does no regular business in New York. D had mailed the collection notice to P at his Pennsylvania address and the notice was forwarded to P in New York. D answered, asserted two affirmative defenses, counterclaimed, and moved to dismiss for improper venue. The district court granted D's motion. P appeals.

Issue. Is venue proper in a FDCPA case in a district where the debtor resides and to which a bill collector's demand for payment was forwarded?

Held. Yes. Judgment reversed and case remanded.

♦   Applying the version of 28 U.S.C. section 1391(b)(2) in force from 1966 to 1990, three district courts have held venue proper in FDCPA cases in a plaintiff's home district if a collection agency had mailed a collection notice to an address in that district or telephoned a number in that district.

♦   Under the current statute, the standard focuses on the location where events occurred.

♦   Here, the most relevant evidence, the collection notice, is located in New York.

♦   If a bill collector seeks not to be challenged for its collection process outside the place of the debtor's original residence, the envelope can be marked "do not forward." The receipt of a collection notice initiates the harmful effect of abusive debt practices and is a substantial part of the events giving rise to a claim.

---

    b.   **Venue in transitory actions.**

        1)   **In general.**

            a)   **Defendant's residence.** Whether federal subject matter jurisdiction is based on diversity or federal question, venue is proper in the district where any defendant resides, if all of the defendants reside in the same state.

            b)   **Substantial part of events, omissions, or property.** Whether federal subject matter jurisdiction is based on diversity or federal question, venue is proper in "a judicial district in which a substantial part of the events or omissions giving rise to the claim occurred, or a substantial part of the property that is the subject of the action is situated."

c) **Alternative venue.** If there is no district in which the plaintiff may otherwise bring the action, when jurisdiction is based on diversity, venue is proper in a "judicial district in which any defendant is subject to personal jurisdiction at the time the action is commenced," and when based on a federal question, venue is proper in a "judicial district in which any defendant may be found."

2) **Residence.** "Residence" has a particular meaning for venue purposes.

a) **Natural persons.** The residence of a natural person who is a citizen is her domicile—the place where she resides with the intent to remain indefinitely.

b) **Aliens.** An alien defendant is not deemed to have a residence and hence may be sued in any district in the country.

c) **Corporate defendant.** A corporate defendant is deemed a resident of each judicial district in which it is incorporated, licensed to do business, or engaged in doing business.

B. TRANSFER OF VENUE IN FEDERAL COURTS

1. **Venue Must Be Proper in Transferee Court--**

Hoffman v. Blaski, 363 U.S. 335 (1960).

Facts. Blaski (P), a citizen of Illinois, sued Hoffman (D), a citizen of Texas, for patent infringement. P served D in Texas and brought the action there. D asked for a transfer of venue to the Illinois court "in the interests of justice." P objected that, since a federal question was involved, the only proper venue was Texas, the state where the cause of action arose and where all defendants resided, that it could not have brought the action in Illinois court itself, and that by the plain words of 28 U.S.C. section 1404, transfer was therefore improper. The trial court granted the change of venue and P appealed. The circuit court reversed and D appeals.

Issue. May a change of venue be granted to a place where the plaintiff could not have brought the suit?

Held. No. Judgment affirmed.

♦ The phrase "in the interests of justice" in section 1404 does not mean that D may transfer a case to venue where P himself could not have brought it. P could not have brought his case in Illinois, so D could not transfer the case there. This is clearly expressed in the "where it might have been brought" section of 1404. The purpose of venue statutes is not to enlarge upon D's rights, or to give him options not open to P. The purpose is only to try to guarantee the cheapest and fairest trial possible in the circumstances.

Dissent (Frankfurter, Harlan, Brennan, JJ.). The statute was intended to obviate hardships resulting from operation of the ordinary rules. It should be interpreted broadly so as to give effect to convenience and justice.

Comment. The text of 28 U.S.C. section 1404 reads, "For the convenience of parties and witnesses, in the interest of justice, a district court may transfer any civil action to any other district or division where it might have been brought."

---

2. **Law of Transferor Jurisdiction Applied.** In the interest of reduction of forum shopping, the Supreme Court has ruled that in federal transfer of venue cases, the substantive law that is applied in the transferee court must be the same substantive law that the transferor court would have applied. This ruling tends to ensure that a transfer of federal venue is only a change of courtrooms rather than a change of law and possibly of outcome.

C. FORUM NON CONVENIENS

1. **In General.** Assuming a court has proper jurisdiction (*supra*) and venue (*supra*) over a cause of action, that court retains the power to refuse to hear the case anyway if, in the opinion of the court, justice would be better served were it to be tried in another venue. This doctrine of discretionary abstention is the doctrine of forum non conveniens, literally, inconvenient forum. Today, some version of this doctrine is standard practice in the federal courts and perhaps half the state court systems.

2. **Forum Non Conveniens in Federal Court--**

Piper Aircraft Co. v. Reyno, 454 U.S. 235 (1981).

Facts. An aircraft manufactured in part by Piper Aircraft Co. in Pennsylvania and Hartzell Propeller, Inc., in Ohio (Ds) crashed in Scotland, killing the pilot and all five passengers instantly. The decedents were Scottish subjects, as are their heirs and next of kin. There were no eyewitnesses. At the time of the crash, the aircraft was registered, owned, and maintained in England by an English company and operated by a Scottish air taxi service organized in the United Kingdom. The wreckage of the plane was in a hangar in England. Reyno (P), a legal secretary to the lawyer who filed the present lawsuit and who was unrelated to and did not know decedents or their survivors, filed separate wrongful death actions against Ds in California Superior Court as the court-appointed administratrix of decedents' estates. Decedents' survivors filed a separate action in England against the pilot, the owner, and the operator of the aircraft. P admits that her lawsuit was filed for the sole purpose of taking advantage of strict liability law, which is recognized under United States law but not under Scottish law. After the case was removed to a California district court and then transferred to a Pennsylvania district court, Ds moved to dismiss on grounds of forum non conveniens. The district court granted the motion but was reversed by the court of appeals on the ground that a forum non conveniens motion could be defeated by a mere showing that the substantive law that would be applied in the convenient forum is less favorable to plaintiff than the present forum. Ds appeal.

Issue. Should the possibility of an unfavorable change in law, by itself, bar dismissal on forum non conveniens grounds, and, if not, did the district court otherwise abuse its discretion in granting dismissal on forum non conveniens grounds?

Held. No. Judgment reversed.

♦ The possibility of an unfavorable change in the substantive law ordinarily should not be given conclusive or even substantial weight in the forum non conveniens decision; otherwise, the doctrine would lose much of its flexibility and, in fact, would become virtually useless. Also, choice-of-law issues that might not otherwise need to be resolved would have to be in order to decide forum non conveniens motions.

♦ On the other hand, if the remedy provided by the alternative forum is so clearly inadequate or unsatisfactory that it is no remedy at all, the unfavorable change in law may be given substantial weight; the district court may conclude that dismissal would not be in the "interests of justice." Here, the remedies provided by Scottish law do not fall within this category.

♦ The forum non conveniens determination is committed to the sound discretion of the trial court and may be reversed only when there is a clear abuse of discretion.

♦ In granting Ds' motion, the district court relied on the balancing test set forth in *Gulf Oil Corp. v. Gilbert*, 330 U.S. 501 (1947). In that case, this Court said that there is ordinarily a strong presumption in favor of the plaintiff's choice of forum, which may be disturbed only when the private interest (affecting the convenience of the litigants) and the public interest (affecting the convenience of the forum) clearly point toward trial in the alternative forum. The presumption, however, applies with less force when the plaintiff is foreign, because, as the central purpose of any forum non conveniens inquiry is to ensure that the trial is convenient, when a plaintiff selects a *foreign* forum, it is not reasonable to assume that this choice is convenient to such plaintiff.

♦ *The private interest factors* weigh in favor of dismissal because fewer evidentiary problems would arise if the trial were held in Scotland. A large portion of the relevant evidence is located in Great Britain. Ds submitted affidavits describing the evidentiary problems they would face if trial were held in the United States, and the aircraft's owner and operator would not be able to be impleaded as third-party defendants in a United States court.

♦ ***The public interest factors*** also weigh in favor of dismissal because of choice-of-law problems (Pennsylvania law would apply to one D and Scottish law to the other D if the case were tried in the Pennsylvania district court) and the fact that Scotland has a very strong interest in this litigation (the accident occurred in Scottish airspace, all decedents were Scottish, and, apart from Ds, all potential plaintiffs and defendants are Scottish or English).

---

3. **Concept of Conditional Dismissal.** The modern prevalence of the doctrine of forum non conveniens has caused some confusion because the operation of the doctrine and the running of the statute of limitations has never been made clear. More than once, a plaintiff has had his case dismissed according to forum non conveniens, only to find that in the interim the statute of limitations had run, so that the defendant was protected from further suit in the more "convenient forum." Indeed, it has happened that the plaintiff has had his case dismissed according to forum non conveniens, only to find that according to statute there is no other forum proper for the bringing of his action. These unnecessary hardships caused the development of the concept of ***conditional dismissal***—dismissal for forum non conveniens is specifically conditioned upon a promise by the defendant to submit to suit in another venue, whether or not that venue is statutorily prescribed and whether or not the statute of limitations has run. Such a doctrine is recognized in the federal courts and perhaps half of those state courts that accept the doctrine of forum non conveniens.

4. **Other Attacks upon Inconvenient Forum.** Forum non conveniens is not the only possible attack upon the plaintiff's choice of venue for his action. Attacks commonly used in those forums that do not use forum non conveniens are:

   a. **Transfer of venue.** In states not explicitly recognizing the full-blown doctrine of forum non conveniens, the void is partially filled by the motion for a transfer of venue. Upon a strong showing that fair trial is impossible in the chosen venue, the defendant may be allowed to defeat the plaintiff's original venue in favor of a more convenient one.

   b. **Collateral injunction.** The defendant may also attack a choice of venue collaterally, in another state court, in an attempt to obtain an injunction against pursuit of a case in a particular forum. Such collateral attacks are rarely used since they are clumsy, expensive, and time-consuming. Moreover, they are enforceable only if the issuing court somehow can subject the plaintiff or his property to its own jurisdiction or contempt power.

c.   **Stay of proceedings.** Finally, a motion by the defendant that proceedings be stayed for an indefinite time in a particular venue often acts as indirect pressure upon the plaintiff to refile his action in another venue. Often, these stays of proceedings are explicitly recognized to be coercive in nature—"back door forum non conveniens"—in those states that refuse to recognize explicitly the doctrine.

VI. ASCERTAINING THE APPLICABLE LAW

A. INTRODUCTION

1. **The Problem.** Litigation that occurs entirely within a state and is between citizens of that state, concerning a cause of action arising within that state, presents no problem of choosing which body of substantive law should govern the outcome. But as soon as litigation concerns citizens of more than one state, or the cause of action arises in an interstate transaction, the forum court must make a conscious choice about which body of substantive law to apply: that of the state of the plaintiff? of the defendant? where the cause of action arose? federal common law? These choice-of-law problems, more closely examined in the course on conflicts of law, are of major importance in federal diversity litigation, where, by the very nature of the case, at least two bodies of state substantive law may be relevant. But choice-of-law problems also arise in state courts, when these courts are called upon to litigate federal questions not brought in the federal courts. This section examines the major premises behind the solution of choice-of-law problems that commonly arise in federal and state courts.

2. **The Goal.** The goal of the choice-of-law rules of the various court systems of the United States is to discourage forum shopping by either of the two parties to a suit. Forum shopping is the conscious choice of one court over another for reasons of more favorable substantive legal doctrines, when either of two possible court systems has jurisdiction and venue. The practice conflicts with the oft-expressed rule that procedure should not be determinative of outcome.

B. STATE LAW IN THE FEDERAL COURTS

1. **Historical Background.** Section 1652 of 28 U.S.C. (formerly section 775 of 28 U.S.C.) provides: "The laws of the several states, except where the Constitution or treaties of the United States or Acts of Congress otherwise require or provide, shall be regarded as rules of decision in civil actions in the courts of the United States, in cases where they apply." In *Swift v. Tyson*, 41 U.S. (16 Pet.) 1 (1842), the Supreme Court interpreted this statute very narrowly, reasoning that state rules of decision had to be applied in the federal courts *only* when the state rules were in the form of statutes. State decisional law did not have to be used in the federal courts. This ruling in effect required federal procedure to duplicate state procedure but allowed federal substantive law to exist apart from state substantive law.

    a. **Shortcomings of *Swift* ruling.** The shortcomings of this ruling soon became evident. The plaintiff with a case ripe for adjudication often had a choice of two distinct bodies of substantive law, one federal, the other state. The plaintiff's counsel could, by choosing the right court, weigh the outcome of the case in his favor. Indeed, it often happened that the federal rule on a legal question was directly the opposite of the state rule. In such a case, the plaintiff's choice of court could all but guarantee the outcome of the case, a circumstance alien to the very theory of civil procedure, that the choice of courtroom should have as little influence upon the eventual outcome of the case as possible.

2.   The *Erie* Doctrine—*Swift v. Tyson* Overruled--

Erie Railroad Co. v. Tompkins, 304 U.S. 64 (1938).

Facts. Tompkins (P) was walking along the Erie Railroad Co.'s (D's) right-of-way in Pennsylvania when he was struck by a bar or mail-hook extending from the side of D's passing train. P was a citizen of Pennsylvania, D a citizen of New York. P sued in New York district court. P argued that "general federal common law" should govern the legal aspects of the case; D argued that "state principles of common law" should govern. The court, following *Swift*, applied general federal common law and found for P; the court of appeals affirmed. D appeals.

Issue. When a federal court has diversity jurisdiction, should it apply federal substantive law in resolving the merits of the case?

Held. No. Judgment reversed.

♦   *Swift* construed the 1789 Judiciary Act to apply only to state statutes and not to state common law. However, the correct construction would have required federal courts sitting in diversity to apply both state statutory and case law. This construction is now the law. There is no longer a federal general common law. The doctrine of *Swift v. Tyson* was an unconstitutional assumption of powers by the federal courts that no lapse of time or respectable array of opinion should make us hesitate to correct.

♦   When a matter is governed by a specific federal statute or when a federal question is involved, federal law will apply to diversity cases.

Dissent (Butler, J.). Both parties assumed that *Swift* applied, and the Court should not overrule *Swift* without the benefit of argument.

Concurrence in part (Reed, J.). *Swift* merely held that the law to be applied in federal courts did not include decisions of local tribunals. This error may be corrected by holding that, under the Judiciary Act, local decisions are part of the law to be applied, thus interpreting a statute instead of the Constitution.

Comment. The purpose of the decision was obviously to eliminate the uncontrolled forum shopping between state and federal courts by compelling federal courts to reach the same result on nonfederal questions as state courts would have reached.

---

3. **Scope of the *Erie* Doctrine.** The essence of *Erie* is that, while federal courts are free to apply their own rules of "procedure," any issue of "substantive" law (other than a federal question) must be determined according to the laws of the state in which the federal court is located. The difficulty in applying the *Erie* doctrine is in determining whether a particular matter or issue is "substantive" (governed by state law) or merely "procedural" (governed by federal rules).

a. **Outcome-determinative test--**

Guaranty Trust Co. v. York, 326 U.S. 99 (1945).

Facts. York (P) sued the Guaranty Trust Co. (D) for alleged failure of D to protect the interests of P and others in a trust. Federal jurisdiction was based upon diversity of citizenship. D moved for summary judgment, on grounds that the state statute of limitations should control the action, and that the statute had run. P argued that statutes of limitations are procedural, hence governed by federal rather than state common law. The trial court granted summary judgment for D; the circuit court reversed, and the case went to the Supreme Court on certiorari.

Issue. When adoption of a federal procedural rule in the federal court will lead to a substantially different outcome than if the case had been brought in state court, should the federal procedural rule still be followed?

Held. No. Judgment reversed.

♦ Generally, procedure in the federal courts is governed by the Federal Rules of Civil Procedure. However, the source of substantive rights enforced by a federal court under diversity jurisdiction is the law of the states. Matters of "substance" and matters of "procedure" are not always clearly distinguishable.

♦ The question is not whether a statute of limitations is a matter of procedure but whether the statute involves a matter of substance in that the outcome of the suit is significantly affected by the federal court's disregard for the state law that would control if the suit were brought in a state court. This test may be stated thus: A rule of law is substantive within the *Erie* mandate if it "has a substantial effect upon the eventual outcome of the case."

♦ Here, the running of the statute of limitations substantially affected the outcome of the litigation. Therefore, it was substantive within the *Erie* mandate, and state law controlled. Since the state statute of limitations had run before the commencement of action, the case was properly dismissed.

Dissent (Rutledge, Murphy, JJ.). Among state courts, whether an action will be barred by a statute of limitations depends not upon the law of the state that creates the substantive right, but upon the law of the state where suit may be brought.

Comment. Under the outcome-determinative test of *York*, federal courts have been required to follow state practice in such quasi-procedural areas as the effect of res judicata, determination of date of official commencement of a lawsuit, sufficiency of minimum jurisdictional contacts, burden of proof, and conflict-of-laws rules.

---

b.   **Basic federal rights--**

Byrd v. Blue Ridge Rural Electric Cooperative, Inc., 356 U.S. 525 (1958).

Facts. Byrd (P), temporarily employed as a line worker by Blue Ridge Rural Electric Cooperative, Inc. (D), was injured in a fall from a telephone pole. In a diversity action in tort brought by P, D claimed P's sole recourse was through workers' compensation (rather than in a negligence action). Under state law, whether P was an employee of D for purposes of workers' compensation would have been decided upon the pleadings by the court alone. Under federal procedure, trial of the issue would have gone to the jury. The question arose whether state or federal law was applicable. The district court presented the question to the jury, which rendered a verdict for P. The circuit court reversed and entered judgment for D. The case came to the Supreme Court on certiorari.

Issue. When questions in a diversity suit in federal court concern the mode and form of remedy, will state procedural rules (when they affect the outcome of the suit) be allowed to override essential federal rights (*e.g.,* trial by jury)?

Held. No. Judgment reversed.

♦   The "outcome-determinative" test of *York*, while generally valid, is not the sole test to be used to separate "substance" from "procedure" for purposes of the *Erie* mandate. The preference for state law is not binding if application of such a law would deprive one party of a strongly protected federal right, even if the standard "outcome" test is met.

♦   In this case, application of state law would deprive P of a jury trial upon a major part of his case. Rather, the district court must determine for itself, using federal guidelines, whether a jury trial upon the issue is proper, keeping in mind the strong federal preference for a jury trial. As a general rule, the preference for state law must be balanced against the deprivation of federal rights resulting from application of state law, a test that is separate from, and intended to augment, the "outcome-determinative" test of *York*.

Comment. The "balance of interests" test of *Byrd* has been applied outside the realm of division of function between judge and jury in only a few cases. Federal evidence rules, contrary to corresponding state rules, were followed in the Fifth Circuit on grounds that the federal rule demonstrated "federal policy of long standing." And a foreign administrator of a domestic estate was permitted to join in an action against the estate, according to Federal Rule of Civil Procedure 43a, despite a contrary state rule, on grounds that the federal rules reflect constitutional federal policy. But state arbitration rules have been held to take precedence over different federal rules on grounds that application of federal rules would have "totally changed the outcome of the case." The most debated subject following the "balance of interests" test of *Byrd* has been whether federal courts are bound to follow state long arm statutes when attempting to obtain long arm jurisdiction over foreign corporations, or whether independent federal standards are applicable. Most decisions have applied relevant state rules, stating that there is no separate federal long arm power in diversity actions, even if due process would not thereby be offended.

---

c.   **Adherence to Federal Rules where they do not affect choice of forum--**

Hanna v. Plumer, 380 U.S. 460 (1965).

Facts. In a diversity negligence action, service of process was made upon Plumer (D) in Massachusetts by leaving process at D's place of residence with his wife. This practice is sanctioned by the Federal Rules of Civil Procedure. However, by Massachusetts law, service of process must be made personally upon the defendant. D moved for dismissal and summary judgment on grounds that state law was controlling and that the statute of limitations had run, so that Hanna (P) could no longer comply with Massachusetts service requirements. The trial court found for D; the circuit court affirmed, finding that the conflict between state and federal law was over a substantive matter. The Supreme Court granted certiorari.

Issue. In a civil action brought in federal court under diversity jurisdiction, must service of process be governed by the Federal Rules, even if the outcome is affected?

Held. Yes. Judgment reversed.

♦   Rule 4(d) of the Federal Rules of Civil Procedure was designed to control service of process in diversity actions. It relates to the practice and procedure of the district courts. D contends that under *Erie* and *York*, Massachusetts procedure should govern because it is outcome determinative. However, the *York* rule is not the sole consideration.

- The constitutional provision for a federal court system carries with it congressional power to make rules governing the practice and pleading in those courts. To hold that the Federal Rules must cease to function whenever they alter the mode of enforcing state-created rights would be to ignore this federal power.

- The difference between the two rules involved here would be of scant, if any, relevance to the choice of a forum. The choice of rule does not alter the outcome at the outset, although at this point the choice will have a marked effect.

Concurrence (Harlan, J.). *Erie* expressed profound policies affecting the notion of federalism. These policies are more significant than the oversimplified outcome-determinative test of *York* and even the forum-shopping rule of *Erie*. The proper approach in determining whether to apply a state or federal rule, whether substantive or procedural, is to inquire if the choice would substantially affect those primary decisions respecting human conduct that our constitutional system leaves to state regulation. If so, the state rule should prevail. Here, application of the federal rule would not substantially impinge on the validity of the state policy; therefore, application of the federal rule is appropriate.

Comment. In essence, the modern rule is that in case of conflict between the Federal Rules and state law, the Federal Rules control; *i.e.,* such matters are presumptively procedural. For example, in *Burlington Northern Railroad Co. v. Woods*, 480 U.S. 1 (1987), the Supreme Court found a direct conflict between an Alabama state statute, which allowed assessment of a 10% penalty on all unsuccessful appeals of money judgments, and Federal Rule of Appellate Procedure 38, which allows a penalty to be assessed only if the appeal was frivolous. The Court held that Rule 38 controlled because the matter could reasonably be classified as procedural.

---

d. No conflict between federal and state laws--

Walker v. Armco Steel Corp., 446 U.S. 740 (1980).

Facts. Walker (P), a resident of Oklahoma, was injured by an allegedly defective nail manufactured and designed by Armco Steel Corp. (D), a foreign corporation. P sued in federal district court on August 19, 1977. Service was not made on D until December, long after the 60 days elapsed that would have brought the filing within the state limitations period. D filed a motion to dismiss on the ground that the action was barred by the state statute of limitations. P claimed Federal Rule of Civil Procedure 3 governs the manner in which an action is commenced in federal court for all purposes including limitations. The district court dismissed, concluding state law applied. The court of appeals affirmed. The Supreme Court granted certiorari.

Issue. In a diversity action, should the federal court follow state law in determining when an action is commenced for the purpose of tolling the statute of limitations?

Held. Yes. Judgment affirmed.

♦   In *Ragan v. Merchants Transfer & Warehouse Co.,* 337 U.S. 530 (1949), we held that we could not give a cause of action longer life in federal court than it would have in state court without adding something to the cause of action. The service of summons statute in *Ragan*, as here, was an integral part of the state statute of limitations and part of the state law cause of action.

♦   Rule 3 is not intended to toll state statutes of limitations or displace state tolling rules. It governs the date from which the various timing requirements of the Federal Rules of Civil Procedure begin to run.

♦   Rule 3 does not replace the policy determinations found in the state law here, *i.e.,* (i) that actual service on or actual notice to the defendant establishes a deadline after which the defendant may have peace of mind, and (ii) after a certain period of time it is unfair to require a defendant to attempt to piece together a defense to an old claim. Thus, Rule 3 and the state statute are not in conflict and a *Hanna v. Plumer, supra,* analysis does not apply.

---

     e.   **Diversity and change of venue--**

Stewart Organization, Inc. v. Ricoh Corp., 487 U.S. 22 (1988).

Facts. Stewart Organization, Inc. (P) sued Ricoh Corp. (D) in district court for the Northern District of Alabama, alleging breach of a distribution contract. The contract contained a clause specifying venue only in Manhattan. D brought a motion for change of venue under 28 U.S.C. section 1404(a). P contended that Alabama law disfavored venue clauses, and that Alabama law should be applied. The district court agreed and denied the motion. The court of appeals reversed. The Supreme Court granted certiorari.

Issue. In a federal diversity suit, should federal rules, rather than state rules, apply in a motion for change of venue?

Held. Yes. Judgment affirmed and case remanded.

♦   In a federal diversity suit federal, not state, rules should apply in a motion for change of venue. When the federal rule to be applied is a statute and the statute applies to the issue before the court, the statute will be applied if it was enacted within the limits of constitutional authority.

♦   Here, section 1404(a) places discretion in the district court to adjudicate motions for transfer according to an individualized case-by-case consideration of convenience and fairness. Section 1404(a) controls the issue before the district court and it must be applied since it represents a valid exercise of Congress's authority under the Constitution to make rules governing the practice and pleading in the federal court system. Therefore the Court of Appeals should be affirmed and the case remanded so that the district court may determine in the final instance the appropriate effect under federal law of the parties' forum selection clause on respondent's section 1404(a) motion.

Concurrence (Kennedy, O'Connor, JJ.). I write to emphasize that enforcing valid forum selection clauses serves to protect the legitimate expectations of the parties and to further vital interests of the justice system.

Dissent (Scalia, J.). The validity of a forum selection clause does not fall within the scope of section 1404(a). Considering the importance of a contractual provision for which the parties bargained, along with the twin aims of the *Erie* Doctrine—discouragement of forum shopping and avoidance of inequitable administration of the laws, I believe that state law should control the question of the validity of a forum selection clause.

---

f.   Review of jury verdicts--

Gasperini v. Center for Humanities, Inc., 518 U.S. 415 (1996).

Facts. Gasperini (P), a journalist who was assigned to cover events in Central America, sold 300 slide transparencies to the Center for Humanities (D) for use in an educational videotape. D was to return the transparencies when it finished using them, but upon completion of the project, it could not locate them. P sued for damages and alleged that the value of each lost transparency was $1,500. The case was filed in federal court due to diversity of citizenship of the parties, but New York law controlled substantive matters. The jury awarded P $450,000 in compensatory damages ($1,500 for each of the 300 slides). Under the law of New York, appellate courts have the power to review the size of a jury verdict and to order new trials when the jury's award "deviates materially from what would be reasonable compensation." D moved for a new trial, arguing that the jury verdict was excessive. The district court denied the motion, but the court of appeals vacated the jury's verdict based on its application of the New York law. The Supreme Court granted certiorari.

Issue. May a federal court, applying a state law that provides for appellate review of a jury verdict, review a jury verdict despite the Seventh Amendment's prohibition of federal court review of a jury's findings of fact?

Held. Yes. Case remanded.

♦   Under the Seventh Amendment, "no fact tried by a jury shall be otherwise re-examined in any Court of the United States, than according to the rules of the common law." P argues that the New York law allowing appellate court review of the size of jury verdicts is procedural and incompatible with the Seventh Amendment, so it cannot be given effect in an action in federal court. D argues that the state law's "deviates materially" standard is a substantive standard that must be applied by federal appellate courts in diversity cases.

♦ To discourage forum shopping, *Erie* precludes a recovery in federal court that would be significantly larger than the recovery would have been in state court. P concedes that a statutory cap on damages would be considered substantive for *Erie* purposes, but argues that application of the state law in this case would shift factfinding responsibility from the jury to the appellate court in violation of the Seventh Amendment.

♦ We find nothing in the Seventh Amendment that prohibits appellate review of a trial court's denial of a motion to set aside a verdict as excessive. New York's law controlling compensatory awards can be given effect without detriment to the Seventh Amendment if the review standard set out by the state statute is applied by the federal trial court judge, with appellate review of the trial court's ruling limited to review for "abuse of discretion."

♦ Because the district court here did not apply the New York standard, the decision must be vacated and remanded to the district court to apply the "deviates materially" standard.

Dissent (Stevens, J.). The Seventh Amendment does not limit the power of a federal appellate court sitting in diversity to decide whether a jury's verdict is excessive as defined by state law.

Dissent (Scalia, J., Rehnquist, C.J., Thomas, J.). Reexamination of facts found by a jury can only be undertaken by the trial court. Appellate review is restricted to review of the verdict for errors of law. The Seventh Amendment provides a specific protection against federal appellate courts reexamining facts found by a jury.

Comment. The majority tries to accommodate *Erie* by applying federal procedural law (the Reexamination Clause) in a way that serves the substantive aims of the New York law.

C. THE PROBLEM OF ASCERTAINING STATE LAW

1. **The Problem in Brief.** Given that federal courts in most diversity cases are required by *Erie* to apply state substantive law, how does a federal court determine precisely what is state law upon an issue? On many issues, state decisions will be poorly reasoned, outdated, or totally nonexistent. The problem of discerning "state law" can be significant.

2. **The Black Letter Rule.** The federal court must apply the law of a state as that law is either (i) declared by statute and interpreted by the highest court of the state or (ii) judicially declared by the highest court of the state. The federal court must refrain from "making" state law by reinterpreting state opinions or by superimposing its own prejudices over those of the state's highest court. When the decisions of the state's highest court are very old or totally nonexistent, the federal court may either turn to lower court decisions (if available) or, as a last resort, try to declare state law as it would be declared by the highest state court if the issue were to be presently tried before it.

3. **Determining Which State's Law Governs.** Federal courts apply the conflicts-of-law rules of the states in which they sit. [*See Klaxon Co. v. Stentor Electric Manufacturing Co.*, 313 U.S. 487 (1941)]

4. **Not Obliged to Apply State Law--**

Mason v. American Emery Wheel Works, 241 F.2d 906 (1st Cir. 1957).

Facts. Mason (P) sued American Emery Wheel Works (D) in federal district court based on diversity. P alleged D negligently manufactured, inspected, and tested a wheel designed for attachment to a bench grinder that caused P's injuries. D manufactured the wheel in Rhode Island, sold it to a New Jersey corporation that manufactured the bench grinder in Massachusetts, and the grinder eventually was purchased by P's Mississippi employer. D answered that P failed to state a claim upon which relief might be granted and that it owed no duty to P as there was no privity of contract between P and D. At the conclusion of P's case, D moved to dismiss under Federal Rule of Civil Procedure 41(b). The order to dismiss was entered. P appeals.

Issue. Is the district court obliged to apply state local law to determine tort liability, if any, of a manufacturer to one not in privity of contract with him?

Held. No. Order vacated and case remanded.

♦ The district court applied state law as declared in *Ford Motor Co. v. Myers,* 117 So. 362 (Miss. 1928).

♦ It is not necessary that a case be explicitly overruled to lose its persuasive force as an indication of what the law is. *Ford* has not been recently reconsidered by the Mississippi Supreme Court, but in *E.I. Du Pont De Nemours & Co. v. Ladner,* 73 So. 2d 249 (Miss. 1954), that court noted the "modern trend in the area" and quoted with approval recent authorities in support of the "modern doctrine."

♦ Should the Mississippi Supreme Court have an occasion to address this issue, we have no doubt it will declare itself in agreement with the overwhelming weight of authority as expressed in *MacPherson v. Buick Motor Co.,* 111 N.E. 1050 (N.Y. 1916).

Concurrence. We present a difficult problem for district judges when they must apply the *Erie* doctrine to situations where the considerations between conflicting holdings and dicta are not as clearly defined as they are here.

---

5. **Forecasting State Decisional Law.** Generally, a federal court sitting in diversity looks to the decisions of the highest court of the forum state as the final authority on state law. In the absence of controlling precedent by the state's highest court, a federal court must ***predict*** how the state's highest court would decide were it confronted with the issue at hand. The decisions of the state's lower courts and other federal courts should be considered, but are not conclusive. [*See* McKenna v. Ortho Pharmaceutical Corp., 622 F.2d 657 (3d Cir.), *cert. denied*, 449 U.S. 976 (1980)] When it appears to a federal court that a cause before it involves determinative issues of state law to which there are no clear controlling decisions of the state's highest court, it may certify the issue to the state's highest court for an answer. This procedure, however, is the exception rather than the rule.

6. **Use of Intermediate Court Decisions.** No general rule about the use of intermediate court decisions in federal cases to determine state substantive law may be laid down. Most courts, faced with a situation in which the only state decision in point is that of an intermediate court, would at the very least find the decision relevant. Many federal courts would find such a decision decisive, unless somehow out of tune with current judicial thinking. This is probably the preferable view, since it saves the federal court from the task of imputing to the state court a certain legal viewpoint, and at the same time takes from the federal court the temptation of "making" state law.

D. FEDERAL "COMMON LAW"

1. **In General.** The *Erie* mandate did not destroy entirely the concept of an independent federal common law, separate from that of any state. *Erie* did not affect the present notion that in federal litigation (and even state litigation in which federal rights, duties, statutes, or mandates are in question) the body of federal law known as federal decisional common law should be determinative. As a rule of thumb, *Erie* is applicable only to actions not involving federal questions, while federal common law is determinative of federal question actions.

2. **Federal Function--**

Clearfield Trust Co. v. United States, 318 U.S. 363 (1943).

Facts. The United States (P) sued Clearfield Trust Co. (D) to recover the value of a stolen government payroll check cashed by D. D had not suspected forgery and P did not inform

D of the forgery until eight months after P learned the intended recipient had not received the check. The district court held the parties' rights were to be determined by state law, and the court dismissed P's complaint based on Pennsylvania law that barred P from recovery because P had unreasonably delayed in giving notice of the forgery. The court of appeals reversed. The Supreme Court granted certiorari.

Issue. Are the rights of the parties to be determined by state law when an important United States interest is at stake?

Held. No. Judgment affirmed.

♦ Under federal precedent, unreasonable delay has been ruled not to bar the bringing of an action for fraud.

♦ When the federal government exercises a constitutional function, the rights enjoyed under the exercise are governed by uniform federal law.

♦ The issuance of commercial paper is on a vast scale with transactions commonly occurring in several states. The application of state law would subject the rights and duties of the United States to exceptional uncertainty. The desirability of a uniform rule is plain.

---

3. **Burden of Proof.** In *Bank of America National Trust & Savings Association v. Parnell,* 352 U.S. 29 (1956), the Court held that federal law does not apply where the federal interests in a suit are incidental and where fundamental federal rights or actions are not in question. Bank of America sued Parnell and Rocco to recover the value of bonds stolen by Rocco and presented for payment by Parnell, acting as Rocco's agent. Under Pennsylvania law the burden of proof fell on Parnell to show a good faith belief in Rocco's good title. Under federal precedent, the burden of proof fell on Bank of America to show Parnell's knowledge that the bonds had been stolen by Rocco. The court indicated that if in the course of litigation it became necessary to determine whether the government bonds were properly presented for payment and properly processed, then federal law governed these issues, since federal rights and actions were directly in controversy.

4. **Choice of Law Where Contract Involves No Federal Liability or Responsibility--**

Miree v. DeKalb County, 433 U.S. 25 (1977).

Facts. Miree (P) and others, the survivors of deceased passengers of an airplane crash, brought this action against DeKalb County (D), the owner of the airport. P sought to impose liability on D as third-party beneficiaries to contracts between it and the Federal Aviation Administration ("FAA"). The terms of the contract stated that D agreed to restrict the use of land adjacent to the airport to activities compatible with airport operations. P asserted that D breached the contract by maintaining a garbage dump adjacent to the airport, and that the cause of the crash was the ingestion of birds swarming from the dump into the jet engines of the aircraft. Applying Georgia law, the district court found that the breach of contract claim was barred by D's governmental immunity and dismissed the complaint. The court of appeals reversed, holding that federal common law, rather than state law, controlled the contract's interpretation. D appealed.

Issue. In interpreting the terms of a contract in which the United States is a party, can a court apply state law when the contract does not involve the liability or responsibilities of the United States?

Held. Yes. Judgment reversed.

♦ The litigation here raises no question regarding the liability or responsibilities of the United States under the contract. The only issue is whether P and the others as third-party beneficiaries to the contract have standing to sue.

♦ While federal common law may govern where a uniform national rule is necessary to further the interests of the federal government, the application of federal common law here would promote no federal interests.

---

5. **Liability of Government Contractors--**

Boyle v. United Technologies Corp., 487 U.S. 500 (1988).

Facts. During a military training exercise, a United States Marine helicopter crashed in water. Its co-pilot, Boyle, could not escape, and he drowned. His father (P) brought a federal court diversity action against the Sikorsky Division of United Technologies Corporation (D), which built the helicopter. P alleged, under Virginia tort law, that D had defectively repaired the device which allegedly malfunctioned and caused the crash and that D had defectively designed the co-pilot's emergency escape system. The jury returned a general verdict in P's favor. On appeal, the court reversed and remanded the case with instructions to enter judgment for D, finding that P had failed to meet his burden of showing that it was D's work as opposed to work done by the Navy that had contributed to the crash. The court of appeals held that D could not be held liable for defective design under a "military contractor defense." P appeals.

Issue. Can a contractor for the United States government be held liable under state law for a design defect in military equipment when it followed the specifications given by the government?

Held. No. Judgment vacated and case remanded.

- The present dispute borders on two areas we have found to involve "uniquely federal interests" that are governed exclusively by federal law: (i) obligations to and rights of the United States under its contracts, and (ii) the civil liability of federal officials for actions taken in the course of their duty. We think the reasons for considering these closely related areas to be of "uniquely federal" interest apply as well to the civil liabilities arising out of the performance of federal procurement contracts.

- Displacement of state law, however, will only occur where a "significant conflict" exists between an identifiable federal policy or interest and the operation of state law, or if the application of state law would frustrate specific objectives of federal legislation. Here, the state-imposed duty of care that is the asserted basis of P's claim (to equip helicopters with the escape mechanism P claims was necessary) is precisely contrary to the duty imposed by the government contract (to manufacture and deliver helicopters with the escape mechanism required by the specifications). Unlike in *Miree*, *supra*, in which the plaintiff sought to enforce a contractual duty, this suit seeks to impose upon the person contracting with the government a duty *contrary* to the duty imposed by the government contract.

- While the Federal Tort Claims Act authorizes recovery of tort damages against the United States in many situations, it expressly excepts claims based on discretionary functions or duties of agencies or employees of the government. We think that the selection of an appropriate design for United States military equipment is assuredly a discretionary function within the meaning of this provision. It involves not merely engineering, but judgment, as to many technical, military, and social considerations. Under the circumstances presented by this case, a "significant conflict" exists between the state law and federal policy applicable in this case, and state law must be displaced.

Dissent (Brennan, Marshall, Blackmun, JJ.). Congress has remained silent as to the liability of government contractors, resisting a sustained campaign by such contractors to legislate for them some defense. Here, the Court, unelected and unaccountable to the people, has stepped in and legislated a rule that denies petitioners such as P the compensation state law assures them. We are judges, not legislators.

Dissent (Stevens, J.). While it is sometimes appropriate for the courts to step in where Congress has not, when the novel question of policy involves balancing the interests in the efficient operation of a governmental program versus the rights of the individual, I believe we should defer to the expertise of Congress.

E. FEDERAL LAW IN THE STATE COURTS

1. **In General.** When state courts are called upon to litigate federal questions, the Supremacy Clause requires application of uniform federal common law. Since

these federal issues may arise in the complaint, or by way of defense, counter-claim, cross-claim, or incidentally to the primary issues of the case, the most bothersome question presented is the separation of federal from nonfederal issues in the complex state case where both types of issues are presented.

2. **Federal Employers' Liability Act--**

Dice v. Akron, Canton & Youngstown Railroad Co., 342 U.S. 359 (1952).

Facts. Dice (P), a railroad firefighter, was injured in the line of duty. He brought suit in state court under the Federal Employers' Liability Act ("FELA"), alleging negligence on the part of Akron, Canton & Youngstown Railroad Co. (D). D produced a signed release, allegedly given for value. P admitted signing several "medical receipts" on advice of his employer, D, but denied the knowing signing of a release. Under Ohio law, the release was valid, since P was negligent in signing what he had not read. Under federal law, there was ample evidence of fraudulent inducement, which would invalidate the release. The state trial judge held that state law controlled and granted judgment n.o.v. for D. The state court of appeals reversed, but the state supreme court reinstated the trial court's decision. P appeals.

Issue. In adjudicating a claim arising out of federal law, may a state court apply state law in determining issues incidental to the adjudication of the federal claim?

Held. No. Judgment reversed.

♦   In question is not only the procedural issue of whether a signature on a release must be knowing to be valid, but also the rights and duties under a major piece of federal social legislation, FELA. An adverse ruling by the state court on the question of fraudulent releases would have emasculated a major portion of the act for all Ohio workers. Since uniformity of federal rights is always a necessary and desirable end, there must be uniform precedent in a federal common law. There-fore, federal rights are directly in question, and federal law controls.

Concurrence and dissent (Frankfurter, Reed, Jackson, Burton, JJ.). We concur in rever-sal but see no inference in the federal law that state procedural arrangements are overrid-den. The questions that remain for decision are whether the validity of the release should be tested by a federal or state standard and, if by a federal one, whether the Ohio courts correctly administered the standard. State courts cannot "depreciate the legislative cur-rency issued by Congress—either expressly or by local methods of enforcement that ac-complish the same result."

---

3. **Federal Rights and State Procedure.** Granted that federal common law con-trols questions of federal rights brought in state courts, to what extent may state

procedural quirks impinge upon the federal law to deprive the plaintiff of some federally protected right? As a general rule, state procedure may infringe upon federal rights only when the state procedure is "reasonable," or "well known and founded in valid state policy," or not "inherently ridiculous."

a. In *Brown v. Western Railway of Alabama*, 338 U.S. 294 (1949), Brown was injured in the line of duty while working for the defendant. He brought a negligence action under FELA in Georgia state court, to which complaint the defendant demurred on grounds that the "complaint does not state specific facts necessary to establish the elements of the cause of action, and is not otherwise sufficient according to state law." Georgia pleading requirements were at that time among the most stringent in the nation. Under federal law, the complaint would have been sufficient to survive a motion to dismiss. The Court held that federal rather than state law controlled the issue. Strict local pleading rules cannot be used to impose unnecessary burdens upon rights of recovery authorized by federal laws. No hard guidelines may be laid down for balancing the value of federal uniformity against the value of state procedural sovereignty; only a case-by-case approach will suffice. But the balance in this case was greatly in favor of federal uniformity—there was no reasonable justification for Georgia's retention of its antiquated rule, and such a rule could not be invoked to defeat a valid federal action.

VII. THE DEVELOPMENT OF MODERN PROCEDURE

A. COMMON LAW PLEADING

At common law, the courts relied on the pleadings exclusively to narrow and define the issues. The pleading process was all-important, and pleading rules were therefore extremely rigid and technical. Errors or mistakes in the pleading process often proved fatal to the pleader's case and prevented a hearing on the merits (*see* below).

1. **Form of Action.** First and foremost, the pleadings at common law had to be drawn according to one of the recognized *forms of action* (trespass, case, trover, assumpsit, etc.), since the common law courts could grant relief only in accordance with these recognized forms. By his initial pleading ("declaration" or "complaint"), the plaintiff was forced to commit himself to one particular theory of substantive law. The plaintiff could recover, if at all, only under the particular form of action pleaded. Since amendments and repleadings generally were not allowed, the plaintiff pleaded "at his peril" in choosing the right form.

2. **Objective.** The basic objective of pleading at common law was to narrow the issues as finely as possible (hopefully, to a single issue), so that it would be easier and quicker to try the case.

3. **Numerous Pleadings.** For this purpose, innumerable distinct pleadings and counterpleadings were employed: declaration, answer, replication, rejoinder, surrejoinder, etc. Each party was required to demur or counterplead to each and every pleading by his adversary. The submission and argument of numerous pleadings was extremely time consuming, and a defendant could utilize the extremely technical pleading rules for purposes of delay.

4. **Court Must Consider Full Record--**

Veale v. Warner, 85 Eng. Rep. 463 (King's Bench 1670).

Facts. Veale (P) brought an action against Warner (D) to collect a £2,000 debt. P alleged that he lent D £2,000, which D was to repay on request, that he had made request of D but that D refused to repay the money, and so P brought this action. D responded that the writing containing the obligation was submitted to arbitrators, who ruled that D owed P £3,169. D further stated that he paid the full amount to P and that P's action against him should be barred because the debt has already been discharged and that he has a writing acknowledged by P that P has been paid. P, however, claimed that he had not been paid. Both parties demurred to the pleadings of the other party.

Issue. On the demurrer must the court look to the whole record and give judgment for the party who, on the whole, appears to be entitled to it?

Held. Yes. A court must look to the whole record when ruling on a demurrer.

♦ Here, D tricked P into demurring to his rejoinder so that the case could be decided before trial. To do this, D pleaded a response in his rejoinder, which was not allowed by the pleading rules. P then demurred to D's rejoinder.

Comment. When the court had the full record before them, they agreed with D that the arbitrators' award was invalid. Since D had used a trick in pleading to get the full record before the court, they would not give judgment to D but allowed P to discontinue his action. In another court D was able to show that P was actually in his debt and that he did not owe P anything.

B. THE FORMS OF ACTION

In ancient England, participants in trials appealed to the supernatural by attempting to convince God of the justice of their cause and relied upon God to show the truth. Proofs were often unilateral acts and consisted of oaths and ordeals. Gradually, there evolved in England three separate courts administered under the King's authority: the King's Bench, the Common Bench, and the Exchequer. With the evolution of these courts came also the development of a group of men professionally learned in the law. Gradually thereafter, the ancient forms of trial by ordeal, trial by battle, wager of law, etc., were abolished and replaced with an ever-growing number of common law writs.

1. **Aspects of the Writ System.** Actions were divided into *real*, *personal*, and *mixed*. Real actions were those brought for the specific purpose of recovery of lands, tenements, or hereditaments. Personal actions were those brought to recover for all other injuries of whatever description, excepting only the specific recovery of lands, tenements, and hereditaments. When a party believed himself aggrieved, he petitioned the King, who issued an original writ. The writ was a letter issuing out of the Court of Chancery under the great seal, and, in the King's name, directing the sheriff of the county where the injury was alleged to have been committed to command the defendant to satisfy the claim and, on his failure to comply, to summon him to appear in one of the superior courts of common law, there to account for his noncompliance. Sometimes the writ merely required the sheriff to enforce the appearance. An original writ existed for every type of case cognizable at common law, and any case that could not be made to fit an existing writ or adapted thereto by analogy was beyond judicial remedy.

2. **Evolution Through Logic-Chopping (Trespass and Case).**

a. **Trespass.** In the original writ of trespass, the plaintiff was required to allege and prove that the defendant "with force and arms" damaged the plaintiff's person or property directly. However, law courts later dispensed with the requirement of alleging and proving "force and arms" as a condition precedent to recovery in a tort action.

b. **The rise of case.** Originally, common law limited trespass actions to direct and unauthorized interference with land, goods, or person. Plaintiffs who voluntarily submitted themselves or their property to a defendant's ministrations (*e.g.,* to a doctor, veterinary, surgeon, farrier, bailee) could not use the trespass writ. Likewise, the writ could not be used by parties whose injury was caused, not directly by, but as a consequence of, the defendant's misfeasance (*e.g.,* the defendant unintentionally flooded neighboring land by operations on his own land) or where injury was caused by a defendant's omission. Gradually, the common law courts of England filled in the gaps with a new form of writ entitled "special trespass" or "trespass on the case" or merely "case."

c. **Drawing the line between trespass and case: directness and indirectness.** If a defendant acted so as to immediately and directly injure another (*e.g.,* he threw a log onto the highway and hit a traveler), the common law writ of trespass would lie; however, if the defendant's act was to create a situation that consequently and indirectly caused another injury (*e.g.,* he threw a log onto the highway and a traveler stumbled over it), the common law action upon the case would lie.

d. **The lines blur--**

Scott v. Shepherd, 96 Eng. Rep. 525 (1773).

Facts. Shepherd (D) threw a lit gunpowder-filled squib from a street into a market house crowded with people. Several persons in sequence hurriedly tossed the squib in an effort to remove it from their area. Finally, it exploded and put out Scott's (P's) eye. P sued D in an action in trespass to recover damages for his injury. D defended with the contention that P erred in bringing an action in trespass instead of on the case. The jury found for P, and D appeals.

Issue. May a plaintiff maintain an action in trespass for an injury that occurred as a result of the defendant's wrongful act?

Held. Yes. Judgment affirmed.

♦ (Nares, J.) A party can maintain an action in trespass for any injury resulting from an unlawful act, whether immediate or consequential. The "wrongfulness" of D's act continued with the squib until it finally exploded and injured P.

♦ (Blackstone, J.) I do not agree with Nares's conclusion that the lawful/unlawful distinction is determinative. A trespass action lay only when an injury is immediate and direct; a party must bring an action on the case when the injury is consequential. In this case, the injury resulted from the new motion of the merchants in the market house—*i.e.,* their plucking up and tossing the squib. Immediately after D threw the squib, it landed and became "at rest," and D's illegality stopped. The intervening merchants' actions of plucking up and tossing the squib were "unnecessary and incautious" and relieved D from any direct liability.

♦ (Gould, J.) I agree with Nares that the original wrongdoer should bear the consequences of an unlawful act and that an injured party can maintain an action in trespass therefor. D was the direct cause of the injury.

♦ (De Grey, C.J.) I concur with Blackstone's representations of the applicable legal principles, but I believe that he has misapplied them. The injury resulted from the direct and immediate act of D, who had intentionally, indiscriminately, and wantonly introduced a dangerous squib, the subsequent tossing of which was a continuation of D's initial act.

Comment. It is not obvious or clear where "direct" injury ends and "consequential" injury begins. The point is well illustrated by the fact that even Blackstone and De Grey, who both agreed that the issue here was whether the accident resulted from a continuation of the original throwing, disagreed on the application of the principle in the case.

---

3. **Evolution Through Fiction (Trover).**

   a. **Writ of debt.** In a writ of debt, the King ordered the sheriff to command the defendant to pay the plaintiff a certain sum of money "which he owes him, and unjustly detains." If the defendant failed to do so, the sheriff was to summon the defendant into the King's common court for him to show why he had not done so.

   b. **Writ of detinue.** In a writ of detinue, the King ordered the sheriff to command the defendant to turn over to the plaintiff a specific chattel or chattels wrongfully withheld from the plaintiff who was entitled to its possession. If the defendant failed to comply, he would be summoned into court to show why he had not done as commanded. The writ of detinue would lie for such circumstances as a bailee wrongfully withholding bailed chattels, or in actions by owners against finders. The deficiency of detinue was that a defendant could, at his option, either return the goods or pay an amount of money equivalent to their value. Even if the goods were injured, the defendant could opt to return them without paying any damages for having injured them.

   c. **Writ of trover.** In the writ of trover, the King ordered the sheriff to command the defendant to pay to the plaintiff the value of personal chattels wrongfully converted by the defendant to his own use. This writ developed to compensate for the inadequacies of the writs of debt and detinue.

d. Limitations on trover--

Bushel v. Miller, 93 Eng. Rep. 428 (King's Bench 1718).

Facts. Bushel (P) and Miller (D) were porters on the Custom-House wharf, each having his own designated space in the building. Bushel put goods belonging to A in the building in such a way that Miller could not get to his space without moving Bushel's goods. Miller moved them about a yard toward the door and, without returning them to their place, went away. The goods were subsequently lost. Bushel paid the value of the goods to A and brought this action in trover against Miller.

Issue. For an action in trover to be proper, must the goods in question be converted?

Held. Yes.

- ◆   Miller had a right to move the goods so that he could get to his designated area in the building. Miller may have been guilty of trespass for not returning the goods to their original location, but what he did did not amount to conversion. Since there was no conversion, the action of trover was not proper.

---

e. Requirement of actual possession for trover--

Gordon v. Harper, 101 Eng. Rep. 828 (King's Bench 1796).

Facts. Gordon (P) brought an action for trover to recover the value of certain household goods. Gordon leased a furnished house to A. Gordon had purchased the furniture in the house from B some time before he leased the house to A. While A was in possession under the lease, Harper (D), the sheriff, seized the furniture in execution of a judgment against B. After Harper seized the furniture, he had it sold. At the time of the trial, A was still in possession of the house under the lease.

Issue. Can a party who does not have actual possession of goods, nor a right to possession of the goods, bring an action of trover to recover the value of the goods?

Held. No.

- ◆   In order to bring an action to trover, the party must have a right to possession of the goods and must actually be in possession of them.

---

4. Development of Remedies for Breach of Promise.

a.   **Inadequacy of debt and covenant.** The early concept of debt was that the debtor was holding back something that he had already granted and that, consequently, already belonged to the creditor. A writ of debt would not lie to recover on a breached contract, since it consisted of merely a promise to do something in the future, not a present grant to the creditor. An exception existed for "debt on a specialty," which would lie for a breach of a promise, made in a sealed instrument, to pay a fixed sum of money. Although a party could bring an ancient form of action called "covenant" for breach of a promise made under a seal other than a promise to pay a fixed sum of money, covenant was deficient because defendants could resort to wager of law to defend themselves at trial and because certain important kinds of defaults in elementary commercial transactions were beyond the range of debt and covenant. These inadequacies led to the development of new forms.

b.   **Rise of special assumpsit to fill lacunae left by debt and covenant.** Assumpsit, or an action against a defendant who undertook to care for the goods properly and later negligently injured those entrusted to his care, was developed to compensate for the inadequacies of debt and of covenant. Assumpsit would also lie for the negligence of barbers, surgeons, and others.

c.   **Assumpsit engulfs simple debt.** In three steps, assumpsit engulfed simple debt. First, courts permitted assumpsit where a defendant who had been indebted to a plaintiff made a fresh promise to pay. Second, the courts permitted assumpsit where a plaintiff pleaded the specifics concerning the original debt, even though the defendant had made no subsequent promise to pay. Finally, the courts developed general assumpsit as the accepted alternative to simple debt. Although the plaintiff still needed to plead a fresh promise to pay, it was now recognized as fictitious and was nontraversable. The plaintiff could make a general, rather than special or completely specific, pleading of the information regarding the original debt.

d.   **Extension of general assumpsit beyond the range of simple debt.** In time, general assumpsit was extended to include maintenance of actions for the recovery of amounts not fixed (reasonable value of compensation as determined by the action). Ultimately, the general assumpsit writ became categorized into: (i) indebitatus or debt counts (money lent, money paid, money had and received, etc.) and other counts (goods sold and delivered, work, labor, and materials, and so on), and (ii) value counts (quantum meruit, for reasonable value of work done; and quantum valebant, for the reasonable value of goods supplied).

e.   **Relation between special and general assumpsit.** General assumpsit would lie as an alternative to simple debt, as a means for recovery of reasonable value under contracts implied in fact, and as a remedy for unjust enrichment. Special assumpsit remained as a remedy for breach of any express promise not under seal.

f. Imputed promise to pay debt--

Slade's Case, 76 Eng. Rep. 1074 (Ct. Exch. 1602).

Facts. Slade (P) brought an action in the King's Bench on the case against Morley (D) for D's failure to pay P for wheat and rye D had agreed to purchase from P. The jurors gave a special verdict that D did agree to purchase from P and there was no other promise or assumption.

Issues.

(i)   Although an action of debt lies upon the contract, may the bargainor have an action on the case?

(ii)   Does every contract executory import in itself an assumpsit?

(iii)   Should P recover only damages for the special loss?

(iv)   Should D have the opportunity to wage his law?

Held. (i) Yes. (ii) Yes. (iii) No. (iv) No.

◆   The bargainor may have an action on the case or an action of debt at his election.

◆   The mutual executory agreement of both parties imports in itself reciprocal actions upon the case, as well as actions of debt.

◆   P should recover for the whole debt, so that a recovery or bar in this action would be a good bar in an action of debt brought upon the same contract.

◆   It is D's folly that he did not take sufficient witnesses with him to prove the payment he made. It would be harm to P to allow D to wage his law, for experience proves that men's consciences grow so large that the respect of their private advantage rather induces men (and chiefly those who have declining estates) to perjury.

g. No promise to pay in defendant's mind--

Lamine v. Dorrell, 92 Eng. Rep. 303 (Queen's Bench 1705).

Facts. J.S. died intestate. D pretended to have a right to be administrator of J.S.'s estate and as such got possession of certain debentures and disposed of them. P became administrator and brought an action in indebitatus assumpsit against D for the money D received for the debentures. D objected that the action would not lie because D sold the debentures as one claiming title and interest in them, not as one receiving the money for P's use. D claims P should have brought trover or detinue for the debentures. The point was saved to D. The court was moved and the same objection made.

Issue. Will an action lie against a defendant who sold debentures as one claiming title and interest in them?

Held.

♦ (Powell, J.). P might have maintained detinue or trover, but P may dispense with the wrong, suppose the sale made by his consent, and bring an action for the money the debentures were sold for as money received to his use.

♦ (Holt, C.J.). If P should bring an action of trover after judgment here, D may plead this recovery in bar to the action of trover. This recovery may be given in evidence upon not guilty in the action of trover, because by this action the plaintiff makes and affirms the act of the defendant in the sale of the debentures to be lawful, and consequently the sale of them is no conversion.

C. THE COMPLEMENTARY SYSTEM OF EQUITY

1. **Development of Equity.** The courts of equity were entirely separate and distinct from the common law courts, and were governed by entirely different procedures. Equitable relief was available only where there was *no* right to recover under any of the forms of action recognized in the law courts. Hence, pleaders in equity were not bound by the form pleading rules applicable in common law actions, although the pleading process was still cumbersome, involving many separate pleadings, each requiring a reply.

2. **Equity Matured.**

   a. **Scope of equity jurisdiction.** The bases of equity jurisdiction were established long ago and include all possible cases that one may properly bring within the cognizance of courts of equity. Those most frequently occurring in practice are: accident, mistake, fraud, trust, specific performance, account, administration, mortgages and liens, partnerships, creditors' bills, partition, injunctions, receivers, interpleader, bills of peace, quia timet, divorce, alimony, infants, persons of unsound mind, and married women.

      1) **Discretionary character of equitable relief.** Even if damages at law are inadequate, courts of equity may still deny relief if the plaintiff drove an unconscionable bargain, because the contract was induced by misrepresentation, concealment, nondisclosure, or mistake,

or because specific enforcement would cause undue hardship to the defendant or third persons or be detrimental to the public interest.

2) **Mutuality of remedy.** This rule came in two forms. Affirmative mutuality of remedy was used as a justification for granting a seller of land a right to specific performance for the price. It was relatively harmless because it merely compelled the buyer to do what he had already contracted to do. Negative mutuality of remedy was used as a justification for denying a plaintiff the right to specific performance because the defendant did not have such right. The injustices caused by negative mutuality of remedy have caused it to be either flatly repudiated or largely nullified by exceptions.

3) **Other uses of equity.** Plaintiffs were able to obtain from courts of equity equitable intervention for misconduct or mistake; equitable relief against torts by recaption or protection of personal property; injunctions against waste, trespass, nuisance, or unfair competition; and labor injunctions and other types of injunctions. Equity could also decree an accounting between debtor and creditor, manage complicated multipartied litigation, and permit discovery.

4) **Flexibility of equity decrees.** Unlike the rigidity of a judgment for damages at law, not only could equity order a person to do or not do specified things, it could also cast its decree in a conditional mold when justice so required, making a certain outcome conditional on certain action or nonaction by the plaintiff or the defendant.

5) **The "cleanup" doctrine.** To save the plaintiff the inconvenience, expense, and delay of beginning a new action in a court of law, when separate law and equity courts operated side by side, equity courts would, after having resolved the equitable issue, retain the case to "clean up" the entire controversy by granting "legal" relief in addition to, or in lieu of, "equitable" relief, provided the plaintiff so desired.

6) **Enforcement of equitable decrees.** Classically, equity courts enforced their decrees through imprisonment for contempt. The recalcitrant party remained under contempt and in prison until he complied with the court's decree.

D. ABOLITION OF THE FORMS OF ACTION—MERGER OF LAW AND EQUITY

1. **Code Pleading.** The New York Code of 1848 (known as the "Field Code") originated modern pleading. This code, or adaptations thereof, was later adopted in the substantial majority of American states, and is retained in many today. It enacted several all-important departures from the former common law pleading rules:

a. **Single form of action.** The fundamental characteristic of code pleading is that there is but one form of civil action. The common law forms of action have been abolished.

1) **Effect.** A plaintiff no longer has to select and set forth in his pleadings the particular legal theory of his case. It is immaterial that he has misconceived the nature of his claim or the theory upon which relief can be obtained. Plaintiff is entitled to recover under *any* legal theory applicable to the facts pleaded and proved.

b. **Merger of law and equity.** Another major accomplishment of code pleading has been the elimination of separate courts of law and equity, and of the separate procedures previously used in each court. Under modern practice, the same court is vested with jurisdiction to grant both equitable and legal relief, the nature of the relief available depending solely on the type of claim involved, rather than on the court in which the claim is filed.

1) However, while the procedural distinctions between legal and equitable actions have been abolished, the *substantive distinctions remain intact*.

a) Thus, equitable relief is generally available only where the legal remedy (damages) is shown to be inadequate.

b) Also, where equitable relief is sought, various defenses are recognized (laches, hardship, unclean hands, etc.) that are not recognized in actions at law.

2) Moreover, while a *jury trial* is almost always available in an action at law, equitable actions are normally tried by the court alone—*i.e.,* there is no right to a jury trial (although the court may empanel a jury for an advisory verdict on disputed questions of fact).

c. **Limited number of pleadings.** Since the issue-framing process is no longer dependent exclusively on the pleadings, far fewer pleadings are allowed under the codes. The following are the only pleadings allowed under the Field Code [*see* Cal. Civ. Proc. Code 422.10]:

Plaintiff's pleadings	**Defendant's pleadings**
Complaint	Demurrer to Complaint
	Answer
Demurrer to Answer	Cross-Complaint
Demurrer to Cross-Complaint	
Answer to Cross-Complaint	Demurrer to Answer to Cross-Complaint

d. **Fact pleading.** Instead of the issue-narrowing function at common law (*see* above), the function of pleading under the codes is to "set forth the *facts* constituting *the cause of action* in ordinary and concise language." This is interpreted as requiring allegation of the "ultimate facts" of the cause of action (or defense) involved.

   1) **Ultimate facts.** "*Ultimate facts*" are those that are deemed to present *legal issues* as distinguished from mere evidentiary facts or conclusions of law. The test is *whether a legal issue can be logically deduced* from that which is pleaded.

   2) **Consequences of improper fact pleading.** Failure to allege by ultimate facts every essential element of the cause of action (or defense) involved renders the pleading subject to general demurrer. If sufficient ultimate facts *are* alleged, then evidentiary allegations and conclusions of law can be treated as surplusage (but are subject to motion to strike).

   3) **Criticism.** The major criticism of the code pleading system is the difficulty encountered in distinguishing the requisite "ultimate facts" from "evidentiary matter" or "legal conclusions" in various fact situations. To avoid such uncertainty, pleaders tend to use stereotyped allegations and form complaints (*e.g.,* the "common counts" in contract or quasi-contract actions), which often reveal very little of the real facts in controversy.

e. **Combining two causes of action in one count--**

Jones v. Winsor, 118 N.W. 716 (S.D. 1908).

Facts. Ps alleged in their complaint that D had been hired by them as their attorney to secure an ordinance from the city council granting Ps a license to secure a franchise for a city railway system. Ps gave D $2,500 on one occasion and $130 on another to be used to secure the franchise. When Ps were not granted the franchise, the city returned $2,500 to D as money belonging to Ps. D sent a draft to Ps in the amount of $1,012.25, along with an itemized bill for $1,250 for his services. Ps claim the fee is unjust, unlawful, and fraudulent and should be no more than $250. Ps claim D has wrongfully converted $1,000. D's demurrer was overruled. D appeals.

Issue. May a complaint combine in one count elements of a cause of action in tort (*i.e.,* conversion) and a cause of action in contract (*i.e.,* an action in assumpsit for money had and received)?

Held. No. Judgment reversed.

♦   The complaint does not allege ownership by Ps of the allegedly converted property at the time the action was brought or at the time it was allegedly converted.

- There are two possible causes of action that may be supported by the allegations, one for money had and received and one for conversion or trover. Such a complaint, framed to unite two distinct and incongruous causes of action in one count, cannot be sustained on demurrer.

- To uphold Ps' contention that the allegations for conversion should be treated as surplusage and the complaint should be held good as one in assumpsit would lead to uncertainty and ambiguity in pleading and would mislead courts and the opposing party.

- If the complaint does not state facts sufficient to constitute a cause of action, the demurrer must be sustained although sufficient facts may be stated to show a different cause of action.

---

f. Tort waived--

Garrity v. State Board of Administration, 162 P. 1167 (Kan. 1917).

Facts. Garrity (P) charged that in 1911 the board of regents of the state university entered P's farm and removed and wrongfully converted a fossil valued at $2,500 for which P received no compensation. The State Board of Administration (D) is the successor to the board of regents. P alleges D is subject to the board of regent's obligations and liable for its debts and contracts. D's demurrer to P's petition was sustained. P appeals.

Issues.

(i) Is P's cause of action one sounding in tort and, therefore, barred by the statute of limitations applicable to torts?

(ii) Can a plaintiff maintain an action against the successor to the board of regents for the board's debts?

Held. (i) No. (ii) No. Judgment affirmed.

- An action in tort is barred by the two-year statute of limitations; however, sufficient facts were alleged to authorize P to waive the tort and rely on an implied promise to pay the value of the fossil.

- When the board, which was a body corporate created by the Legislature, was replaced by D in 1913, D was not made a body corporate. Power was conferred on D to "execute trusts and other obligations now or hereafter committed to any of . . . said institutions." D or its members are not liable for a tort committed by the board and P cannot make them liable on the theory of an implied promise.

VIII. MODERN PLEADING

A. INTRODUCTION

Traditionally, the purposes of the pleading rules were: (i) to provide notice of the nature of a claim or defense; (ii) to identify baseless claims; (iii) to delineate each party's view of the facts; and (iv) to narrow the issues. Under the codes and rules of modern pleading, only the first of these traditional purposes is retained. Further, the Federal Rules attempt to deter baseless claims (Rules 11 and 12) and ensure judicial efficiency without thereby influencing trial upon the true merits of any issue. Under the Federal Rules, there are only three pleading stages: a *complaint*, an *answer*, and a *reply*.

B. THE COMPLAINT

1. **In General.** The modern complaint has five essential parts: the caption, the pleading of jurisdiction, the body, the prayer for relief, and the subscription or verification.

2. **The Caption.** The caption of a complaint is simply the reference preface to the complaint. While the exact requirements for a valid caption are usually statutorily prescribed in each jurisdiction, the most commonly required elements are: name of the court in which the action has been brought; docket number assigned to the action by the clerk of the court; name and official residence of both parties to the action; and the general nature of the action (action for damages, action for injunction, action for declaratory judgment, etc.). A defect in the caption does not render the complaint vulnerable to demurrer or motion to dismiss as long as the pleading party makes a prompt motion to correct the defect.

3. **Pleading Jurisdiction.**

   a. **Federal Rule of Civil Procedure 8(a):** "A pleading which sets forth a claim for relief . . . shall contain (1) a short and plain statement of the grounds upon which the court's jurisdiction depends, unless the court already has jurisdiction and the claim needs no new grounds. . . ."

   b. **Pleading jurisdiction in state courts.** State courts are usually said to be courts of general jurisdiction in that their subject matter jurisdiction is not specifically delimited by statute. Therefore, in state courts the plaintiff usually does not need to plead jurisdiction, unless she is bringing her action in a special state court, that is, one of limited jurisdiction. This is true both in the code states and the rules states.

4. **Detail Required Under the Codes.**

a. **Black letter requirements.** The black letter requirements for a valid pleading under the codes are:

1) Pleading of all the major elements constituting the cause of action of the plaintiff;

2) Pleading of the ultimate facts that lead the pleader to conclude these elements are present;

3) Pleading of the statutorily prescribed elements such as docket number, identity of parties and their attorneys, name of action, etc.; and

4) Pleading of the relief sought by the plaintiff.

b. **Requirement of ultimate facts.** In pleading the ultimate facts underlying the elements of her cause of action, the plaintiff must not plead either mere "evidentiary facts" or "legal conclusions" without their supporting ultimate facts.

c. **Alleging legal conclusions.** A complaint must contain a statement of facts sufficient to give the opposing party notice and to enable the court to declare the law upon the facts stated. Mere legal conclusions are insufficient. In *Gillispie v. Goodyear Service Stores*, 128 S.E.2d 762 (N.C. 1963), a complaint that stated that the defendants "maliciously came upon and trespassed upon the premises . . . and by the use of harsh and threatening language and physical force . . . assaulted the plaintiff . . ." was found to be insufficient because it alleged legal conclusions rather than ultimate facts. The court was concerned that the complaint did not indicate what had actually occurred, when and where it occurred, and who was involved. The court in *Gillispie* concluded that the plaintiff had not pleaded sufficient facts to support her cause of action. Yet if she had pleaded more minute facts, it is quite possible that her complaint would have been vulnerable as replete with "evidentiary facts" rather than ultimate facts. This points up the fatal weakness with the Code pleading requirements—lack of flexible application by overly formalistic courts. If the plaintiff concentrates on the facts of "what happened," her complaint may very well be vulnerable as too evidentiary. If the plaintiff concentrates on the broad sweep of the action, a hostile court may strike her pleading as not detailed enough. On an a priori basis, a plaintiff can never be secure in the knowledge that her complaint has successfully "threaded the needle," especially if she is facing a hostile court.

5. **Detail Required Under the Federal Rules.** Much less detail is required for a pleading under the Rules to survive a motion to dismiss than is required under the codes to survive a demurrer. There is no requirement that a Rules complaint state the elements of a cause of action, or confine itself to so-called ultimate facts. Indeed, it is commonly said that a complaint under the Rules is

sufficient if the court is satisfied that the plaintiff is attempting to set forth a transaction that has the possibility of resulting in relief, no matter how unskill-fully the actual complaint sets forth the cause of action.

    a.   **Federal Rule of Civil Procedure 8(a):** "A pleading which sets forth a claim for relief . . . shall contain (1) a short and plain statement of the grounds upon which the court's jurisdiction depends . . . , (2) a short and plain statement of the claim showing that the pleader is entitled to relief, and (3) a demand for judgment for the relief the pleader seeks.

    b.   **Short and plain statement--**

Dioguardi v. Durning, 139 F.2d 774 (2d Cir. 1944).

Facts. Dioguardi (P), an Italian exporter-importer, filed a home-drawn complaint against Durning (D), the Collector of Customs at the Port of New York. The complaint was in Italian-laden English and was extremely difficult to understand. The general tone of the complaint was that D had confiscated P's imports without paying just compensation therefor, but the complaint failed to allege exactly who, what, why, when, or where. On motion to dismiss, P was given leave to amend his complaint. This he did by substituting a more detailed description of the confiscated goods—but in all other respects the new complaint was identical to the old one. D again moved to dismiss. The district court granted the motion. P appeals.

Issue. Is a complaint containing a short and plain statement of the claim asserting that the pleader is entitled to relief, but not stating facts sufficient to constitute a cause of action, adequate under the Federal Rules?

Held. Yes. Judgment reversed.

♦   P obviously felt strongly aggrieved by D's action. The general subject of the griev-ance, while inarticulately expressed, was clear enough. P's case should not have been dismissed. However, in fairness to D, P must further amend his complaint, this time to include the various temporal descriptions that would allow D to pre-cisely identify the series of transactions in question.

---

    c.   **Motion for a more definite statement.**

        1)   **Federal Rule of Civil Procedure 12(e):** "If a pleading to which a responsive pleading is permitted is so vague or ambiguous that a party cannot reasonably be required to frame a responsive pleading, the party may move for a more definite statement before interposing a responsive pleading. The motion shall point out the defects com-plained of and the details desired. . . ."

2) Example. In *Lodge 743, International Association of Machinists v. United Aircraft Corp.*, 30 F.R.D. 142 (D. Conn. 1962), Lodge 743 sued United Aircraft Corp. for breach of a strike settlement contract. The plaintiff alleged that not all workers had been returned to their jobs. The defendant moved for a more definite statement, asking for the names of the workers involved and their respective job qualifications. The plaintiff countered that it could not fulfill the defendant's request because the defendant's personnel files were unavailable. To grant the defendant's motion would effectively dismiss the plaintiff's case. However, the court granted the defendant's motion, with special permission for the plaintiff to complete its own discovery proceedings before being required to answer the defendant's motion. The court thereby recognized the strong policy argument behind Rule 12(e).

6. **Pleading the Right to Relief—the Body of the Complaint.** A complaint in federal court must contain a "short and plain statement of the claim showing that the pleader is entitled to relief." State statutes are phrased either in the same way or in terms of "pleading the elements of plaintiff's cause of action." These allegations constitute the body of the complaint.

   a. **Stating the essential elements.** A proper complaint must adequately show that the plaintiff has a right to relief. Determining which factors are essential and which are not can be difficult, however.

      1) **Burden of pleading.** It is a handy and virtually universally valid rule of thumb that the party who has the burden of proving a given issue at trial also has the burden of pleading that issue. Therefore, what the plaintiff must prove to establish her case she must also plead. What the defendant must prove to establish his defense he must first plead. In practice, only one consideration complicates the rule: Several states require a plaintiff to allege the nonexistence of a certain defense as a part of the complaint. This means in effect that the plaintiff has the burden of pleading an issue that the defendant has the burden of proving. Thus, for example, a plaintiff in a negligence action may be required to plead no contributory negligence, an issue that the defendant must prove if he is to establish his defense. But such exceptions to the rule that the burden of pleading follows the burden of proof at trial are rare and well known. For the most part, the rule holds true.

      2) **Effect of omission of an essential allegation.** Under the "fact pleading" theory of the codes, accidental omission from the complaint of an averment of one of the essential elements of a cause of action renders the complaint vulnerable to demurrer. Under the liberal "notice pleading" of the Federal Rules, however, rarely does such omission constitute sufficient grounds for the court to grant a motion to dismiss the complaint.

3) Omission of essential element--

Garcia v. Hilton Hotels International, Inc., 97 F. Supp. 5 (D. P.R. 1951).

Facts. Garcia, (P), a bellboy at the Hilton Hotel (D), was discharged in front of the staff, allegedly roughly and abusively, for procuring for a ring of prostitutes working the hotel. He brought this action for slander and defamation of character. Publication is an essential element of such a cause of action, but the complaint failed to formally allege such publication. D filed a motion to dismiss and a motion for a more definite statement of the allegedly defamatory words used to discharge P.

Issue. Does failure to specifically allege an essential element of the cause of action require that the complaint be dismissed?

Held. No. Motion to dismiss denied.

♦ Under the codes, omission of such an essential element of a cause of action might have rendered the complaint vulnerable. But under the Federal Rules in effect in Puerto Rico, a motion to dismiss is denied if the complaint, construed in its entirety, shows reasonable probability that the plaintiff may eventually prevail upon the merits, even if an essential element of the cause of action is not formally pleaded.

♦ Dismissal for failure to state a claim should be used only in those rare cases where the complaint totally lacks merit or otherwise is unfair to the defendant. For these reasons, the complaint is deemed sufficient. The motion for a more definite statement is granted, and several paragraphs of the complaint are stricken.

7. **Allocating the Burden of Pleading Between Plaintiff and Defendant; Other Considerations.**

   a. **In general.** The party with the burden of producing evidence at trial is usually assigned the burden of pleading an issue.

   b. **Other considerations.**

      1) **Utilization of pretrial conference.** Many legal theorists believe that pleading under neither the codes nor the Rules can ever accomplish the traditionally defined goals of pleading. They favor adoption of widespread use of pretrial conferences, informal in nature, to accomplish many of the issue-defining functions of modern pleading. It is their belief that pretrial conferences would acquaint both parties, and the court, with the general nature of the case, thus saving much time and expenditure of energy. Indeed, there is some evidence that in

jurisdictions where pretrial conferences are regularly used, fewer frivolous cases actually go to trial, and those that do go to trial seem more satisfactorily presented.

2) **Use of official forms.** The Appendix to the Federal Rules of Civil Procedure provides a group of official forms illustrating generally acceptable pleadings. Many state codes of civil procedure also supply such illustrative forms. Included are blank form complaints and answers for each major type of legal action. Some commentators believe that the widespread use of well-drafted official forms would substantially minimize the "luck" now so much a part of pleading in many jurisdictions, and at the same time would ensure that each party is supplied with the information necessary for him to appreciate the major aspects of his opponent's case. Currently, official forms enjoy only limited use in the courts—most practicing lawyers consider them too inflexible and poorly drafted for the tasks at hand.

3) **Concept of judicial notice.** When an essential element of a cause of action is not pleaded by a plaintiff, upon motion the court may take judicial notice of the existence of that element if such element is a "fact objectively ascertainable, commonly known, and a matter of public record." Such judicial notice has the effect of stipulating for the duration of the action the existence of that fact and obviating either party's pleading its existence.

4) **Alleging matters of defense in the complaint.** Ordinarily, in her complaint, the plaintiff need not anticipate and deny any defenses she expects the defendant to raise by answer. Therefore, it is rarely grounds for dismissal that a plaintiff has failed to affirmatively show that she is entering the action with "clean hands" or has failed to show the initiation of her action within the statute of limitations. In those rare cases in which the plaintiff must avoid a defense in her complaint, this requirement is specifically spelled out by statute, and a careful reading of the statute will usually suffice to alert the pleader.

5) **Doctrine of ineffective avoidance.** As indicated, a plaintiff need not anticipate and avoid a defense in her complaint. However, if the plaintiff does attempt to avoid such an anticipated defense, her attempted avoidance must be legally effective, or the entire complaint is rendered subject to dismissal. This is the doctrine of ineffective avoidance.

   a) **Example.** The plaintiff in a negligence action attempts to anticipate and avoid the defendant's plea of contributory negligence. Therefore, in her complaint she alleges that she used "all care to be expected of her in her condition," therefore concluding that she was not contributorily negligent. Legally, the attempted avoidance is bad—tort law teaches that negligence is an objective rather than a subjective concept. The ineffective avoidance renders the entire complaint defective and subject to dismissal on motion by the defendant.

8. Pleading Special Matters.

a. **Fraud.** A plea of fraud is probably the more perilous plea for the novice pleader, as each state tends to approach the problem differently. In a few states, and under the Federal Rules, a general averment of fraud is sufficient, without more, to withstand a motion to dismiss. But in most states, the pleader of fraud must specifically aver malice, or the circumstances of the discovery of the fraud, or the bringing of an action within the statute of limitations, or the specific workings of the alleged fraud, or all at the same time. The pleader is advised to investigate carefully the specific state rules before attempting to plead fraud.

1) **Specificity of complaint--**

Denny v. Carey, 72 F.R.D. 574 (E.D. Pa. 1976).

Facts. Denny (P) brought a proposed class action against Carey and other officers and directors (Ds) of First Pennsylvania Corp. for securities fraud. P alleged that Ds conspired to conceal First Penn's true financial condition by including improper accrued interest, misleading sales figures, inadequate provision for loan losses, and by failing to reveal loan defaults in its financial statements. Ds moved to dismiss for failure to allege facts constituting fraud with sufficient particularity.

Issue. Must a complaint based on fraud specifically allege facts constituting fraud on the part of the defendant?

Held. No. Motion denied.

♦ A complaint alleging fraud must state the circumstances with particularity so that the defendant can prepare an adequate answer to the allegations. However, requiring the plaintiff to meet a rigorous burden of pleading fraud, especially where many of the matters are peculiarly within the defendant's knowledge, would be unfair. The requirement of Rule 9(b) is met when there is sufficient identification of the circumstances constituting fraud so that the defendant can prepare an adequate answer to the allegations.

---

2) **Pleading fraud in securities litigation.** The Private Securities Litigation Reform Act of 1995 ("PSLRA") imposes a "super-heightened"

standard of pleading fraud in securities cases. The complaint must specify each misleading statement and state the reasons why it was misleading. All facts upon which an allegation made on information and belief is formed must be stated with particularity, and facts giving rise to "strong inferences" of scienter must be stated with particularity.

b. Employment discrimination not a special matter--

Swierkiewicz v. Sorema N.A., 534 U.S. 506 (2002).

Facts. Swierkiewicz (P), a native of Hungary and 53 years old at the time of the complaint, began working for Sorema (D), a reinsurance company, in 1989 as senior vice president and chief underwriting officer. Nearly six years later, Chavel, D's chief executive officer, demoted P to a marketing and services position and transferred the bulk of his underwriting responsibilities to Papadopoulo, a 32-year-old who, like Chavel, was a French national. One year later, Chavel appointed Papadopoulo as the chief underwriting officer, although he had only one year of underwriting experience next to P's 26 years. After unsuccessful attempts to discuss the situation and a request for a severance package, D gave P the option of resigning without a severance package or being dismissed. P refused to resign, and was fired. P filed suit alleging national origin and age discrimination. The district court dismissed the complaint for P's failure to allege sufficient circumstances to support an inference of discrimination. The court of appeals affirmed. The Supreme Court granted certiorari.

Issue. Must a complaint based on employment discrimination contain specific facts establishing a prima facie case of discrimination?

Held. No. Judgment reversed.

◆ The prima facie case is an evidentiary standard, not a pleading requirement. Moreover, in some cases, an employment discrimination plaintiff may prevail without proving all of the elements of a prima facie case.

◆ The court of appeals' heightened pleading standard conflicts with Rule 8(a)(2)'s standard, which requires only a "short and plain statement" of the claim showing that the pleader is entitled to relief, and which applies to all but limited contexts, such as those involving fraud.

◆ P's complaint satisfies the requirements of Rule 8(a) because it gives D fair notice of the bases of his claims.

---

c. Defamation. State statutes governing the plea of slander or defamation of character vary from state to state. Occasionally it is sufficient if the plaintiff

generally avers slander. But more characteristically, the plaintiff may have to recount in the complaint the exact words alleged to be slanderous. In such a case, the plaintiff's attorney has the delicate task of trying to coax the plaintiff into recalling the events upon which the cause of action is based in detail that is almost humanly impossible.

d. Conditions. In pleading the performance of conditions precedent in a contract, it is usually sufficient to state that all the conditions have been performed. Only if the defendant controverts this general assertion must the plaintiff then produce, at trial, evidence showing that all conditions have actually been performed. Under many state codes, the defendant may controvert the performance of conditions precedent generally, therefore putting the plaintiff to his proof in almost every case. But under the Federal Rules, the defendant is required specifically and with particularity to controvert those conditions not performed. This tends to narrow down the true issues of disagreement and speed up trial.

9. Pleading Alternate or Inconsistent Allegations.

a. Common law and early codes. At common law and under the early codes, pleading of either inconsistent legal theories or inconsistent facts was fatal to the complaint or the answer, if the opposing party challenged the inconsistency by demurrer. Under the early codes, the only justification to be found for the rule that pleading of inconsistent legal theories rendered a pleading subject to demurrer was historical inertia, a holdover from earlier practice.

b. Modern code pleading. Under modern code authority, a party may plead inconsistent legal theories of recovery or defense, without rendering his pleading subject to demurrer, as long as each alternative legal theory is set forth separately in a separate count of the complaint or answer. But under the modern codes a party may not plead inconsistent facts—it is assumed that the pleader will have done sufficient investigation prior to pleading to be able to deduce the true state of affairs.

c. Pleading under the Rules. It is not grounds for dismissal of a pleading under the Rules that a pleader has stated alternative, inconsistent, or even hypothetical allegations, whether legal or factual. Rather, in pleading in the alternative, the pleader is only constrained by a requirement that he plead in "good faith." Further, under the Rules, an admission for purposes of hypothetical or alternative pleading in one count may not be held to be an admission for purposes of the other hypothetical alternatives—the pleader is "entitled to have every claim or defense considered upon its own merits alone, by the trier of fact."

d. The separate statement requirement. Federal Rule of Civil Procedure 10(b) requires that, as much as possible and practical, each count or paragraph of a pleading be limited to "a statement of a single set of circumstances" or advancement of a single legal theory. Most state codes of civil procedure based upon the Rules have similar requirements. However, while under the codes, violation of this separate statement requirement is often grounds for demurrer, under the Rules violation of the requirement, if objected to by the opposing party, may be cured by a motion to separate. Such a violation under the Rules is almost never grounds for dismissal or demurrer, unless the entire pleading is so hopelessly confused that the court deems it advisable to force repleading.

10. Pleading Damages.

a. **General vs. special damages.** For purposes of pleading, damages are divided into "*general damages*" and "*special damages*." General damages are said to be those damages that "flow expectedly and naturally" out of the nature of the cause of action. Special damages are said to be those actual damages that "are the natural, but not the necessary and inevitable result of the wrongful act." It is the prevailing rule in most courts that general damages need not be specifically alleged in detail to be recoverable—a general summation of such damages is sufficient—but that special damages, to be recoverable, must be set out with particularity. Problems arise when courts attempt to decide whether a specific element of the plaintiff's damages is general or special.

b. **Failure to plead special damages--**

Ziervogel v. Royal Packing Co., 225 S.W.2d 798 (Mo. 1949).

Facts. Ziervogel (P) was injured in a collision with a delivery van owned by Royal Packing Co. (D). In her complaint P alleged as general damages "injuries to neck, back, spine, and central nervous system." At trial, she attempted to prove that, in addition to the damages generally enumerated in her complaint, her blood pressure had been permanently raised and her life expectancy thereby shortened. D stipulated that the medical injuries originally enumerated were elements of general damages, but protested the incorporation of the new element of damage, since it was "special," and not pleaded with particularity. The trial resulted in a verdict and judgment in favor of P. D appeals.

Issue. Must recovery for special damages be denied if such damages were not pleaded in the complaint?

Held. Yes. Judgment reversed.

♦   Admission of evidence relating to the blood pressure issue was improper. A rise in blood pressure was not "generally to be expected" following minor traffic accidents; therefore, such damages are special and must be specifically pleaded. A general allegation of "injuries to the spine and central nervous system" was not sufficient as a special plea of change in blood pressure, even though blood pressure is directly regulated by the central nervous system.

11. **Prayer for Relief.** Every complaint, under both the codes and the Rules, must contain a statement of the relief to which the plaintiff deems herself entitled. This is the prayer for relief. Omission of such a prayer makes the average complaint meaningless, and unless motion to amend is granted, such an omission renders the complaint subject to dismissal without prejudice.

    a. **Federal Rule of Civil Procedure 8(a).** "A pleading . . . shall contain . . . a demand for judgment for the relief the pleader seeks. Relief in the alternative or of several different types may be demanded."

    b. **Amending prayer for relief--**

Bail v. Cunningham Brothers, Inc., 452 F.2d 182 (7th Cir. 1971).

Facts. Bail (P) sued Cunningham Brothers, Inc. (D) for damages suffered by P as a result of the collapse of a scaffold. P originally sought damages for $100,000, but on the morning of the trial, P sought to increase the ad damnum clause to $250,000. P's motion was denied, but the jury awarded P $150,000. P was granted leave to amend the clause to $150,000 in a post-trial motion; D appeals.

Issue. May an ad damnum clause be amended post-trial to correspond to the jury's verdict?

Held. Yes. Judgment affirmed.

♦ The clear majority of authorities permit awards of damages in excess of those pleaded. It is not an abuse of discretion to permit a post-trial motion to amend the pleadings. D argues that it was prejudiced by the trial court's initial denial of P's motion; *i.e.,* D thought that it was subject only to $100,000 in damages. If D had known that the exposure was greater, it claims that it would have handled the case differently. However, D was never confronted with an insignificant amount; there was no real prejudice involved here, as there might have been had the original pleadings alleged only $1,000.

---

    c. **Effect of the prayer.**

        1) **Contested cases.** In those cases in which the defendant makes an answer to the complaint or otherwise contests the action, the plaintiff

is **not** limited in final recovery by the actual amount or type of relief originally prayed for. It is said that the plaintiff is entitled to damages according to the proof rather than according to her pleadings. Usually, if the jury awards an amount greater than was prayed for in the complaint, the court will grant a motion to conform the pleadings to the proof, and allow amendment of the original prayer.

2) **Default cases.** A defendant defaults when he fails to answer a complaint, and otherwise does not appear to contest adjudication of the action against him. By the prevailing rule, alluded to above, recovery allowed by a plaintiff against a defaulting defendant *is* limited by the amount prayed for in the complaint. Under the codes, recovery allowed against a defaulting defendant must equal that prayed for. Under the Rules, the prayer acts as a maximum limit to recovery, but actual default recovery may be less than the prayer if, in the estimation of the court, the plaintiff should not reasonably be awarded the full amount of her prayer. In either case, however, it is improper for default recovery to exceed the prayed-for amount, even if the prayer seriously underestimates the real damages sustained.

a) **Federal Rule of Civil Procedure 54(c).** "A judgment by default [in favor of the plaintiff] shall not be different in kind from or exceed in amount that prayed for in the demand for judgment. Except as to a party against whom a judgment is entered by default, every final judgment shall grant the relief to which the party in whose favor it is rendered is entitled, even if the party has not demanded such relief in the party's pleadings . . . ."

3) **Constructional limits.** Despite the wording of Rule 54(c), above, the federal courts have been reluctant to extend the liberality of the Rules to such an extent that they will allow the plaintiff to recover under a legal theory entirely different in scope and context from that adjudicated. The rationale is that Federal Rule 8(a), requiring that the plaintiff set out the relief to which she deems herself entitled, would be rendered meaningless if such a liberal construction were adopted. [*See* Convertible Top Replacement Co. v. Aro Manufacturing Co., 312 F.2d 52 (1st Cir. 1962)]

d. **Amendments.** Some state courts require that the eventual recovery given to the plaintiff conform exactly with the formal prayer in the complaint. Many other courts are uneasy if there is a great difference between recovery and the prayer. Therefore, as a tactical matter, most courts will grant as a matter of course a request, after trial, to conform the prayer to the recovery. In this way the formal prayer and the recovery are made to "balance," and the chances of reversal are lessened. [*See* Haney v. Burgin, 208 A.2d 448 (N.H. 1965)]

C. RESPONDING TO THE COMPLAINT

1. **Time Permitted for a Response.** Generally, defendants have 20 days from service of the complaint to respond by a motion pursuant to Rule 12 or by answer. However, counsel generally request, and usually are granted, extensions by opposing counsel. Rule 6(a) authorizes the court to grant such extensions.

2. **Motions to Dismiss.**

   a. **Rule 12(b) defenses.** Rule 12(b) provides that the following defenses may at the option of the pleader be made by motion:

      1) Lack of jurisdiction over the subject matter.

      2) Lack of jurisdiction over the person.

      3) Improper venue.

      4) Insufficiency of process.

      5) Insufficiency of service of process.

      6) Failure to state a claim upon which relief can be granted.

      7) Failure to join a party under Rule 19.

   b. **Rule 12(b)(6)—counterpart to common law demurrer.**

      1) **Motion to dismiss for failure to state a claim.**

         a) **Degree of specificity required--**

American Nurses' Association v. Illinois, 783 F.2d 716 (7th Cir. 1986).

Facts. The American Nurses' Association (P) brought a class action against the state of Illinois (D), claiming sex discrimination in employment. An essential element of the complaint was that D paid workers in predominantly male job classifications a higher wage than workers in comparable predominantly female job classifications. The trial court dismissed the complaint because a comparable worth violation does not violate federal antidiscrimination law. P appeals claiming the suit is not a comparable worth case.

Issue. Must a complaint be dismissed if it does not set forth a complete and convincing picture of the alleged wrongdoing?

Held. No. Judgment reversed.

♦ If P is merely suing because D has not implemented a comparable worth study, the suit was properly dismissed, but if it contains an allegation of an actionable wrong, it should not have been dismissed. Unfortunately, P's complaint was not drafted as a plain and short statement of the claim.

♦ In practice, few complaints follow the models included in the Federal Rules of Civil Procedure Appendix of Forms. In this case, P's complaint was 20 pages long, with an appendix consisting of a 100-page comparable worth study. A long, detailed complaint may contain enough facts to show that the plaintiff's legal rights were not invaded, which is what the district court held in this case.

♦ Rather than merely alleging that D intentionally discriminated against female employees because of their sex, which would clearly constitute a claim, the complaint alleges numerous facts based on a theory that D failed to adopt a wage scale based on comparable worth, which is not a claim under federal law. The list of discriminatory practices alleged contains no actionable claims; it is merely illustrative.

♦ Another paragraph of the complaint alleges willful failure to take any action to correct the alleged discrimination, but under federal law the only basis for a claim is if D did not correct the alleged discrimination because of the sex of the employees; *i.e.,* that D thought men should be paid more than women despite the lack of difference in the skill, effort, or conditions of the work. But P did not allege such a motivation. It is not a violation that the male jobs are higher paying if D's wages reflect the market wages.

♦ A complaint should not be dismissed for failure to state a claim "unless it appears beyond doubt that the plaintiff can prove no set of facts in support of his claim which would entitle him to relief." [Conley v. Gibson, 355 U.S. 41 (1957)] But a complaint does not need to allege evidence. Therefore, although P's complaint makes a series of allegations that do not constitute a valid claim, it also could be alleging intentional discrimination, so that it does state a claim.

♦ To prevail on the merits, P must prove that D is intentionally discriminating by paying workers in predominantly male jobs more than the market rate because most of those workers are male. This burden of proof may not be inferred by evidence of a comparable worth study.

---

3. **Motion to Strike.** This motion is used to challenge pleadings that include "scandalous," "impertinent," or "irrelevant" matter. The general rule today is that allegations will not be stricken from a complaint unless their presence will prejudice the adverse party. The question of prejudice turns on whether the contents of the pleadings will be disclosed to the jury. Pleadings filed late are challenged by a motion to strike the pleadings or to dismiss the claims that they contain.

4. **Answering the Complaint.** The answer is the defendant's formal response to the allegations of the plaintiff's complaint. It, too, is filed with the clerk of the court and delivered to the plaintiff, usually within a period set by the statute. The general function of the answer is to somehow avoid the allegations of the complaint, either by denying the allegations themselves or by introducing new facts that avoid the legal consequences prayed for in the complaint.

   a. **Denials.** The defendant may attempt to escape the legal consequences of the complaint by denying that the allegations of the complaint are true, thereby putting the plaintiff in the position of having to prove at trial the truth of her allegations. Such an answer is a denial. Denials may be either general denials or specific denials of specific allegations.

      1) **General denials.** Many codes provide that a defendant may file as a general denial an answer reading substantially as follows: "For his answer to the complaint of the plaintiff herein, the defendant denies each and every allegation of the complaint, and asks that the plaintiff be put to her proof upon each and every allegation before a court of law." There is usually a requirement that such a general denial of "each and every allegation" be in good faith.

      2) **Improper use of general denial--**

Zielinski v. Philadelphia Piers, Inc., 139 F. Supp. 408 (E.D. Pa. 1956).

Facts. Zielinski (P) sued Philadelphia Piers, Inc. (D) for injuries sustained when a forklift with the initials "PPI" painted on the side ran P down on a Philadelphia dock. D, all of whose forklifts had PPI stenciled on the side, generally denied "each and every allegation of the complaint." P proceeded with discovery, during which the statute of limitations for filing of a new negligence action ran. At a pretrial conference D indicated that the forklift in question had been long-term leased to another firm not connected with PPI, and demanded that P sue that other firm rather than PPI. P went to court seeking a pretrial ruling that, because D had exercised bad faith in not alerting P to the mistake in party, D should be considered the owner of the forklift for purposes of the negligence action. Otherwise, P argued, he would be permanently barred from recovery, since the statute of limitations had run while he was relying on D's vague general denial of liability.

Issue. When the defendant makes a general denial when a specific denial was called for, and the result is that the plaintiff learns he has sued the wrong defendant, may the plaintiff be granted a declaratory judgment that the defendant is the proper defendant?

Held. Yes. Ruling for P granted.

♦ Compliance with the good faith spirit of pleadings makes a general denial improper in situations like this. D should have alerted P of the mistake in party as soon as D was aware of the mistake. By not doing so, D was estopped from denying liability once the statute of limitations ran. D's actions positively misled

P into sacrificing proper recovery against the real negligent party. For this reason, D can be held as surrogate for the real negligent party.

---

3) **Denials for lack of information.** Under Federal Rule of Civil Procedure 8(b), a party may deny an allegation in a complaint on the ground that he does not have sufficient knowledge or information necessary to determine the truth of the allegation. However, courts have held that some facts are "presumptively within the knowledge" of a party. [*See* Oliver v. Swiss Club Tell, 35 Cal. Rptr. 324 (1963)] For example, if a complaint alleges that the defendant is an unincorporated association, the defendant cannot deny the allegation based on lack of information, as this is a fact that is presumptively within the defendant's knowledge. [Oliver v. Swiss Club Tell, *supra*]

4) **Specific denials.** Whereas the general denial denies every allegation of the complaint, a specific denial picks out specific allegations of the complaint, lists them by paragraph number or count, and denies only those listed allegations. The defendant may negate a specific allegation, or go through the complaint line by line, admitting and denying where appropriate, or simply allege a fact contrary to a fact alleged in the complaint. Whatever method is chosen, the specific denial tends to focus attention upon a finite number of controverted issues at an early stage of the pleadings, thereby narrowing the scope of discovery and making it more efficient. [*See* Fed. R. Civ. P. 8(b) and (d)]

   a) **Negative pregnant.** Although negating a specific allegation is an effective denial, if carelessly done, it may be deemed "pregnant" with an admission of what the defendant is attempting to deny. Thus, if the plaintiff's complaint alleges that "the defendant struck and kicked the plaintiff," the defendant's answer that "the defendant did not strike and kick the plaintiff" is pregnant with an admission that he may have struck *or* kicked the plaintiff. To avoid this, the defendant should make his denial in the disjunctive; *i.e.,* "The defendant did not strike or kick the plaintiff."

   b) **Example.** In *Wingfoot California Homes Co. v. Valley National Bank*, 294 P.2d 370 (Ariz. 1956), in an action for payment of some notes, the plaintiff alleged that $150 was a reasonable value of attorneys' fees due from the defendant to the plaintiff's attorney. The defendant denied specifically that $150 was reasonable. The trial court deemed the answer as an admission that $100 was reasonable, and awarded $100 for attorneys' fees regarding each note. The supreme court affirmed. By his denial that the plaintiff's attorney was entitled to exactly $150, the defendant had in effect admitted that any amount under $150 was reasonable value for such fee, and the court deemed that amount admitted by the defendant.

b. **Affirmative defenses.** In addition to denying the allegations of the plaintiff, the defendant may also introduce new matter by way of answer if that matter tends to "avoid" the legal consequences sought by the plaintiff. Under a denial, only the allegations of the plaintiff are put in issue. If the defendant pleads affirmative defenses that tend to avoid liability, these must be adjudicated by the court in addition to the allegations of the plaintiff, and the scope of the trial is considerably broadened.

1) **Definitions and traditional tests.** It is often difficult to determine whether a specific defense is only a "denial" of liability or an affirmative defense that must be pleaded and proved by the defendant. This acquires crucial importance if one realizes that most codes of civil procedure deem affirmative defenses not pleaded by the defendant to be waived. Generally, defenses are admissible under a denial only if they tend to destroy, rather than confess and avoid, the bases of liability. As a practical matter, courts view as new matter those issues that place the burden of proof on the defendant—if the defendant carries the burden of proof on a defense, that defense is an affirmative defense, which he must plead.

2) **Must be pleaded timely--**

Ingraham v. United States, 808 F.2d 1075 (5th Cir. 1987).

Facts. Ingraham and others (Ps) separately sued the United States (Ds) under the Federal Tort Claims Act for injuries caused by the negligence of government physicians. After entry of adverse judgments, the government moved for relief from the judgment to the extent that the damages exceeded the limit imposed by the Medical Liability and Insurance Improvement Act of Texas on medical malpractice awards (this issue was not raised at trial). The respective district courts denied the post-trial motions, and D appeals.

Issue. May an affirmative defense be raised for the first time on appeal?

Held. No. Judgment affirmed.

♦ Federal Rule of Civil Procedure 8(c) requires that a party plead affirmative defenses when pleading to a preceding pleading. Failure to raise an affirmative defense timely constitutes a waiver of that defense. Since D failed to plead the defense limiting damages or raise it at trial, it was waived and may not be raised on appeal.

Comment. In *Taylor v. United States*, 821 F.2d 1428 (9th Cir. 1987), the court held that a statutory limitation on damages was not an affirmative defense, reasoning that, unlike the affirmative defenses listed in Rule 8(c), the statute limits, but does not bar, recovery for noneconomic damages.

D. THE REPLY

1. **Under the Codes.** Under the codes, when the answer of the defendant sets forth new matter (as an affirmative defense), the plaintiff is usually given the right to file a reply to the answer, setting at issue the new matters alleged in the answer. If the answer merely denies the allegations of the complaint, rarely is the plaintiff afforded the right to reply to the answer, since the issues for trial are deemed sufficiently defined by the first two pleadings alone. However, even if the plaintiff has the right to reply to new material in the defendant's answer, but fails to do so, most courts under the codes will deem the new material of the answer controverted rather than admitted. Thus the reply is rendered superfluous.

2. **Under the Rules.** The reply generally is not used under the Federal Rules or their state counterparts, although in rare circumstances the court may allow it. This reflects an attitude in the courts that less emphasis should be placed on pleadings and more emphasis on discovery and preparation of factual material. This attitude tends to prevail both when new material is contained in the answer and when the answer is merely a denial of liability. However, if the answer contains a counterclaim against the plaintiff, the federal courts freely allow the reply as an answer to the counterclaim.

   a. **Federal Rule 7(a).** "There shall be a complaint and an answer; a reply to a counterclaim denominated as such; an answer to a cross-claim if the answer contains a cross-claim; a third-party complaint, if a person who was not an original party is summoned [as a third party]; and a third-party answer, if a third-party complaint is served. No other pleading shall be allowed, except that the court may order a reply to an answer or a third-party answer."

3. **Doctrine of Departure.** At common law a plaintiff could not by reply or supplemental pleading set forth a new cause of action against a defendant. Such a new cause of action was a departure, and rendered the reply vulnerable to a motion to strike. Since the common law also tended to restrict the right to amend a complaint, the practical effect of such a doctrine was to require the plaintiff to very carefully draw her complaint so as to contain every possible cause of action against the defendant. However, with the advent of the later codes and the Rules, the doctrine of departure has been largely laid to rest—the reply that introduces a new cause of action against the defendant is usually taken as a request to amend the complaint. Such requests are often granted.

E. AMENDMENTS

1. **In General.** Once a party has filed her pleading, she may be allowed to correct defects, oversights, or other deficiencies in the pleading through amendment or supplemental pleading. At common law, the right to amend was quite severely limited—it could be utilized only to correct documentary difficulties. However, as pleading rules have become more and more liberal, first under the codes, later under the Rules, the rules governing amendment have also become more and more liberal. It is probably not overstating the case to say that, in most instances, it is incumbent on the opposing party to demonstrate good cause why an amendment should *not* be allowed rather than on the requesting party to show why it should be allowed. Under the Rules there is no requirement that the amendment confine itself either to the same legal theory originally sued on, or even to the same transaction or occurrence that formed the basis of the original cause of action. Within certain ill-defined boundaries, an amendment under the Rules may totally change both the nature of the cause of action sued on and the factual base underlying the cause of action.

2. **Number of Amendments Allowed.** Federal Rule 15 allows a party to amend once as a matter of course at any time before a responsive pleading is filed. Under the Rules, amendments should be allowed by the court until there is a reasonable certainty that the plaintiff will find it impossible to set forth a cause of action or that the defendant will find it impossible to avoid the consequences of the complaint. The actual number of amendments is therefore not relevant.

3. **Amendments and the Statute of Limitations.**

    a. **Amendments to the claim for relief.** Under the Rules, an amendment may add a new cause of action, predicated on a transaction or occurrence different from that originally sued upon in the complaint. The question arises whether such an added cause of action should "relate back" to the time of the original complaint for purposes of the statute of limitations (*i.e.,* should the plaintiff's added claim be barred when the statute of limitations, otherwise applicable, has run between the time the original complaint was filed and the time that the cause of action was added by amendment?). If the amendment relates back to the time of filing of the complaint, the cause of action meets the statute of limitations. If it does not relate back, the cause of action is barred by the statute. The relation back doctrine is elastic, depending largely on the court's view of the scope of the transaction or occurrence.

        1) **Federal Rule 15(c).** Whenever "the claim or the defense asserted in the amended pleading arose out of the conduct, transaction, or occurrence set forth or attempted to be set forth in the original pleading," the amendment relates back to the date (of filing) of the original pleading.

2) Failure to name correct defendant--

Beeck v. Aquaslide 'N' Dive Corp., 562 F.2d 537 (8th Cir. 1977).

Facts. Beeck (P) sued Aquaslide (D), claiming that he was severely injured on July 15, 1972, while using a water slide allegedly manufactured by D. P sought to recover damages on theories of negligence, strict liability, and breach of implied warranty. The statute of limitations on P's personal injury claim expired on July 15, 1974. In its initial answer, D admitted manufacture of the slide. After the statute had run, D conducted an investigation and determined that the slide was not manufactured by D. Consequently, D moved to amend its answer to deny manufacture; P resisted the motion. The district court granted D's motion to amend, finding that D's initial answer admitting manufacture was based in good faith on the conclusions of three insurance companies that investigated the accident and that P failed to show that it would be unable to proceed against any other party. Pursuant to D's request, a jury trial was held on the issue of whether D manufactured the slide. The court dismissed P's complaint after the jury returned a verdict in D's favor. P appeals.

Issue. Was it an abuse of discretion for a court to grant D's motion to amend after the statute of limitations ran on P's personal injury claim?

Held. No. Judgment affirmed.

♦ Federal Rule 15(a) provides that leave to amend should be freely granted so as to do substantial justice. The burden is on the party opposing the amendment to show prejudice, bad faith, or undue delay.

♦ Allowance or denial of leave to amend a pleading lies within the sound discretion of a trial court and is reviewable only for an abuse of discretion.

♦ The trial court did not abuse its discretion in granting D leave to amend its answer to deny manufacture of the water slide. P failed to show that he would be precluded from recovering from any other party and that D acted in bad faith.

Comment. *Beeck* illustrates that the burden is on the party opposing amendment to show actual prejudice. It is an abuse of discretion for a court to deny amendment in the absence of some justification for doing so.

---

b. **Amendments adding parties.** Pretrial amendments may add new parties to the action as well as correct oversights in the original pleadings. Under the codes, while such amendments are allowed, they may never relate back to the time of the filing of the original action to toll the statute of limitations against the new party. Under the Rules, however, an amendment adding a new party may relate back to toll the statute of limitations against the new party if, prior to the running of the statute, the new party had actual notice that except for a mistake in identity she herself would have been named in the original complaint.

1) **Federal Rule 15(c).** Effective December 1, 1991, Rule 15(c) was amended to provide that the party to be added must receive notice within the period for *service of process*, rather than that for commencing the action. [Fed. R. Civ. P. 15(c)] This amendment allows a plaintiff an additional 120 days to notify a party against whom she has a claim.

2) **Mistake concerning party identity--**

Worthington v. Wilson, 790 F. Supp. 829 (C.D. Ill. 1992).

Facts. During an arrest in Peoria Heights on February 25, 1989, Worthington's (P's) wrist was injured by police. On February 25, 1991, the day the statute of limitations expired, P filed suit in circuit court against the village of Peoria Heights and "three unknown named police officers," claiming a violation of his constitutional rights under 42 U.S.C. section 1983. The village removed the action to this court. On June 17, 1991, P amended his complaint and named Wilson and Wall (Ds) as the officers who arrested him; the amended complaint contained no claim against the village. Ds moved to dismiss on the grounds that the statute of limitations had run and the complaint failed to state a proper claim under section 1983. A magistrate recommended Ds' motion be granted. P objected. This is an additional hearing on the motion.

Issue. Where a complaint is filed against "unknown" defendants and subsequently amended to name actual defendants, does the amended complaint relate back if the failure to name the defendants in the original complaint was not due to a mistake but rather to being unaware of the identities of the defendants?

Held. No. Motion to dismiss granted.

♦ Under Federal Rule of Civil Procedure 15(c) as amended, P's complaint is not timely filed because, even though Ds received notice of the action within 120 days of the original filing, P's original use of fictitious names did not involve a "mistake concerning the identity of the proper party."

♦ Relation back in this case is not governed by section 2-413 of the Illinois Code of Civil Procedure because it is not necessary to borrow the state rule unless there is no similar federal provision. Here, the state law would dictate a contrary result, and when state law is at odds with federal law, federal law governs.

---

4. **The Variance Problem.** Pleadings are intended to limit the scope of proof offered at trial. When a party, therefore, attempts at trial to offer a line of proof

not alluded to in the pleadings, there is a variance between the pleadings and the proof. At common law, such a variance automatically excluded the proffered evidence. Under later pleading rules, however, variance need not automatically preclude introduction of the new line of proof. Under certain conditions the trial court will allow the introducing party to amend her pleadings to encompass the attempted proof.

a. **Variance under the codes.** In code pleading, the trial court will exclude evidence from trial only if there is a "total variance" between the pleadings and the attempted proof. If there is only a "partial variance," most trial courts as a matter of course will allow the introducing party to amend her pleadings to encompass the attempted line of proof.

   1) **Total variance.** In code pleading, there is said to be a total variance between pleading and proof when the "fundamental theory of recovery" or the "fundamental nature of the action" sought to be proved at trial is alien to that introduced by way of the pleadings. Preclusion of such a fundamentally different theory of recovery is automatic on grounds that there is bound to be prejudice to the opposing party in his not having time to prepare an adequate defense to the new cause of action.

   2) **Partial variance.** In code pleading, partial variances between the pleadings and the offered proof at trial are deemed immaterial, unless actual prejudice to the opposing party is demonstrated. A partial variance is a variance that seeks to introduce concrete facts not alluded to in the pleadings, but that does not fundamentally change the nature of the action.

b. **Variance under the Rules.** Under the Federal Rules and their state counterparts, a variance between pleading and proof almost never is grounds for automatic exclusion of the proffered evidence. Rather, leave to amend pleadings to conform to the proof is almost totally within the discretion of the trial court, with the added proviso that amendments must be granted freely unless there is undue surprise to the opposing party. There is purposefully omitted from the Federal Rules any mention of "partial variance" or "total variance"—the only criterion by which propriety of an amendment to correct a variance may be judged is that of surprise to the opposing party.

   1) **Federal Rule 15(b).** "When issues not raised by the pleadings are tried by express or implied consent of the parties, they shall be treated in all respects as if they had been raised in the pleadings. Such amendment of the pleadings as may be necessary to cause them to conform to the evidence and to raise these issues may be made upon motion of any party at any time, even after judgment; but failure so to amend does not affect the result of the trial of these issues. If evidence is objected to at trial on the ground that it is not within the issues made

by the pleadings, the court may allow the pleadings to be amended and shall do so freely when the presentation of the merits of the action will be subserved thereby and the objecting party fails to satisfy the court that the admission of such evidence would prejudice the party in maintaining the party's action or defense upon the merits. The court may grant a continuance to enable the objecting party to meet such evidence."

2) Notice to opposing party--

Moore v. Moore, 391 A.2d 762 (D.C. Ct. App. 1978).

Facts. Mr. Moore (P) and Mrs. Moore (D) were divorced. P filed a complaint for custody. After trial, D moved to conform the pleadings to the evidence; the court granted the motion and awarded D custody, plus child support, separate maintenance, and attorneys' fees. P received visitation rights subject to a bond. P appeals.

Issue. May D be granted relief where none was claimed in the pretrial pleadings?

Held. Yes. Judgment affirmed in part and reversed in part.

- ◆ Issues not raised in pleadings may be added by amendment when the issues are tried by express consent of the parties. Where consent is to be "implied," careful examination of the record is required to see whether the party contesting the amendment received actual notice of the injection of the unpleaded matters and had adequate opportunity to litigate.

- ◆ Although D did not plead custody, P had adequate notice that the court would determine not merely whether he should have custody but also whether D should have custody.

- ◆ The trial judge indicated that a grant of support was necessary to provide complete relief. This and P's failure to object to the introduction of evidence on the issue indicates that P had adequate notice and had impliedly consented.

- ◆ The grant of separate maintenance does not appear justified. Such issues are not normally involved in custody cases; the evidence presented, although not objected to by P, was introduced late in the trial and could have been relevant to the child support issues. Amendment to include this issue was improper.

- ◆ Awarding attorneys' fees is not uncommon in custody suits. In addition, the trial judge held a separate hearing on the issue. Therefore, it was permissible to allow amendment on this issue.

- ◆ Visitation rights resolution is obviously part of a custody suit. The bond requirement is well within the court's power to impose.

F. SUPPLEMENTAL PLEADINGS

1. **Introduction.** A supplemental pleading is distinct from an amendment in both purpose and scope. The function of a supplemental pleading is to call to the attention of the court and the opposing party occurrences directly related to the cause of action sued upon that have transpired after the filing of the original pleading—to "update" the pleading to include relevant items unknown at the time of the original filing.

2. **Supplemental Pleadings Under the Rules.**

   a. **Federal Rule 15(d).** "Upon motion of a party the court may, upon reasonable notice and upon such terms as are just, permit the party to serve a supplemental pleading setting forth transactions or occurrences or events which have happened since the date of the pleading sought to be supplemented. Permission may be granted even though the original pleading is defective in its statement of a claim for relief or defense. If the court deems it advisable that the adverse party plead to the supplemental pleading, it shall so order, specifying the time therefor."

   b. **Code and Rules pleading compared.**

      1) **Cure of defects.** Under code pleading, a supplemental pleading may not alter the cause of action sued upon, nor may it be used to cure pleading defects in the original pleading. Such goals may be accomplished, if at all, only through the use of amendments to the pleading. However, the Rules are specifically more liberal in their use of supplemental pleadings—they may be used to cure defects in the original pleading as long as the entire nature of the cause of action set forth in the original pleading is not changed. Under the Rules, it seems, the traditional sharp distinction between amendments and supplemental pleadings is being slowly devolved in favor of a general battery of "curative measures" designed to make the pleadings subserve the goal of efficient adjudication upon the merits.

      2) **Introduction of new causes of action.** It is generally stated, both under the codes and under the Rules, that the purpose of supplemental pleadings is to aid a cause of action already averred, not to introduce a cause of action accrued since the plaintiff filed his original action. As a rule of thumb, this is probably still true today—amendments rather than supplemental pleadings are the proper vehicles for the introduction of new causes of action into an existing action. But under Rule 15(d), it has been ruled that a supplemental pleading may "cure" a defective cause of action to the extent that it may introduce a cause of action acquired only subsequent to the supplemented pleading.

G. PROVISIONS TO DETER FRIVOLOUS PLEADINGS

1. **Federal Rule 11—Signing of Pleadings.** Every pleading of a party represented by an attorney must be signed by at least one attorney of record. Except when otherwise specifically provided by rule or statute, pleadings need not be verified or accompanied by affidavit. The signature of an attorney constitutes a certificate by the signer that it is not interposed for any improper purpose such as to harass or to cause unnecessary delay or needless increase in the cost of litigation, the claims and defenses are warranted by existing law or by a nonfrivolous argument for the extension, modification, or reversal of existing law, or the establishment of a new law, and that the allegations and factual contentions have or are likely to have evidentiary support. [Fed. R. Civ. P. 11] The 1993 amendment to Rule 11 imposes an ongoing duty on counsel to evaluate the position taken in earlier documents to determine whether counsel can continue to advocate the earlier position taken. Under prior Rule 11, the certification that a claim was not frivolous applied only at the time of signing. The Rule further provides that unsigned pleadings, or those interposed for delay, may be stricken as sham and false and the action may proceed as though the pleading had not been served. In addition, for a willful violation of Rule 11, an attorney may be subjected to appropriate disciplinary action, including sanctions and attorneys' fees.

2. **Verification in State Courts.** "Verification" is the practice of submitting, with a pleading, a separate affidavit from the party on whose behalf the pleading is filed, to the effect that to the best of the party's knowledge and belief the material contained in the pleading is true or based upon reasonable grounds. It is a practice designed to forestall specious pleadings—the pleading party is liable for breach of affidavit if it is shown that the material pleaded is patently false. Under the codes, verification is optional except in certain statutorily prescribed types of cases. Under the Rules, the signature of the attorney is itself verification, so separate verification is superfluous. Therefore, separate verification of a pleading is much more common in state procedure under the codes than under the Federal Rules or corresponding state rules.

3. **Verification by Nominal Plaintiff in Class Action--**

Surowitz v. Hilton Hotels Corp., 383 U.S. 363 (1966).

Facts. Surowitz (P) was nominal plaintiff in a class action by shareholders against the board of directors of Hilton Hotels (D). P, in a long, highly technical, carefully drafted, and well-researched complaint prepared for her by a staff of corporate attorneys, alleged that the board of directors had been illegally withholding dividend funds. D, by deposition, showed that P personally did not understand the meaning of the complaint, even though she had verified it under Federal Rule 23(b). Therefore, D moved under Federal Rule 11 that the pleading be stricken as a sham and as falsely verified. The motion was granted by the district court and affirmed by the court of appeals. P appeals.

Issue. Is dismissal of a class action proper on the grounds that the nominal plaintiff does not fully understand the charges, although the suit is based on reasonable beliefs growing out of careful investigation?

Held. No. Judgment reversed.

♦ The purpose of provisions such as Rules 11 and 23.1 is to discourage obviously specious pleadings, not to discourage complex class actions brought by nominal plaintiffs in good faith. The complaint was filed after long, detailed, arduous investigation by a staff of skilled lawyers and accountants. It was obviously not specious—in fact the complaint was so thorough that there was more than a small chance that the allegations were correct. Under such circumstances, the fact that the nominal shareholder did not personally have the educational training to understand the legal ramification of the complaint was immaterial.

Concurrence (Harlan, J.). The complaint was supported by an affidavit of P's counsel. Rule 23(b) does not specify that the complaint need be verified by the plaintiff shareholder. Under a reasonable interpretation of Rule 23(b), I believe that the counsel's affidavit amounts to an adequate verification.

---

4. **Reasonable Inquiry into Evidentiary Support.** Rule 11 now requires that an attorney conduct an inquiry that is "reasonable under the circumstances" into whether facts asserted by a client have evidentiary support in the record. At least one court has held that an attorney is entitled to rely on the objectively reasonable representations of his client.

   a. **Reliance on information client provides--**

Hadges v. Yonkers Racing Corp., 48 F.3d 1320 (2d Cir. 1995).

Facts. Hadges (P) was a racehorse driver, trainer, and owner who had had his license suspended by the New York State Racing Board. P claimed that, because of a conspiracy against him, he was being denied the ability to work at a number of racetracks even after his license had been reinstated. P filed suit in federal court against Yonkers Racing Corporation (D), the owners of one of the tracks that had banned him. P was also involved in a state action against D that alleged D conspired with other state racetracks to "blackball" him. During the course of the federal litigation, P submitted to the court an affidavit stating that P had not worked in over four years. The affidavit was signed by both P and his attorney, Kunstler, neither of whom mentioned the state court litigation. In response to the affidavit, D provided evidence that P had raced five times in 1991 and seven times in 1993. D then moved to dismiss the case and requested sanctions against P and his attorney for misrepresentation and for failing to disclose the state action to the district court. The court imposed a Rule 11 sanction of $2,000 on P for misrepresenting his racing history. The court also censured Kunstler for failing to adequately inquire as to the truth of P's affidavit and for failing to inform the court of the state court litigation. P and Kunstler argued that the district court abused its discretion in imposing sanctions on them.

Issue. Did the court abuse its discretion in imposing Rule 11 sanctions on P and his attorney?

Held. Yes. Sanctions reversed.

♦ D failed to comply with the procedural requirements of Rule 11. Specifically, D did not serve P with the request for sanctions 21 days before presenting it to the court. This 21-day "safe-harbor" period is specifically mandated by Rule 11. If P had received notice of the request for sanctions, he would have had the benefit of 21 days to correct or withdraw any misstatements in his affidavit. Therefore, the sanctions against P must be reversed.

♦ Kunstler also did not receive the benefits of the safe harbor provision. In addition, we find that his reliance on his client's statements was reasonable under the circumstances. While it is clear that he made no attempt to verify the statements, there is no evidence to indicate that Kunstler had any independent knowledge of the misrepresentations in his client's affidavit. At the time of the affidavit, Kunstler had in his possession an affidavit from Meadowlands, another racetrack, which stated that D's ban on P would provide the basis for a ban at Meadowlands as well. In light of this, it was reasonable for Kunstler to believe that his client was telling the truth about not being able to work.

♦ Further, there would be no tactical advantage in not mentioning the pending state court litigation to the district court since D was a party to both actions, and would certainly have informed the court of the state action if it were to its advantage. For these reasons, we reverse the imposition of censure.

---

b. Contrast. In *Business Guides, Inc. v. Chromatic Communications Enterprises, Inc.*, 498 U.S. 533 (1991), a magistrate had found that the plaintiff's complaint and application for a temporary restraining order ("TRO") were completely baseless. Both the plaintiff and its attorneys had signed the TRO application, and both were sanctioned. The Supreme Court upheld the sanctions finding that the plaintiff's attorneys had failed to conduct a reasonable and proper inquiry, which resulted in the presentation of unreasonable and false information to the court. Note that *Business Guides* was decided under the 1983 version of Rule 11, in which an attorney violated the Rule by failing to make a reasonable investigation of the facts. The 1993 version appears to relax the rule somewhat.

IX. JOINDER OF CLAIMS AND PARTIES: EXPANDING THE SCOPE OF THE CIVIL ACTION

A. JOINDER OF CLAIMS

1. **At Common Law.** The common law allowed the plaintiff to join, in one action, several separate and distinct claims against a defendant only when each of the separate claims was of the same quality, legal or equitable. Each claim was pursued in the same action through a separate plea—the pleas themselves could be joined in the same document only when all the claims were of the same quality, and the relief sought from each count was of the same type—*e.g.,* money damages.

2. **Early Code Provisions.** Early codes did away with the necessity for all of the plaintiff's joined actions to be of the same quality, legal or equitable, and substituted instead a series of "classes" of causes of action. Two distinct causes of action within the same class could be united in the same claim and the same plea, but causes of action in two different classes could not be so united.

   a. **Typical classification system.** The classes of legal actions used for purposes of joinder of claims under the early codes were typically: (i) actions on contract, express or implied; (ii) injuries to the person; (iii) injuries to personal reputation; (iv) injuries to property; (v) actions to recover real property; (vi) actions to recover personalty; and (vii) all actions arising out of the same transaction or occurrence.

   b. **Different actions arising from same transaction--**

Harris v. Avery, 5 Kan. 146 (1869).

Facts. Avery (P) sued Harris (D) to recover damages for false imprisonment and slander. P possessed causes of action against D for false imprisonment and slander, both of which arose from the same series of transactions. The Kansas Code read, in part, that the "plaintiff may unite in a single action in the same petition several causes of action . . . arising out of the same transaction connected with the same subject of the action." P sought to join his causes of action in a single petition.

Issue. May a plaintiff prosecute two causes of action in the same proceeding if they arose out of the same transaction?

Held. Yes. Judgment affirmed.

- At common law, joinder would not have been allowed since the two claims were of different quality.

- The Kansas State Code abolished the old common law rules of joinder. Joinder of pleas is proper whenever the same transaction forms the basis of two or more causes of action.

- Since the same transaction forms the basis for the slander claim and the false imprisonment claim, joinder of both actions in a single plea was proper.

Comment. State codes and the Federal Rules of Civil Procedure have greatly modified the common law of joinder of claims. In *M.K. v. Tenet* (*infra*), the court recognized that Rule 18 removes all restrictions to the joinder of claims in federal court (outside of subject-matter jurisdiction requirements).

B. ADDITION OF CLAIMS

1. Counterclaims.

a. Historical analysis. A counterclaim is an offensive weapon that a defendant may use against a plaintiff—as a part of her answer, the defendant may set forth certain causes of action that she herself possesses against the plaintiff. At common law, the counterclaim as we know it today did not exist, although a practice known as "equitable setoff of claims" existed in the courts of chancery. The original version of the first New York Code provided that a defendant could counterclaim against a plaintiff if:

1) The defendant's cause of action arose out of the same transaction or occurrence that also formed the bases of the plaintiff's claims against the defendant, or was "otherwise integrally related" to the bases of the plaintiff's cause of action; and

2) In a counterclaim based on contract, the defendant's asserted claim arose out of a contract existing at the time of the plaintiff's commencement of action against the defendant.

b. Compulsory and permissive counterclaims in modern law.

1) **Jurisdiction of court over counterclaims.** Under most modern statutes, including the Federal Rules, counterclaims are either compulsory or permissive. In federal courts, compulsory counterclaims, those counterclaims that a defendant must set out in her answer, require no basis of jurisdiction independent from that which supports the plaintiff's claim—compulsory counterclaims are deemed ancillary

to the plaintiff's jurisdiction. But permissive counterclaims, those that the defendant may or may not bring, as she desires, require independent, adequate grounds for federal jurisdiction before they can be entertained.

2) **Compulsory and permissive counterclaims.** A defendant may state against a plaintiff *any* cause of action that she possesses against the plaintiff at the time that she files her answer, but she is required to counterclaim on any such causes of action that arose out of the same "transaction or occurrence" that formed the basis of the plaintiff's complaint. This is a characteristic that runs throughout the modern codes, the Federal Rules, and their state counterparts. It reflects a policy decision that the small risk of confusion (*i.e.,* the scope of the litigation is expanded by the joining of many causes of action in the same suit) is outweighed by the risk of undue expansion of the judicial workload if such counterclaims are severely limited.

a) **Federal Rule of Civil Procedure 13(a):** "A pleading shall state as a counterclaim any claim which at the time of serving the pleading the pleader has against any opposing party, if it arises out of the transaction or occurrence that is the subject matter of the opposing party's claim and does not require for its adjudication the presence of third parties of whom the court cannot acquire jurisdiction."

b) **Federal Rule 13(b):** "A pleading may state as a counterclaim any claim against an opposing party not arising out of the transaction or occurrence that is the subject matter of the opposing party's claim."

c. **"Transaction or occurrence."** Compulsory counterclaims are those that arise out of the same "transaction or occurrence" that the plaintiff has sued on. Generally a counterclaim is said to arise out of the same "transaction or occurrence" as that underlying the plaintiff's cause of action only if there is a "compelling logical relationship" between the plaintiff's and the defendant's claims.

1) **Compulsory counterclaim--**

United States v. Heyward-Robinson Co., 430 F.2d 1077 (2d Cir. 1970).

Facts. D'Agostino Excavators, Inc. (P) contracted with Heyward-Robinson Co. (D), the general contractor, for certain construction work to be done at federal and nonfederal sites. P sued D and D's surety to recover payments alleged to be due on the federal job. A single insurance policy covered both jobs. D counterclaimed on the basis that P was liable for overpayments and costs of completion on both jobs. D also argued that P had breached the subcontracts by allowing the insurance policy to lapse. A verdict was returned in favor of P. D appeals on the basis that the court lacked jurisdiction over that portion of the counterclaim dealing with the nonfederal job.

Issue. Is a counterclaim compulsory, and therefore not requiring an independent basis of federal jurisdiction, if it arises out of the transaction or occurrence that is the subject matter of the opposing party's claim?

Held. Yes. Judgment affirmed.

♦ The claims arising out of both the federal and nonfederal jobs are closely and logically related.

♦ Both jobs were covered by a single insurance policy and were entered into by the same parties for the same type of work.

♦ The controversy in this case arose from occurrences affecting both jobs. The two jobs are so intertwined that it is impossible to separate them.

Concurrence. The counterclaim here is permissive, not compulsory. The rule requiring permissive counterclaims to have an independent jurisdictional basis should be changed.

---

2) **Ancillary jurisdiction.** In *Great Lakes Rubber Corp. v. Herbert Cooper Co.*, 286 F.2d 631 (3d Cir. 1961), the court recognized that the issue of whether ancillary jurisdiction exists is answered by the same test that determines whether a counterclaim is compulsory.

d. **Consequences of failing to plead a counterclaim.** If the defendant fails to include in her action a compulsory counterclaim, by majority rule the omission bars her from ever asserting the same claim in another action. The omission of the compulsory counterclaim carries full res judicata effect on the issues that should have been included. For this reason, almost every court is very liberal in allowing omitted counterclaims to be added by amendment to the answer, even at late stages of the trial itself. Of course, omission of a permissive counterclaim carries no such res judicata effect.

2. **Cross-claims.**

a. **General definition.** In her answer, a defendant may assert not only counterclaims against the plaintiff but also any independent claims that she has against co-defendants when such claims have arisen out of the same "transaction or occurrence" as that which gave rise either to the plaintiff's original cause of action or to a counterclaim against the original plaintiff. As with counterclaims, the rationales behind cross-claims are reduction of the judicial workload and a belief that all segments of a disagreement should be simultaneously considered if true justice upon the merits of the disagreement is to be obtained. [*See* Fed. R. Civ. P. 13(g)]

b. **Jurisdiction over cross-claims.** As a general rule, cross-claims need no independent grounds of jurisdiction in the federal courts. Since cross-claims are always closely related either to the original cause of action of the plaintiff or a jurisdictionally supported permissive counterclaim of the defendant, cross-claims always have ancillary jurisdiction.

c. **New parties brought in by cross-claims.** As a general rule, a cross-claim between co-parties may not directly involve persons not parties to the original action of the plaintiff or the counterclaim of the defendant. However, if for the fair adjudication of a cross-claim the presence of a new party is required, the court has the right to summon the new party if within the jurisdiction of the court.

d. **Cross-claims in state courts.** Cross-claims in federal courts are freely allowed—there is a policy favoring the validity of a cross-claim "in the interests of full adjudication of an entire dispute upon the merits." In many state courts, however, cross-claims are disfavored, although allowed occasionally. The rationale behind this hesitance to permit cross-claims is that multidirectional claims in the same suit unduly confuse the jury and tend to obscure the legal issues involved in any one of the claims.

e. **Cross-claims involving different legal theories--**

Lasa Per L'Industria Del Marmo Societa Per Azioni v. Alexander, 414 F.2d 143 (6th Cir. 1969).

Facts. Lasa (P) had a contract to supply marble to Alexander (D1) for use in a construction project. P sued D1, who was a subcontractor, and Southern Builders (D2) and others for the balance due on the contract. D1 filed a cross-claim against D2, who filed a cross-claim against D1. D1 also filed a third-party complaint against the architect. D1's claims were based mostly on negligence and injury to D1's business reputation. The district court dismissed all but the original claim. D1 appeals.

Issue. Where cross-claims involve legal theories different from the original claim and arise out of related, but not identical, transactions, should they be permitted?

Held. Yes. Judgment reversed.

♦ Under the Federal Rules, the rights of all parties generally should be adjudicated in one action. The words "transaction or occurrence" should be liberally interpreted; here, there is a logical relationship between P's claim and D's cross-claims, since all relate to the same project and to problems involving the use of marble.

Much of the evidence to be presented in these claims is similar. If the trial is too complex, the trial judge may order separate trials.

Dissent. P's claim is essentially contractual, while the cross-claims are actions in tort. The proof in the separate claims would consist of entirely different evidence. The basic issues are different, and different contracts and relationships are involved. The trial court's opinion should be affirmed.

C. IDENTIFYING PARTIES WHO MAY SUE AND BE SUED

1. Real Party in Interest Rule.

    a. The black letter rule. A civil action may be prosecuted only by the "real party in interest" and not by any other acting in her behalf. The real party in interest in a civil action is that party to whom the substantive law assigns the right to secure a remedy against an offending party. This is not in every case identical with the party who may derive a benefit from the prosecution of the action—it often occurs that the real party in interest secures no benefit from the bringing of the action, although one or more collateral parties, not real parties in interest, may derive such benefit.

    b. Common law. At common law, the real party in interest was required to bring the action, but not necessarily in her own name. The equitable holder of title to real estate was deemed a real party in interest in any civil action concerning title to that real estate, but could not sue in a court of law under her own name. She could, however, bring an action under the name of the legal title holder—a nominal plaintiff—and thus gain access to the courts of law.

    c. Code pleading. Under modern code pleading, the real party in interest to a civil controversy is the only party allowed to institute the action on the controversy, and further, she must institute the action in her own name. However, a few courts now allow the real party in interest to be joined only as a nominal plaintiff in an action prosecuted by one not traditionally considered a real party in interest—suit is allowed as long as the real party in interest's name is used to institute the action.

    d. Federal Rules. Under Federal Rule 17(a), the following parties have the right to sue on claims, even though they may have no beneficial interest therein:

        (i) Executor, administrator, guardian, bailee, or trustee of an express trust;

(ii) A party with whom or in whose name a contract has been made for the benefit of another, *e.g.,* principal-agent; and

(iii) The United States Government, when expressly authorized by statute to maintain the action for the use or benefit of another.

In all other cases, the real party in interest in a federal action is determined by reference to applicable state law.

e. **Creation of diversity jurisdiction.** The citizenship of the real party in interest governs the action for purposes of diversity of citizenship jurisdiction in the federal courts. Many plaintiffs have attempted to "manufacture" diversity of citizenship by assigning their rights to another, by subrogating their rights to another, or by creating fictitious agencies or "transparent" trusts. In determining whether such a transfer of interest actually changes the real party in interest to the claim, the court uses a good faith test: only good faith transfers of interest, as determined by reasonableness of motive, may change the real party in interest of a cause of action.

f. **Insurance subrogation actions--**

Ellis Canning Co. v. International Harvester Co., 255 P.2d 658 (Kan. 1953).

Facts. Ellis Canning Co. (P), insured by Potomac Insurance Co., filed a negligence action against International Harvester Co. (D) for damages allegedly due for injury to one of P's packing plants. Potomac had paid all of P's losses from the accident prior to P's filing of suit, but under terms of the insurance contract, P was required to institute a civil action against any negligent party causing damage to the insured property. D's answer alleged, inter alia, that P was not the real party in interest and so had no legal right to maintain the action. P's motion to strike this portion of D's answer was overruled. P appeals.

Issue. Is an insured plaintiff, reimbursed for damages caused by the defendant, the real party in interest in a subsequent suit against the defendant?

Held. No. Judgment affirmed.

♦ Because all of P's losses had been paid by insurance, P no longer had any real interest in the outcome of the action. The real party in interest to the prosecution of the civil action against the negligent party was the insurance company, to whom would accrue all the recovery gained from prosecution of the action. Therefore, the action must be dismissed, and Potomac Insurance must institute an action in its own name.

D. CLAIMS INVOLVING MULTIPLE PARTIES

1. **Permissive Joinder of Parties.** Frequently, the most difficult problem encountered at the outset of a lawsuit is determination of which parties are to be joined therein as plaintiffs or defendants. Rules of permissive joinder apply to those parties who may be joined ("proper parties"). Compulsory joinder rules apply to parties who must be joined ("indispensable parties") and those who should be joined ("conditionally necessary parties") if possible.

   a. **Early state code application of joinder rule--**

Ryder v. Jefferson Hotel Co., 113 S.E. 474 (S.C. 1922).

Facts. Ryder (P) sued Jefferson (D) for damages for personal injuries. P and his wife rented a room in D's hotel. During the night, the room clerk, convinced that they were not married, entered without knocking, accused them of immoral conduct, and ejected them from their room. D demurred to the causes of action for defamation of character and assault (which the wife had joined with her husband's claim) on grounds that joinder was improper. The trial court overruled D's demurrer. D appeals.

Issue. When two or more plaintiffs allege that a defendant committed a tort of a personal nature against them, must each of them serve and try their right of action separately?

Held. Yes. Judgment reversed.

♦ Each of the two plaintiffs, husband and wife, held a different and distinct personal cause of action against D. By state law, "united causes of action" must "affect equally all the parties joined in suit . . . and must be separately stated." The personal causes of action held by the joint plaintiffs were not "united" or imbued with instinctive similarity of nature. Therefore, joinder of the causes of action was improper.

Dissent. This was a joint injury like an injury to a co-partnership.

---

   b. **Modern approach.** In response to the restrictiveness of the original code approach, modern rules are extremely liberal. Basically, all persons may join in one action as plaintiffs, or be joined therein as defendants, if: (i) a right to relief is asserted by (or against) them jointly, severally, or in the alternative; (ii) the right to relief arises out of the same transaction or series of transactions; and (iii) there is at least one question of law or fact common to all parties sought to be joined. [Fed. R. Civ. P. 20(a)]

   c. **"Logically related" claims--**

M.K. v. Tenet, 216 F.R.D. 133 (D.C. 2002).

Facts. Six former CIA employees (Ps) sued the CIA, its director, and other parties (Ds) alleging violations of the Privacy Act of 1974 and various constitutional claims based on the obstruction of Ps' right to counsel. Specifically, Ps asserted that they were victims of employment discrimination but had been unable to effectively bring their discrimination claims because Ds continually denied Ps and/or Ps' counsel access to employee and agency records. Ps sought to amend their complaint to add nine named Ps, to identify "John Doe" Ds, and to provide information about existing claims in order to cure deficiencies of their original complaint. Ds filed a motion to sever the claims of the initial Ps under Rule 21.

Issue. Should plaintiffs' claims be joined if the defendants' acts and omissions pertaining to the plaintiffs' claims are logically related events that arise out of the same series of transactions or occurrences and if the plaintiffs' claims are related by a common question of law or fact?

Held. Yes. Ps' motion to amend is granted, and Ds' motion to sever is denied.

♦ Citing Rule 20(a), Ps assert that Ds' acts and omissions pertaining to Ps' claims are "logically related" events that the court can regard as "arising out of the same transaction, occurrence or series of occurrences." "Logically related" events may consist of an alleged consistent pattern of obstruction of security-cleared counsel by Ds. The court concludes that the alleged repeated pattern of obstruction of counsel is "logically related" as a "series of transactions or occurrences" that establishes an overall pattern of policies and practices aimed at denying Ps the effective assistance of counsel. Each P claims to have been damaged by Ds' actions and requests declaratory and injunctive relief. Thus, the court finds that Ps have satisfied the first prong of Rule 20(a).

♦ Ps' claims are related by common questions of law or fact, including whether a certain notice restricting Ps' counsel from accessing records intruded on Ps' substantial interest in freely discussing their legal rights with counsel, whether Ds engaged in a common scheme or pattern of behavior effectively denying Ps' legal right to discuss their claims with counsel, and whether Ds' alleged policy or practice is implemented through a concert of action among the CIA management and the newly named Ds. Furthermore, Ps allege common claims under the Privacy Act. Thus, Ps have also met the second prong of Rule 20(a).

♦ The joinder or non-severance of the six existing Ps and their new claims under Rule 20(a) will promote trial convenience, expedite the final resolution of disputes, and act to prevent multiple lawsuits, extra expense to the parties, and loss of time to the court and the litigants in this case.

d.   No identity of duty or contract necessary--

Tanbro Fabrics Corp. v. Beaunit Mills, Inc., 167 N.Y.S.2d 387 (1957).

Facts. Three parties are involved in this litigation: Tanbro (P), buyer of a defective lot of yarn; Beaunit (D), bulk seller of the lot of yarn; and Amity (D), independent processor of the yarn. At the outset of the suit, it was indeterminate when the defect had been introduced into the yarn. Therefore, P sought to join both Ds in a single action for breach of implied warranty. Ds both resisted the joinder on the grounds that their separate rights were unrelated to each other. The state statute was identical to Rule 20, above. The trial court denied P's motion to consolidate. P appeals.

Issue. When there exist claims involving multiple parties to an action, must there exist among these parties an identity of duty or contract before the court will permit a consolidation of various claims?

Held. No. Judgment reversed.

♦   To avoid multiplicity of suits covering the same grounds, we must construe the "series of transactions or occurrences" requirement of the state statute liberally— as there was a common connection of all parties with the defective yarn, there was enough of a common interest that joint suit was proper. It was no bar to joinder of the actions against Ds that the exact warranty sued on was not identical for each of them or that they might not be jointly liable to P.

Comment. This case illustrates the tactical importance of consolidation. Consolidation here allowed P to avoid the possible necessity of prosecuting civil litigations to discover who breached which warranty in causing the yarn to be defective.

e.   **Effective joinder of claims.** As long as the requirements for the joinder of parties (above) are met, each of the parties joined may assert as many claims as she has against any opposing party. [*See* Fed. R. Civ. P. 18] The policy of the law is to allow unlimited joinder of claims, providing only that among the claims joined there is at least one "common question of fact or law" involving all the parties.

f.   **Power of the court to order separate trials.** To curb any extra expense, delay, or other prejudice to any party that might result from the joinder of numerous parties asserting numerous separate claims against one another, the court is empowered to order separate trials for the various claims joined, or otherwise regulate the proceedings to minimize the prejudice, delay, or expense involved. [*See* Fed. R. Civ. P. 20(b)]

g.   How to attack improper joinder. If parties are joined who do not meet the requirements above ("common question," "same transaction," etc.), the defect must be raised at the outset by appropriate motion or demurrer. Failure to raise it waives the nonraising party's right to later object to the defect.

2.   Mandatory Joinder of Persons.

   a.   In general. It is generally acknowledged that the court must compel joinder of any nonparty whose interests are so identified with those interests being litigated that either fair adjudication on the merits requires her presence or failure to join her will prejudice her interests. If the nonparty sought to be joined is outside the jurisdiction of the court, however, compulsory joinder is not possible. When joinder is not possible, if the action cannot in good faith proceed, the nonjoined party is considered indispensable to the action. Otherwise, the nonjoined party is considered necessary but not indispensable, and the action may proceed without her joinder. [*See* Fed. R. Civ. P. 19(a) and (b)]

   b.   Modern approach—practical considerations. Modern rules focus on the practical considerations arising if a party with an interest in the action is not before the court. Rule 19(a) provides that any person with an interest in the subject of a pending action shall be joined as a party thereto if:

   1)   In the person's absence complete relief cannot be afforded among those already parties; or

   2)   The person's interest is such that to proceed without the person would be substantially prejudicial because it would:

      a)   Impair the person's ability to protect that interest in later proceedings, or

      b)   Expose the parties before the court to the risk of double liability or inconsistent obligations.

   c.   Indispensable parties in will contests--

Bank of California National Association v. Superior Court, 106 P.2d 879 (Cal. 1940).

Facts. Bank of California (D) was appointed administrator of the Boyd estate. St. Luke's Hospital was residuary legatee, and received 75% of the estate. Before probate, however, Smedley (P) brought an action claiming that Boyd had executed a contract with her, in which Boyd had promised to make a new will leaving the entire estate to her. In the action, only D, as administrator, and the hospital, as primary legatee, were served or appeared. The remaining legatees were all outside the jurisdiction of the court. D obtained an injunction against the further pursuance of the Smedley action until the other legatees under Boyd's will were served and appeared. P obtained a dissolution of the injunction on grounds that the interests of all parties were adequately protected by P's and the hospital's appearance—therefore all other parties were necessary but not indispensable. P sought a writ of prohibition to restrain the trial until the other parties were brought in. P appeals from denial of the writ.

Issue. Are all legatees indispensable parties in a suit by one legatee against the residuary legatee?

Held. No. Judgment affirmed.

♦ The tendency of the courts is to limit expansion of the number of indispensable parties to a suit if at all possible. The claims of the other legatees under the Boyd will were easily separable from the specific claims being adjudicated in the Smedley action, the validity of the gift to the hospital. From this aspect, then, the other legatees were necessary but not indispensable parties to the action.

♦ The other legatees' long-run interest in the protection of the validity of the Boyd will would be quite adequately handled by the two parties appearing in the action, the administrator and the primary legatee. Therefore, the secondary legatees under the Boyd will were necessary but not indispensable parties to the Smedley action, and there was no reason to hold up prosecution of the action because they could not immediately be joined.

------

d. **Waiver of right to compel joinder.**

1) **Not indispensable.** If the absentee is not "indispensable," his nonjoinder must be raised at the earliest possible opportunity by the parties to the action. The defect must be raised in the initial pleading (motion or answer) of those who are parties to the action. Otherwise it is waived. [Fed. R. Civ. P. 12(h)]

2) **Indispensable.** If, however, the absentee is determined to be "indispensable," there is no such waiver. The nonjoinder of an "indispensable" party can be raised at any time by pleading or motion . . . even at the trial of the action. [Fed. R. Civ. P. 12(h)(2)] However, delay in raising the objection is one of the factors that the court may properly consider in exercising its discretion as to whether to dismiss the action.

e. **Effect of absence of indispensable party--**

Provident Tradesmens Bank & Trust Co. v. Patterson, 390 U.S. 102 (1968).

Facts. In 1958, Cionci, Lynch, and Smith died when Cionci negligently drove Dutcher's car over the median line on a highway and collided with a truck driven by Smith. After first obtaining a $50,000 judgment against Cionci's penniless estate, Lynch's estate, represented by Provident (P), filed suit against the insurer of Dutcher's auto, Lumbermen's Mutual (D). P sought a declaratory judgment as to D's liability to Lynch. The trial court awarded judgment to P. The appellate court reversed because of P's failure to join Dutcher, whom the appellate court believed an "indispensable" party. The United States Supreme Court granted certiorari to determine whether failure to join under the circumstances was automatically fatal.

Issue. When parties to an action fail to raise before or at the trial the issue of failure to join an indispensable party, does the absence of that indispensable party render the judgment invalid?

Held. No. Judgment vacated and case remanded.

♦   When there is no objection at trial to the nonjoinder of an "indispensable party," a verdict is rendered, and when the court determines in equity and good conscience that it may proceed without the party whose presence could have been compelled, a federal appellate court will not retroactively dismiss a lawsuit for failure to join an "indispensable party."

♦   Federal Rule 19(a) compels joinder only if the overriding interests in the case make such feasible. The court may determine "feasibility" under Rule 19(b) only by reference to the plaintiff's interest in the forum, the defendant's interest in avoiding a multiplicity of suits, the interests of the parties who potentially may be joined, and the court's interest in efficient and economic judicial administration.

♦   In the instant case, the court of appeals failed to examine these considerations before dismissing the suit. Therefore, its judgment should be reversed and that of the district court reinstated.

Comment. The policy behind Rule 19(a) is to establish flexible criteria designed to encourage the joinder of parties where feasible without subjecting parties to harsh and inflexible penalties for failure to join. Thus, though common law would render void for lack of subject matter jurisdiction any judgment in an action where the court failed to join all of the indispensable parties, under Rule 19(a), even where a court mistakenly refuses to join a party to an action, such court does not lose the power to adjudicate the controversy.

E. IMPLEADER

1. **General Definition.** Once a defendant has been sued in a civil action, he may cause a summons and complaint to issue to a third party, thereby impleading that third party into the action, as long as that third party is, or may be, liable to the original defendant for all or part of the claim that the plaintiff has filed against him. Use of impleader is rather limited in many codes, but the practice of impleader enjoys wide use under all versions of the Rules, and under several modern codes. [*See* Fed. R. Civ. P. 14(a)]

2. **Characteristics of Impleader.**

   a. **Right to indemnity.** Impleader is proper only in those limited situations where the third-party defendant is or may be liable to the original defendant by indemnification, subrogation, or recompensation. Where no possible right to indemnity exists, but the defendant still desires to bring in a third party, he must advance some theory other than impleader—*e.g.*, that the third party is a necessary party to the action.

   b. **Jurisdiction.** Impleader in no way affects the jurisdiction of a federal suit. An impleaded claim is always considered "ancillary" to the original cause of action running from the plaintiff to the defendant, and therefore requires no independent federal jurisdiction of its own.

   c. **Use of impleader.** Use of impleader is restricted to bringing a nonparty into an action—a nonparty who may ultimately be liable for the damage that has befallen the plaintiff. Any other use of impleader, such as in an attempt to realign existing parties to an action, is improper.

3. **Impleader a Procedural Matter--**

Jeub v. B/G Foods, Inc., 2 F.R.D. 238 (D. Minn. 1942).

Facts. Jeub (P) and several others were poisoned by ham served in B/G Foods, Inc.'s (D's) restaurant. D impleaded Swift & Co., from whom it had bought the canned ham that was served, seeking complete indemnity from Swift for any recovery allowed P. P and the others declined to amend their complaints to include Swift & Co. as an original defendant. Minnesota state law allowed impleader only on a "demonstrated right to indemnity." Federal law allows impleader when there "may be" a right to indemnity. Swift & Co. moves to vacate the order making it a third-party defendant.

Issue. Is the right to implead procedural and therefore governed by federal law in diversity cases?

Held. Yes. Motion denied.

♦ While the extent of indemnity between parties should be determined by reference to state law, the right to implead is a "procedural" matter in the district court and as such is governed by the Federal Rules. Therefore, since Swift & Co. might have been liable to the defendant for indemnity, the defendant had the right to implead Swift into the primary action.

♦ Only if the state law had recognized no right to indemnity at all would impleader have been improper—"the fact that federal impleader procedure is available does not act to create a substantive state right of indemnity." But Minnesota recognized a limited right to indemnity; therefore, federal impleader procedure governed the application of that state doctrine.

---

4. Indemnification and Contribution Claims--

Too, Inc. v Kohl's Department Stores, Inc., 213 F.R.D. 138 (S.D.N.Y. 2003).

Facts. Too, Inc. (P) filed an action against Windstar Apparel, Inc., (D), alleging copyright infringement, trademark infringement, and unfair competition. D filed a motion for leave to file a third-party complaint seeking contribution and indemnification from two of Windstar's former employees, DeCaro and Abraham. DeCaro allegedly designed the girls' sleepwear at issue, and Abraham allegedly sold the sleepwear to Kohl's, knowing that it contained designs infringing on P's copyrights and trademarks.

Issues.

(i) May a party bring a third-party complaint for contribution if the interests of judicial economy outweigh the risks of prejudice and undue delay?

(ii) May a party bring a third-party complaint for indemnification if it most likely cannot succeed on such a claim?

Held. (i) Yes. (ii) No. Motion granted in part and denied in part.

♦ Impleader is appropriate when the third-party defendant's liability to the third-party plaintiff is "dependent upon the outcome of the main claim" or the third-party defendant is "potentially secondarily liable as a contributor to the defendant." The purpose of this rule is to promote judicial efficiency by eliminating the necessity for the defendant to bring a separate cause of action against a third party for contribution.

♦ A court has considerable discretion in deciding whether to permit a third-party complaint. If the court determines that a third-party complaint would be appropriate and would foster the interest of judicial economy, the court then considers: (i) whether the movant deliberately delayed or was derelict in filing the motion; (ii) whether impleading would unduly delay or complicate the trial; (iii) whether impleading would prejudice the third-party defendant; and (iv) whether the third-party complaint states a claim upon which relief can be granted. These factors help the court balance the benefits of settling related matters in one suit with the potential prejudice to the plaintiff and third-party defendants.

♦ The proposed third-party complaint for contribution clearly arises from the same core of facts that is determinative of P's claim, because DeCaro and Abraham would be potentially liable for contribution if Windstar were found liable to P, and their potential liability is derivative of Windstar's liability. Also, since DeCaro and Abraham are material witnesses in Too's action, the purpose of judicial economy would be served by allowing the complaint because a separate action would entail repeating much of the discovery and proceedings that has already occurred in this case.

♦ Windstar states a claim upon which relief may be granted, and the claim does not appear to be unmeritorious. Furthermore, the concerns of prejudice and undue delay are not grave enough under these circumstances to sufficiently outweigh the interest of judicial economy. Thus, Windstar's motion to file a third-party complaint for contribution is granted.

♦ Windstar's proposed indemnification complaint, however, is without merit. Windstar has no contractual claim for indemnification, leaving common law as its only theory. Under New York law, common law indemnity is barred where, as is most likely the case here, the third party seeking indemnification was itself at fault and both tortfeasors violated the same duty to the plaintiff. Thus, Windstar's motion to file a third-party complaint for indemnification is denied.

F. INTERPLEADER

Interpleader is a procedure whereby a party, against whom several mutually exclusive claims have been asserted with respect to the same debt, fund, or property, may join the claimants in the same action and require them to litigate among themselves their rights, if any, to the debt, fund, or property.

1. Historical Limitations on the Use of Interpleader--

Hancock Oil Co. v. Independent Distributing Co., 150 P.2d 463 (Cal. 1944).

Facts. Hancock Oil Co. and another corporate lessee of real property (Ps) filed a suit seeking interpleader against two groups, each of which claims the right to receive rents and royalties reserved under the terms of Ps' lease. One group of defendants filed an answer alleging they are the property owners and the other group holds title to the property in trust for them. Both groups filed demurrers on the ground of uncertainty. Each demurrer was sustained without leave to amend on the sole ground that it is a violation of a fundamental principle for a tenant to be allowed to question the title of his landlord. Ps appeal, asserting that a suit in interpleader is merely a means by which the tenant may discharge his lease obligation without becoming involved in Ds' conflicting claims.

Issue. May lessees of real property bring an interpleader action against two groups who have conflicting claims concerning the right to receive the rents and royalties reserved in the lease?

Held. Yes. Judgment reversed.

♦ The common law bill of interpleader had four elements: (i) the same thing, debt, or duty must be claimed by all parties against whom relief is sought; (ii) all adverse titles or claims must be dependent, or be derived from a common source; (iii) the interpleader must not have nor claim any interest in the subject matter; and (iv) the interpleader must have incurred no independent liability to either of the claimants.

♦ Ps assert that there are conflicting claims concerning Ps' obligation to pay rents and royalties. Both groups of defendants must answer, and if they agree that each claims the right to the rents and royalties, Ps should be discharged from liability upon payment of their obligation under the lease.

♦ If conflicting claims are mutually exclusive, interpleader cannot be maintained, but the fact that an identical right is not asserted by each of the claimants does not preclude the use of the remedy. In addition, there is no requirement of privity between the claimants.

♦ Ps stand in the position of a disinterested stakeholder. Ps have no personal obligation to either group of claimants. The relations between the parties is such that a decision will determine the liability of Ps to each group of Ds.

Comment. Once interpleader is granted, the stakeholder, after depositing the disputed money or property with the court, is decreed to have withdrawn from the suit and the claimants are enjoined from further proceedings against the stakeholder. Then, the respective rights of the claimants are determined.

---

2. **Jurisdictional Problems--**

New York Life Insurance Co. v. Dunlevy, 241 U.S. 518 (1916).

Facts. Dunlevy (P) brought an action against New York Life (D) in California for the surrender value of a life insurance policy on her father. D asserted as a defense a prior interpleader action instituted by D in Pennsylvania after a garnishment by a third party of the policy proceeds. However, P was never personally brought within the personal jurisdiction of the court in Pennsylvania. Therefore, the judgment in the interpleader action, notwithstanding the payment of the policy proceeds into the court by D, was held not binding on P, such that P was permitted to recover against D in the California action. D appeals.

Issue. Must a court have personal jurisdiction over the parties affected in an interpleader action?

Held. Yes. Judgment affirmed.

♦ Any personal judgment rendered by a state court against one who did not voluntarily submit to its jurisdiction and who is not a resident of that state is void for lack of personal jurisdiction.

♦ Since only P's property was in Pennsylvania and Pennsylvania could exercise no personal jurisdiction over P, D could not meet the interpleader requirement of personal jurisdiction, and the Pennsylvania interpleader action could have no binding effect on the California proceedings.

━━━━━━━━━━━━━━━━━

3. **Interpleader in the Federal Courts.**

   a. **Federal statutory interpleader.** Partly in response to *Dunlevy*, Congress enacted the Federal Interpleader Act of 1917, which, in its current form, (i) permits venue in any district where a claimant can be found; (ii) permits nationwide process; (iii) requires two or more claimants, any two of whom have diverse citizenship, with adverse claims of at least $500 in the same debt, instrument or property; and (iv) requires the plaintiff to deposit the fund into court or give bond therefor. These rules are found in 28 U.S.C. sections 1335, 1397, and 2361.

   b. **Federal Rule 22 interpleader.** This is a broader form of interpleader than the federal statutory interpleader, but includes the jurisdictional, venue, and procedural requirements of an ordinary federal civil action. There must be complete diversity between the plaintiff and all adverse claimants or there must be a federal question involved; the jurisdictional amount is in excess of $75,000 if based on diversity; and process may be served only within the state in which the district court is located.

   c. **Liability of stakeholder--**

Pan American Fire & Casualty Co. v. Revere, 188 F. Supp. 474 (E.D. La. 1960).

Facts. A large tractor-trailer collided head-on with a bus carrying schoolchildren, killing the bus driver and three children and injuring 23 others. A few moments later, two cars following the bus collided. The insurance carrier for the tractor-trailer, Pan American (D), having three suits already filed against it, instituted this interpleader action, depositing with the court a bond in the full amount of its policy limits, $100,000, stating that it had no interest in the insurance proceeds, being merely a "disinterested stakeholder." The carrier, however, also denied that it was liable to anyone on the theory that to admit liability would be conclusive on its insured and expose the insured to a deficiency judgment.

Issue. Is interpleader available where the stakeholder also claims no liability?

Held. Yes. Interpleader granted.

♦ Historically, strict interpleader required that the stakeholder make no claim to the fund, whereas a bill in the nature of interpleader permitted the stakeholder to be a claimant directly or by denying the validity of some or all of the other claims. Both Rule 22 and statutory interpleader provide for strict interpleader as well as actions in the nature of interpleader. While an equitable ground is necessary for the granting of interpleader, the threat of a multiplicity of suits is not sufficient, unless, as here, the claims are against the same fund and the aggregate demand would exceed the fund.

♦ The court finds the plaintiff "exposed" to "double or multiple liability" in satisfaction of the requirement of Rule 22 even though the policy limits liability to a fixed sum. The court finds the element of "adversity" in the fact that it is in the interest of each claimant to defeat the claims of the others since the fund is insufficient to satisfy all demands.

♦ The court also finds that, although interpleader is an equitable remedy, the questions of liability and damages should be put to a jury, leaving to the court the task of apportioning the recoveries in the event they exceed the fund.

♦ The court notes that the only proper venue under Rule 22 when all claimants do not reside in the same state is the plaintiff's residence, unless venue objections are waived by the nonresident claimants, and that process is limited to the boundaries of the state in which the court sits. Since the plaintiff was domiciled in Texas, and the claimants were not, they could not have been validly served and interpleader could not be maintained under Rule 22. However, the Interpleader Act has no such requirement and, in the instant case, suit is therefore maintainable under it (at the residence of any defendant).

♦ An injunction is issued restraining the prosecution of all other pending suits against the plaintiff or its insured because of the accident.

---

d. Improper use of interpleader--

State Farm Fire & Casualty Co. v. Tashire, 386 U.S. 523 (1967).

Facts. A Greyhound bus collided with a pickup truck in California, killing two passengers on the bus and injuring the truck driver and 34 others. State Farm (D), the insurer of the truck driver, brought an interpleader action in federal district court in Oregon, paying the $20,000 policy limit into court to require all claimants to establish their claims against the truck driver in this single proceeding and in no other. Joined as defendants were the truck driver, his passenger, Greyhound, and all the prospective claimants who had been passengers on the bus. The district court issued an injunction requiring all parties to prosecute their suits in the interpleader action in Oregon. On appeal, the circuit court held that federal interpleader was not available in states like Oregon, which do not permit direct action suits against the insurance company until judgments are obtained against the insured, and that the insured may not invoke federal interpleader in such states until claims against the insured are reduced to judgment. The case then went to the Supreme Court on certiorari.

Issues.

(i)   Must the insurance company wait until persons asserting claims against its insured have reduced those claims to judgment before seeking to invoke the benefits of interpleader?

(ii)   May a district court, through interpleader jurisdiction, compel all of the tort plaintiffs, even those whose claims are not against the insured and could not be satisfied out of the insurance proceeds, to litigate the case in a single forum of the insurance company's choosing?

Held. (i) No. (ii) No. Judgment reversed.

♦ The 1948 revision of the Judicial Code removed whatever requirement there might previously have been that the insurance company wait until at least two claimants reduced their claims to judgment.

♦ The modern federal interpleader device is not a "bill of peace" capable of sweeping dozens of lawsuits out of the various state and federal courts in which they were brought and into a single interpleader proceeding. The interpleader statute did not authorize the injunction entered in the present case. The court may restrain claimants from seeking to enforce against the insurance company any judgment obtained against its insured, except in the interpleader proceeding itself. To the extent that the district court sought to control the claimants' lawsuits against the insured and the other alleged tortfeasors, it exceeded its powers.

Dissent (Douglas, J.). The litigants in this action are not "claimants" under the terms of the Federal Interpleader Act. The insurance policy provided that actions could not be brought against the insurance company until the obligation of the insured was determined, and further, neither Oregon nor California law permits direct actions against an insurer until final judgment against the insured has been rendered.

Comment. Where the stakeholder initiates the interpleader, the adverse claimants can, and usually do, file cross-claims against each other to obtain a judicial determination of their respective rights in the fund or property interpleaded.

G. INTERVENTION

1. **Definition.** Intervention is a procedure whereby a nonparty, upon timely application, may interpose himself into a lawsuit pending between other parties to protect his interests from being adversely affected by any judgment in that action. Intervention is favored whenever necessary to avoid a multiplicity of actions.

2. **Types of Intervention.** There are two distinct types of intervention under Federal Rule 24:

    a. **Intervention of right: Federal Rule 24(a).** Intervention is granted as a matter of right where:

        1) A federal statute confers an unconditional right to intervene (*e.g.*, 28 U.S.C. section 2323—suit to enforce an order of the Interstate Commerce Commission); or

        2) Disposition of the pending action would, as a practical matter, "impair or impede" the applicant's interest in the subject matter of that action (unless the existing parties are adequately representing his interests).

    b. **Permissive intervention: Federal Rule 24(b).** The court has discretion to permit a nonparty to intervene if:

        1) A federal statute confers a conditional right to intervene; or

        2) The applicant's claim or defense has a common question of law or fact with the main action.

3. **Effective Intervention.**

    a.   **Jurisdiction.** If the intervention is a matter of right, the intervenor's claim is deemed "ancillary" to the main litigation and no jurisdictional problem is presented. Thus, the fact that the intervenor is of the same citizenship as one of the existing parties, or that the amount of his claim is $75,000 or less, does not destroy diversity jurisdiction. However, permissive intervention is in effect a new claim, and hence is proper only if independent grounds of jurisdiction—both with regard to citizenship and jurisdictional amount—exist as to the intervenors.

    b.   **Judgment.** Any judgment rendered subsequent to intervention is as conclusive on the rights of the intervening party as though he originally had been a party; and, of course, he also has the right of appeal.

4. **State Rules.** State rules on intervention are similar to the federal requirements, allowing "any person who has an interest in the matter in litigation" to intervene, either by joining the plaintiff in claiming what is sought in the complaint, by joining the defendant in resisting the plaintiff's claims, or by demanding something adverse to both the plaintiff and the defendant.

5. **Intervention After Judgment--**

Smuck v. Hobson, 408 F.2d 175 (D.C. Cir. 1969).

Facts. Hobson (P) brought a class action against a local Board of Education and its individual members for racial and economic discrimination in the operation of the schools. P won, and the Board voted not to appeal. However, Smuck (D), one of the individual Board members named as a defendant in the original suit, appealed. The former school superintendent also appealed and moved to intervene. Twenty parents of affected schoolchildren moved to intervene as well. The district courts granted the motions to intervene, and the court of appeals considered both the motions and the merits of the appeal.

Issue. Is intervention possible when the third parties do not seek to intervene until after the initial judgment?

Held. Yes. Judgment affirmed in part and reversed in part.

♦   The superintendent, who resigned following the initial judgment, has no interest that will be affected by the appeal and therefore can neither appeal nor intervene. D, as a member of the Board, has no separate interest as an individual in the litigation and cannot appeal. The parents' motion requires a detailed examination of the requirements for intervention of right.

♦   While Rule 24(a) is titled "Intervention of Right," it does involve the exercise of judicial discretion. The three requirements are that a potential intervenor have an "interest" in the transaction, that he be impeded in protecting his interest by the action, and that his interest is inadequately represented.

♦ The "interest" requirement is merely a prerequisite, not a determinative criterion, for intervention. These parents' interests satisfy this requirement. The burden is on the party opposing intervention to show that the applicant's interest is adequately represented by existing parties.

♦ The disposition of the action might impair these parents' ability to protect their interests unless they are allowed to intervene.

♦ Although the Board may have adequately represented these parents at trial, the decision not to appeal may not have adequately represented their interests. The Board's desire to avoid publicity, costs, etc., could have conflicted with the parents' interests. Therefore, the parents are permitted to intervene to pursue resolution of their interests; namely, that the school board be free to exercise the broadest discretion constitutionally permissible in deciding upon educational policies affecting schoolchildren.

Comment. Inadequate representation for purposes of intervention as of right under Rule 24(a)(2) may also be argued when there is collusion between the applicant's representative and the adverse party, or when the applicant and his attorney are antagonistic. Note, however, that intervention ***after judgment*** as in *Smuck* will be allowed only in very unique situations.

———————————

X. CLASS ACTIONS

A. HISTORY AND PHILOSOPHY OF THE CLASS ACTION

1. **English Origins.** The class action can be traced to the English "Bill of Peace" in the 17th century. The "Bill of Peace" was a procedural device that was permitted only in equity, and then only if it was shown that: (i) the joinder of all parties having similar interests was impractical, because the parties were too numerous, were presently unascertainable, or were not yet in being; (ii) the named parties could fairly represent all the parties in the litigation; and (iii) all of the parties possessed a joint interest in the issues under litigation. The chancellors in equity permitted suit to be maintained by or against representatives of the class and, in some instances, held that the decree rendered in such an action was binding on all members of the class.

2. **Early United States Applications.** The Federal Equity Rules and various state codes generally included provisions for class actions modeled after the English procedure. However, Federal Rule 23, enacted in 1938, was the first effort to specifically define class actions. As originally adopted, Rule 23 provided for three different kinds of class actions: (i) a "true" class action wherein the rights of all members of the class were "joint" or "common" and a judgment rendered in such an action bound all members of the class, including absent parties; (ii) a "hybrid" class action wherein a specific fund or property was the subject of the action and the members of the class had "separate" rights therein, which were determined by the judgment in the litigation; and (iii) a "spurious" class action wherein a "common question of law or fact" affected all members of the class, the claims of each member were separate, and the judgment bound only those members of the class actually before the court.

3. **Present Federal Class Action Rules.** In 1966, Federal Rule 23 was completely revised, eliminating the distinctions noted above and providing that the members of the class could sue or be sued with binding effect on the entire class.

4. **State Rules.** Federal Rule 23 has been adopted (sometimes with modifications) by most states.

B. OPERATION OF THE CLASS ACTION DEVICE

1. **Requirements for Bringing a Class Action.** Under Federal Rule 23(a), all four of the following conditions must be established:

   a. **Numerous parties.** The class must be so numerous that joinder of all members individually is impracticable. Although there are no fixed minimums or maximums, some commentators feel that at least 60 members should be involved. However, the class cannot be so large as to be unmanageable.

b.   **Common question.** There must exist a common nucleus of law or fact upon which the issue of liability to the entire class depends—even though the damage claims of each member may be separate.

　　1)   Some courts have interpreted this requirement rather liberally. For example, where the defendant made separate misrepresentations to various groups of stock purchasers, the defendant's "common and consistent course of conduct" was held to satisfy the common question requirement. [Green v. Wolf Corp., 406 F.2d 291 (2d Cir. 1968)]

　　2)   It is not enough that there exists a common question of law or fact; the question must be essential to the recovery of all members of the class.

c.   **Typical claim.** The claim of the person or persons suing on behalf of the class must typify the class generally, so that the representative will be motivated to protect the interests of the class generally.

　　1)   The *size* of the plaintiff's personal claim is relevant to the issue of whether she is properly motivated to protect the interests of the class generally. Some courts require the plaintiff's claim to be coextensive with the interest of the class generally.

　　2)   In any event, the plaintiff is not allowed to maintain a class action unless she can allege and prove specific individual injury to herself. A claim of injury to the class generally and potential injury to herself is not enough. The pleadings must show a "clear and specific link" between the plaintiff's claim and the claims of the purported class. [*See* General Telephone Co. v. Falcon, 459 U.S. 147 (1982)]

d.   **Adequate representation.** This is akin to the typical claim requirement, but is directed also to the question of whether there is any actual or potential conflict of interest between the representative and the class she seeks to represent. In other words, the named representative cannot be expected to "fairly and adequately protect the interests of the class" unless her interest is similar to that of all members of the class. This requirement is based on the requirements of due process, *i.e.,* that the interests of any party not before the court but bound by the adjudication will be adequately represented.

2.   **Certification.**

a.   **Certification hearing.** At an early practicable time after commencement of a class action, a hearing is held to decide whether the action should proceed as a class suit. If the district court finds that the class action requirements (*see supra*) are met and that the class action is "superior" to other means of litigating the interests of the parties, the district court then certifies the action as a class action. If, on the other hand, the district court finds that no class action is possible, the suit may be continued by the "representatives," but it will have no res judicata effect for or against any absent class members.

b. **Evidence.** The district court, during the certification process, can take evidence on any of the issues raised by the litigation. The court is not restricted to the pleadings. However, the court may not consider the merits of the litigation, although it may make a preliminary inquiry as to whether the plaintiff has a "realistic chance" of recovering, since this matter is relevant to deciding whether to go through with a class action.

c. **Modification.** At any time before trial, the district court may limit or reduce the class to that of the named parties if it becomes convinced that a class action is unmanageable or inappropriate.

d. **Conditional certification--**

Castano v. American Tobacco Co., 84 F.3d 734 (5th Cir. 1996).

Facts. Plaintiffs brought a class certification motion in an action against tobacco companies (Ds) seeking compensation for the injury of nicotine addiction. The class of plaintiffs was to include all nicotine-dependent persons, estates, representatives, and administrators of nicotine-dependent smokers, and the spouses, children, relatives, and significant others of these smokers as heirs or survivors (Ps). Ps claimed that Ds failed to inform consumers of the addictive nature of nicotine, and that Ds manipulated the amount of nicotine in cigarettes to sustain their addictive properties. Using its power to sever issues for certification under Rule 23(b)(3), the district court conditionally certified the class pursuant to Federal Rule of Civil Procedure 23(c)(1) on the issues of core liability and punitive damages. Ds claimed the court abused its discretion in certifying the class.

Issue. Did the district court err in conditionally certifying the class?

Held. Yes. Judgment reversed and case remanded.

♦ Conditional certification is not a device to allow a district court to sidestep the question of whether the plaintiffs meet the requirements for class certification. The court abdicated its duty to decide whether common questions predominate over individual questions by failing to consider how variations in state law would affect predominance, superiority, and practical administration of the case.

♦ The court also failed to consider how Ps' addiction claims would actually be tried, either individually or on a class basis. A fraud class action cannot be certified when individual reliance would be an issue. However, the court sidestepped this issue by failing to even reach the issue of reliance.

♦ We believe that a specific mass tort such as this cannot be properly certified without a prior track record of trials from which the court could draw information in order to make the predominance and superiority analysis required by Rule 23. The issues in this case are too novel and allege an immature tort. There is little prior litigation to allow the court to assess the relative superiority of a class action in this type of case.

♦ Finally, the class fails the superiority requirement of Rule 23. The district court reasoned that judicial economy would be served by certifying the class to prevent millions of individual trials. It is improper for the court to base its decision on such a speculative basis. The court cannot presume that all or any of the potential plaintiffs will actually file suit.

---

3. **Notice.**

   a. **Form of notice.** In class actions, the form of notice required depends on the type of class action. In class actions under Federal Rule 23(b)(1) or 23(b)(2) (*i.e.,* where the basis of the class is to avoid inconsistent adjudications or the claim is for injunctive or declaratory relief), the appropriate form of notice to class members is left to the discretion of the court. In class actions for damages under Rule 23(b)(3) where there is a question common to the class, "the best notice practicable under the circumstances, including individual notice to all members who can be identified through reasonable effort," must be given. [Fed.R.Civ.P. 23(c)(2)(B)]

   b. **Contents of notice.** The notice must advise the class members of the existence of a suit, the nature of the claim and the relief requested, provisions for costs of maintaining this suit, and the identity of the person or persons suing on behalf of the class. If the suit is based on Rule 23(b)(3), the notice must also advise that judgment in the suit will bind each class member unless, after receiving notice, the proposed member requests to be excluded from the class.

   c. **Costs.** The plaintiff initially must pay the costs of notifying all members of the class. If the plaintiff wins the action, the expenses of notice may be recovered from the defendant as necessary court costs.

4. **Orders Appointing Class Counsel.** Under Federal Rule 23(g), after certifying a class, a court must designate an attorney as class counsel, taking into consideration such factors as knowledge of the relevant law and prior class action experience. This attorney must "fairly and adequately represent the interests of the class."

5. **Interlocutory Appeals from Certification Orders.** Courts of appeals can accept interlocutory appeals from orders denying or granting class certification.

6. **Orders Regulating the Conduct of Pretrial and Trial.** Under Federal Rule 23(d), the court may create a timetable for discovery and presentation of issues at trial, set limits on oral presentations by attorneys, regulate discovery, and establish a committee of counsel to make decisions about the way in which the class's case will be prosecuted. For purposes of discovery, class members are treated as "quasi-parties." The opposing party may proceed with "fair" discovery of the "typicality" of claims, the factual basis for determining inclusion in the class, individual damages, and similar matters. However, full rights to depose each class member are not given. Note that if depositions of all class members are necessary, this indicates that common questions do not predominate and that the action should be decertified.

7. **Proving Class Claims and Administering Class Relief.** Ordinarily, any funds obtained by settlement or judgment in a class action will be held for distribution to the members of the class, who will be notified to file individual claims to establish their shares. However, where the class is large and claims are small, such an approach may be impractical and some courts have therefore adopted the "fluid recovery" approach (*i.e.,* the recovery will be distributed to those persons who are members of the class at the time of judgment or in the future— *e.g.,* distribution of overcharges to former taxi customers accomplished by reducing rates to future customers).

8. **Settlement.** Because of the fiduciary nature of a class action, it may not be dismissed or compromised by the class representative without court approval. Notice of any proposed dismissal or compromise must be given to all members of the class before the court can give its approval.

9. **Attorneys' Fees.** The court may award reasonable attorneys' fees as agreed among the parties or as authorized by law.

C. DUE PROCESS CONSIDERATIONS

1. **Notice and Opportunity to Be Heard--**

Hansberry v. Lee, 311 U.S. 32 (1940).

Facts. Lee (P) brought this suit to enjoin a sale of land to Hansberry (D), a black man, by a party who had signed a restrictive covenant not to sell to blacks. D contended that the covenant was not in force, since it required that 95% of the landowners sign, and only 54% had actually signed. P pleaded that the issue was res judicata, because a decree in an earlier suit on the restrictive covenant had found that 95% of the landowners had signed. To this D rejoined that he and his seller were not bound by the prior judgment, since they had not been a party to the prior action. The Supreme Court of Illinois found that the prior action was res judicata as to D and his seller, since it had been a class action wherein D and his seller's interests were represented. D appeals to the United States Supreme Court, alleging that his rights to due process had been violated, since his interests had not been properly represented in the prior litigation.

Issues.

(i)   Was D, whose rights have been thus adjudicated in a class action, afforded such notice and opportunity to be heard as are requisite to the due process that the United States Constitution prescribes?

(ii)   Were D's interests adequately represented by other members of the class in the previous action so as to bind D by the decision?

Held. (i) No. (ii) No. Judgment reversed.

♦   It is a general principle that one is not bound by a judgment in personam in litigation in which he is not designated as a party or to which he has not been made a party by service of process. The exception is that the judgment in a class action, to which some members of the class are parties, may bind members of the class or those represented who were not made parties. There has been a failure of due process only in those cases where it cannot be said that the procedure adopted fairly ensures the protection of the interest of absent parties who are to be bound by it.

♦   Those who had sought to enforce the restrictive covenant could not be said to be in the same class with or to represent those whose interest was in resisting performance. If those who seek to enforce the agreement are the members of a class, those who are interested in challenging the validity of the agreement are not of the same class in the sense that their interests are identical with those who seek to enforce it. It is impossible to say, solely because they are parties to the agreement, that any two of them are of the same class. A selection of representatives for purposes of litigation, whose substantial interests are not necessarily the same as those whom they are deemed to represent, does not afford that protection to absent parties that due process requires.

D. CLASS ACTIONS AND JURISDICTION

1.   Subject Matter Jurisdiction in Class Actions.

    a.   Diversity. Only the residence of the representative is considered for purposes of establishing federal diversity jurisdiction.

    b.   Amount in controversy. In the federal courts, all class members must have claims in excess of the jurisdictional minimum of $75,000 (except in cases involving violation of a federal statute or a federal question), though aggregation has been permitted where (i) a single plaintiff seeks to aggregate two or more of his own claims against a single defendant or (ii) two or more plaintiffs unite to enforce a single title or right in which they have common and undivided interest.

      c.   **All members must meet jurisdictional amount.** In *Snyder v. Harris*, 394 U.S. 332 (1969), the Court held that each of several plaintiffs asserting separate and distinct claims must satisfy the jurisdictional amount requirement if his claim is to survive a motion to dismiss; *i.e.,* there may be no aggregation of claims. Although in *Snyder*, none of the plaintiffs had an individual claim over $10,000, the holding clearly requires dismissal of any plaintiff whose claim cannot satisfy the jurisdictional amount, even though others allege sufficient claims.

  2.   **Personal Jurisdiction.**

      a.   **Minimum contacts in class actions--**

Phillips Petroleum Co. v. Shutts, 472 U.S. 797 (1985).

Facts. Shutts and other persons entitled to royalties under natural gas leases (Ps) brought a class action in Kansas against Phillips Petroleum Co. (D), a Delaware corporation, seeking interest payments on suspended royalty payments. Each class member was provided notice of the action by mail. The notice stated that members would be included in the class and bound by the judgment unless they "opted out" by executing and returning a "request for exclusion." Fewer than 1,000 of the 28,000 members of the class resided in Kansas, and a minuscule number of the involved leases were on Kansas land. The trial court applied Kansas law and found D liable to all class members for interest on the suspended royalties. D appealed, claiming that Kansas lacked jurisdiction over the absent class members and that the trial court should have considered the laws of each state where the leases were located to determine, under conflict of law principles, where interest was due. The Kansas Supreme Court affirmed. The Supreme Court granted certiorari.

Issues.

(i)   May a forum state exercise jurisdiction over the claims of absent class action plaintiffs even though the plaintiffs (not unlike absent defendants in an ordinary long arm case) may not possess the minimum contacts with the forum that would support personal jurisdiction over a defendant?

(ii)   May the forum state apply its own law to every claim in a class action even though the forum has no significant contacts to such claims?

Held. (i) Yes. (ii) No. Judgment affirmed in part and reversed in part.

♦   The forum state may exercise jurisdiction over the claims of absent class action plaintiffs under certain circumstances.

Substantial burdens are placed by the state upon absent defendants. The out-of-state defendant is faced with the full powers of the forum state to enter judgment against it. The defendant must generally travel to the forum, retain counsel, and defend itself or suffer a default judgment. The minimum contacts requirement of the Due Process Clause prevents the forum state from unfairly imposing these burdens on the defendant.

The Due Process Clause need not and does not afford as much protection to absent class plaintiffs because fewer burdens are placed on them. An absent class plaintiff is not required to do anything. The court and the named plaintiffs protect the absent plaintiffs' interests. The class action is an exception to the rule that one cannot be bound by a judgment in personam unless one is fully made a party in the traditional sense.

To bind an absent plaintiff, the forum state must provide minimal procedural due process protection. The plaintiff must receive notice (the best practicable to apprise parties of the action) plus an opportunity to be heard and participate in the litigation. The plaintiff must have an opportunity to "opt out." The named plaintiff must at all times adequately represent the interests of absent class members.

◆　　　The forum state may not, however, apply its own law to every claim.

The Due Process Clause and Full Faith and Credit Clause require that the forum state have a significant contact or aggregation of contacts to the claims of the plaintiff class that create state interests in order to ensure that the choice of forum law is not arbitrary or unfair.

There are material conflicts between the forum law and other law that could apply. There is no indication that the parties intended the forum law to apply. Ps' failure to "opt out" of the class did not constitute a consent to the application of forum law. Ps' desire for forum law is rarely, if ever, controlling. There is no identifiable res in the forum. Over 99% of the leases and 97% of Ps had no apparent connection to the forum except the lawsuit.

Given the forum's lack of interest in claims unrelated to the forum and the substantive conflict with the law of other jurisdictions, the application of forum law to every claim is sufficiently arbitrary and unfair as to exceed constitutional limits.

Comment. The key to understanding this case is to understand D's basic argument, that absentee members of a *plaintiff* class are in the same boat as (and hence should be treated like) absentee defendants in an ordinary long arm jurisdiction case. The Supreme Court rejects this analogy but recognizes that absentee class members have constitutional rights and that Kansas procedural law—which requires notice and an opportunity to opt out—satisfies the constitutional standards.

3.   **Venue.** Only the residences of the class representatives are important for purposes of venue; the residences of absent class members and intervenors are irrelevant.

E. SETTLEMENT CLASSES

1.   Certification of Class for Settlement--

Amchem Products, Inc. v. Windsor, 521 U.S. 591 (1997).

Facts. Ps represent an extremely large class (potentially hundreds of thousands) suing asbestos manufacturers (Ds) for damages stemming from asbestos-related injuries or wrongful death. The parties eventually reached a mass settlement agreement. The settling parties filed a joint motion for conditional class certification under Rule 23(b)(3) for the purpose of gaining court approval for the proposed settlement. The proposed settlement seeks to settle not only the claims of the present class with cash payments, but also the claims of future claimant parties, who have yet to be identified via a system of medical examinations and a payment schedule. The settlement also puts forth a notice system that employs individual notice, and also uses public media to notify any future claimants. Significantly, the settlement proposes to bind anyone who does not opt out. Some of the members of the currently identified class opposed the terms of the settlement because it seeks to settle claims of unknown parties, and because the same counsel was used to represent both the present and future plaintiffs. The district court certified the class as a Rule 23(b)(3) action and declared the settlement fair. The court of appeals reversed, holding that intra-class conflict precluded the class from satisfying the adequate representation requirement. The Supreme Court granted certiorari.

Issue. When a class is certified for settlement purposes only, must it comply with the certification requirements of common issue predominance and adequacy of representation as if it were to be litigated?

Held. Yes. Judgment affirmed.

♦   Settlement-only class actions have become a standard device for addressing numerous claims. Some circuits have held that a class cannot be certified for settlement when certification for trial would be unwarranted. Others have held that settlement reduces the need to comply fully with Rule 23 requirements.

♦   We find that for settlement-only class certification, the court need not consider whether the case, if tried, would present management problems under Rule 23(b)(3)(D). However, the provisions of Rule 23 that are designed to protect absentees remain applicable and are vitally important.

♦   Among the safeguards of Rule 23 are the requirement of notice to all class members and the requirement of unity among class members so that absent members can fairly be bound by the decisions of the class representatives. The federal courts have no authority to apply a more lenient standard in settlement-only cases, even if they determine that the settlement is fair.

♦ The proposed settlement class cannot be certified because it does not satisfy the Rule 23(b)(3) requirement that common questions of law predominate. The fact that all class members were exposed to asbestos products supplied by Ds is insufficient. There are many more issues peculiar to the several categories of class members and individuals within each category, such as the nature and extent of exposure, the type of symptoms of disease suffered, whether they smoked cigarettes, etc.

♦ In addition, Rule 23(a)(4)'s requirement of adequate representation is not satisfied in this case because the present Ps' claims were traded off against the future Ps' claims. The named parties who have already manifested medical problems are interested in generous immediate payments. Class members who were merely exposed are more interested in having an ample, inflation-protected fund for the future, when symptoms develop. This disparity between the plaintiff categories makes it unlikely that the named Ps could adequately represent the other class members.

Concurrence and dissent (Breyer, Stevens, JJ). I agree that settlement is relevant to class certification. However, now that the Court has clarified the law, the case should be remanded rather than the Court making factual determinations regarding predominance and adequacy of representation requirements.

---

2. **Mandatory Class—Limited Fund Class Actions--**

Ortiz v. Fibreboard Corp., 527 U.S. 815 (1999).

Facts. Fibreboard (D), a manufacturer of asbestos products, had settled some 45,000 personal injury claims. D proposed a plan for a global settlement of its remaining liability. Under this plan, D and its insurers would create a trust fund of $1.535 billion for asbestos claimants who would file a Rule 23(b)(1)(B) class action, based on D's assertion that there was a "limited fund" to pay class members. The plan provided claimants with a process of settling their claims with the trust. If no agreement could be reached, claimants were required to engage in mediation and arbitration. If the claim could still not be settled, claimants could file suit against the trust, but there was a $500,000 cap on recovery, and a bar on punitive damages and prejudgement interest. There would be no ability for a claimant to opt out of the settlement. The district court found that the class action met the requirements of Rule 23(a) and the requirements of mandatory class treatment under Rule 23(b)(1)(B). The court of appeals affirmed. The Supreme Court granted certiorari.

Issue. Is mandatory class treatment under Rule 23(b)(1)(B) appropriate to settle the mass tort claims in this case?

Held. No. Judgment reversed and case remanded.

♦ Rule 23(b)(1)(B) provides certification of a class where the prosecution of individual actions would be dispositive of the interest of other similarly situated persons not party to the adjudications or would substantially impair or impede their ability to protect their interests. Such is the case when numerous claims are made against a limited fund insufficient to satisfy all claims. Unlike Rule 23(b)(3) class members, under Rule 23(b)(1)(B) objectors have no inherent right to opt out. The legal rights of absent class members are resolved regardless of their consent.

♦ To satisfy Rule 23(b)(1)(B), it must be demonstrated that: (i) the fund is insufficient to satisfy all of the claims; (ii) the whole of the inadequate fund is to be devoted to satisfying the claims; and (iii) the claimants identified by a common theory of recovery will be treated equitably among themselves.

♦ Although Rule 23(b)(1)(B)'s legislative history indicates that the Advisory Committee did not contemplate the Rule being used to aggregate tort claims on a limited fund rationale, we do not decide the ultimate issue of whether it may ever be used in this context. We only find that it is inappropriate in this case as the requirements of the Rule have not been met.

♦ First, the parties presented little evidence to demonstrate the fund was in fact insufficient. Prior claim amounts could have been used to demonstrate the expected total liability of D, but no such evidence was presented. The district court and court of appeals simply adopted the figures agreed upon by the parties in showing the fund's inadequacy without any analysis of the evidence. This is not sufficient.

♦ Second, the court did not determine the value of the assets available. The court concluded that D had a sale value of $235 million that could be devoted to the fund. However, the court failed to hear evidence or make an independent finding of the value of the two insurance policies involved. Even if D's assets would clearly be insufficient to satisfy the claims, the value of the insurance policies must also be considered. Also, under the agreement, D would have been allowed to retain nearly all of its net worth, which is inconsistent with a limited fund analysis.

♦ Finally, the settlement agreement failed to provide equity among members of the class. Class counsel agreed to exclude from the class those who had previously settled with D while retaining the right to sue again upon the development of a future malignancy. It is unknown how many claimants settled with a reservation of rights, but it could be almost one-third of the claimants. Thus the class was underinclusive. Furthermore, the agreement failed to provide the structural protection of independent representation for subclasses with conflicting interests.

Such an agreement must contain procedures to resolve the difficult issues of treating differently situated claimants with fairness among themselves. As we indicated in *Amchem*, a class divided between holders of present and future claims requires division into homogenous subclasses with separate representation to eliminate conflicting interests of counsel.

F.   THE PRECLUSIVE EFFECT OF A CLASS ACTION JUDGMENT

1.   Later Individual Claims Not Barred--

Cooper v. Federal Reserve Bank of Richmond, 467 U.S. 867 (1984).

Facts. Cooper and three other employees (Ps) intervened in a civil action against the Federal Reserve Bank (D) commenced by the Equal Employment Opportunity Commission ("EEOC") for alleged violations of Title VII of the Civil Rights Act of 1964, including refusing to promote black employees because of race. After Ps were allowed to intervene, the district court conditionally certified the following class pursuant to Federal Rule of Civil Procedure 23(b)(2) and (3):

> All black persons who have been employed by the defendant at its Charlotte Branch Office at any time since January 3, 1974 . . . who have been discriminated against in promotion, wages, job assignments and terms and conditions of employment because of their race.

Notice was published and mailed to each member of the class. The notice described the status of the litigation and stated that any members of the class who did not exclude themselves in writing to the Clerk "will be bound by the judgment or other determination." Six members of the class made no attempt to exclude themselves and testified at trial. Later, after the district court had found no proof of class-wide discrimination above grade 5 and that these six members were not entitled to participate in Stage II proceedings, they filed a separate action against D, alleging violations of 42 U.S.C. section 1981. D moved to dismiss on the grounds that each of the six was a member of the Cooper litigation and that they were bound by the determination that there was no proof of discrimination above grade 5. The district court denied D's motion but certified its order for interlocutory appeal. The interlocutory appeal was consolidated with D's appeal in the Cooper litigation. The court of appeals reversed the judgment on the merits in the Cooper litigation in part and held that the six members were precluded by res judicata from maintaining their individual race discrimination claims. Thus, the order denying D's motion to dismiss was reversed. The Supreme Court granted certiorari.

Issue. Does a judgment in a class action determining that an employer did not engage in a general pattern or practice of racial discrimination against the certified class of employees preclude a class member from maintaining a subsequent civil action alleging an individual claim of racial discrimination against the employer?

Held. No. Judgment reversed.

- The Cooper litigation adjudicated the individual claims of each of the four intervening Ps, deciding in D's favor. This does not foreclose other individual claims. The litigation also decided the "policies and practices" of discriminating against employees claim on which the res judicata analysis is based.

- A judgment in a properly entertained class action is binding on class members in any subsequent litigation between them on any issue actually litigated and determined, if its determination was essential to that judgment.

- The significant difference between an individual's claim of discrimination and a class action alleging a general pattern or practice is obvious. The first requires an inquiry into a particular employment decision, while the second requires a focus on a pattern of discriminatory decisionmaking. Discrimination against one or two individuals may not prove the existence of a company-wide policy.

- Two of the intervening plaintiffs here established that they were victims of racial discrimination, but they were employed in grades higher than 5 and the finding regarding them provided no support to conclude there was a practice of discrimination.

- The six class members are barred, as the court of appeals held, from (i) bringing another class action against D alleging a pattern or practice of discrimination during the relevant time period, and (ii) relitigating that issue in any other litigation with D. The six members are not barred from individual claims.

- If the six members each establish a prima facie case of discrimination, D will be required to articulate a legitimate reason for each of the challenged decisions.

G. THE PROBLEM OF THE MASS TORT CASE

1. **History.** Mass tort litigation is a relatively new legal phenomenon. Critics argue that these actions are responsible for increased product prices and insurance costs, corporate bankruptcies, and huge legal fees. Proponents argue that they are efficient methods of adjudicating the rights of multiple litigants with common claims against the same defendant.

2. **Early Cases.** One of the first mass tort cases was a product liability case involving the Dalkon Shield contraceptive device, which was alleged to cause infertility. [*See In re* Northern District of California, Dalkon Shield IUD Products Liability Litigation, 693 F.2d 847 (9th Cir. 1982), *cert. denied*, 459 U.S. 1171 (1983)] The Ninth Circuit decertified the class, stating that the prevalence of individual issues outweighed any potential efficiency the class action

device could provide. However, in another product liability action involving exposure to Agent Orange, the Second Circuit upheld certification of a class containing over 15,000 named members and 2.5 million potential members. [*See In re* Agent Orange Product Liability Litigation, 597 F. Supp. 740 (E.D.N.Y. 1984), *affirmed*, 818 F.2d 145 (2d Cir. 1987), *cert. denied*, 484 U.S. 1004 (1988)]

XI. PRETRIAL DEVICES FOR OBTAINING INFORMATION: DEPOSITIONS AND DISCOVERY

A. THE GENERAL SCOPE OF DISCOVERY

1. **Definition of "Discovery."** Once the pleadings of the parties to a civil action have been filed and the case docketed for trial, each party prepares for trial by attempting to ferret out information and witnesses that support his side of the case or destroy the case of the opponent. It is the role of the various modern discovery devices to aid in this search for evidence.

2. **Purposes of Modern Discovery Procedure.** Modern discovery attempts to balance three major goals to ensure that each trial is truly "upon the merits" of each controverted issue.

   a. **Preserve information.** Modern discovery devices tend to preserve information that otherwise might not be available for trial. Thus, if a vital witness is leaving the jurisdiction of the court, her testimony may be preserved for presentation at trial through sworn depositions.

   b. **Narrow scope of trial.** Traditionally, it was the function of the pleadings to narrow the scope of the legal dispute to a finite number of controverted issues. However, as pleading rules have become more liberal, the modern discovery procedures isolate those issues of law or fact that are truly points of dispute. This reflects a policy decision that only when all the facts of a controversy are known to each side—through discovery procedures—can each party make a reasoned decision about the substance of his case.

   c. **Uncover information.** Finally, modern discovery procedures concentrate on making visible to all concerned parties each aspect of the coming litigation and on making the keeping of secrets of minimal value in modern litigation.

   d. **Discovery prior to commencing a lawsuit--**

In re **Petition of Sheila Roberts Ford,** 170 F.R.D. 504 (M.D. Ala. 1997).

Facts. Ford (P) filed a petition under Federal Rule 27 for leave to proceed with the deposition of a sheriff whom she believed would be able to identify the parties and facts involved in the shooting death of her father. P wanted to preserve the testimony of the sheriff before his memories faded or became distorted by publicity, and she wanted to determine whether and what parties to sue.

Issues.

(i) Does Rule 27 permit a pre-complaint deposition simply to discover or uncover information related to the potential action?

(ii) Should Rule 27 be read in conjunction with Rule 11 to allow a party to conduct discovery for the purpose of uncovering sufficient evidentiary support to file a complaint that complies with Rule 11?

Held. (i) No. (ii) No. Petition denied.

♦ Rule 27 allows depositions to be taken prior to the filing of an action "to perpetuate testimony" under certain conditions. The phrase "to perpetuate testimony" suggests preserving testimony that might otherwise be lost before trial. Here, P seeks to discover or uncover testimony rather than to perpetuate it. Nothing before the court indicates that the sheriff's testimony is in danger of being lost. Thus, Rule 27 does not provide for the discovery P seeks.

♦ Rule 11 requires certification that, to the best of the person's knowledge, information, and belief, formed after a reasonable inquiry, the allegations are supported by evidence or are likely to be supported by evidence after a reasonable opportunity to discover or uncover such evidence. P asserts that Rule 27 should be read in conjunction with Rule 11, because she is otherwise without the means to uncover information upon which to file a complaint under Rule 11. While the court is not without sympathy for P, Rule 27 does not permit the type of discovery she seeks.

---

3. **Relevance.**

   a. **Limiting scope of interrogatories--**

Kelly v. Nationwide Mutual Insurance Co., 188 N.E.2d 445 (Ohio 1963).

Facts. Kelly (P) sued to recover under the terms of a comprehensive insurance policy for damage to his truck. Nationwide Mutual (D) generally denied liability and submitted to P a complex of interrogatories that inquired into the substance of P's case: witnesses' names; testimony to be offered; circumstances surrounding the incident; etc. P answered the interrogatories, but D moved to require more complete answers. P opposed the motion on grounds that under state law discovery could not be used to inquire into material pertinent only to the opponent's preparations for trial.

Issue. May interrogatories be directed toward material pertinent only to the opponent's trial preparation?

Held. No. P's motion granted.

♦ This court concludes that, under its code, interrogatories to an opposing party are proper only when: (i) the information sought was a general issue in the action, not an evidentiary issue of one or the other pleader; (ii) the interrogatory did not seek "privileged" information; and (iii) the information sought would be admissible per se as evidence at the coming trial.

♦ To be excluded from the scope of discovery is all information related merely to the opposing party's preparation for trial—*i.e.,* witnesses' statements, concrete evidence not placed in issue by the pleadings, information obtained through independent investigation, etc.

---

b. Discovery of inadmissible evidence--

Lindberger v. General Motors Corp., 56 F.R.D. 433 (W.D. Wis. 1972).

Facts. Lindberger (P) sued General Motors Corp. (D) for injuries caused by an allegedly negligently manufactured and designed front-end loader. D refused to answer certain interrogatories relating to subsequent design changes, on grounds that such evidence is privileged because it is inadmissible at trial. P filed a motion to compel discovery.

Issue. May evidence that would not be admissible at trial be subject to pretrial discovery?

Held. Yes. Motion granted.

♦ D claims the evidence is privileged because evidence rules prohibit introduction of evidence of subsequent remedial measures to establish negligence or culpability. The rule is based on external policy, *i.e.,* promoting public safety by not discouraging subsequent repairs. However, protection against discovery of traditionally privileged material is justified by the fact that disclosure by itself, even outside of trial, might harm the parties. Here, the only possible harm would arise from disclosure at trial.

♦ P need not establish that the evidence sought would be admissible at trial. If the evidence is relevant—which it clearly is—and is not protected by traditional privilege theories, it is subject to discovery by P.

---

4. Limitations.

Marrese v. American Academy of Orthopaedic Surgeons, 726 F.2d 1150 (7th Cir. 1984) (en banc).

Facts. After unsuccessful state court actions against the American Academy of Orthopaedic Surgeons (D), two orthopaedic surgeons (Ps) filed an action in federal district court alleging that D's denial of their membership applications constituted a boycott in violation of section one of the Sherman Act. Discovery began and D refused Ps access to certain files relating to membership applications for the years 1970-1980. The district court entered a protective order allowing Ps to read the files and to discuss with D's counsel the contents of all other files and to depose anyone named therein. After D persisted in its refusal despite the protective order, the district court held D in criminal contempt and fined D $10,000. D appeals.

Issue. Was the district court's discovery order an abuse of discretion under Federal Rule of Civil Procedure 26(c)?

Held. Yes. Judgment reversed.

♦ Federal Rule 26(c) empowers a district court to "make any order which justice requires to protect a party or person from annoyance, embarrassment, oppression, or undue burden or expense, including . . . that discovery not be had." Also, Federal Rule 26(d) allows the court to control the sequence and timing of discovery. However, even though a district judge has broad discretion in conducting discovery, he commits reversible error if he abuses his discretion.

♦ When ruling under Rule 26(c) to limit discovery, the court must compare the hardship to the party against whom discovery is sought if it is allowed with the hardship to the party seeking discovery if it is denied. Not only the magnitude of the hardship, but also its nature, must be considered. Purely private interests deserve less weight than social values such as the First Amendment's protection of freedom of association, which protects D's membership application files here.

♦ In light of D's First Amendment interest in its membership files, the district court's discovery order was impermissibly broad. The district judge had several more appropriate alternatives available. For example, he could have examined D's membership files in camera and, if he found no evidence of anticompetitive practices by D, he could have determined that it was inappropriate to continue. Or he could have edited the files, deleting the names of the applicants, and if P found favorable evidence, then P could have requested access to the names. Finally, the district judge could have controlled the sequence of discovery by implementing Rule 26(d).

Dissent. I would affirm the district court's order holding D in contempt, but on remand would direct the court to examine D's membership files in camera and consider possible redaction (*i.e.,* removing the names of the applicants) before enforcing any discovery order.

Comment. Federal Rule 26 was amended in 1983 to allow greater judicial involvement in the discovery process, thus acknowledging that discovery often does not work on a self-regulating basis.

---

b. Constitutional considerations--

Seattle Times Co. v. Rhinehart, 467 U.S. 20 (1984).

Facts. Rhinehart (P), spiritual leader of a religious group, the Aquarian Foundation, brought a defamation and invasion of privacy action against the *Seattle Times* (D) in a Washington state court, alleging that D published several false articles about P's religious group. In the course of performing extensive discovery, the court, on D's motion, entered a discovery order compelling P to identify all donors who made contributions during the five years preceding the complaint, along with the amounts donated. The court also required P to divulge any information substantiating his claims of diminished membership. Finally, pursuant to the state counterpart of Federal Rule 26(c), the court prohibited D from publishing or otherwise using this information in any way except to prepare their case. This protective order did not apply to information gained by means other than the discovery process. The Washington Supreme Court affirmed both the production order and the protective order, commenting that P had adequately shown that public release of the donor and membership lists would adversely affect group membership and subject members to harassment. D appealed the protective order and the United States Supreme Court granted certiorari.

Issue. Did the trial court's protective order violate the First Amendment?

Held. No. Judgment affirmed.

♦ Pursuant to Rule 26(b)(1), the only express limitations on a litigant's discovery request are that it not seek privileged information and that it be relevant to the subject matter of the pending action. A litigant may request the court to issue an order directing compliance that can be enforced by the court's contempt powers. Thus, the rules allow for extensive intrusion into the affairs of others.

♦ Rule 26(c) confers broad discretion on a trial court to decide when a protective order is appropriate and to what degree protection is required. This is because a trial court is in the best position to weigh the competing interests of those affected by discovery.

♦ Here, the protective order was valid and did not offend the First Amendment, since (i) it was entered on a showing of good cause as mandated by Rule 26(c);

(ii) it was restricted to the context of pretrial civil discovery; and (iii) it did not restrict the dissemination of information gained from other sources.

Comment. The Supreme Court's decision in *Seattle Times* illustrates the broad discretion that a trial court has in directing the discovery process. It recognizes that the trial court is in the best position to fairly weigh the competing needs and interests of parties affected by discovery.

B. MANDATORY DISCLOSURE AND THE DISCOVERY PLAN

1. **Mandatory Disclosure.** Under Federal Rule of Civil Procedure 26(a), the discovery process initially begins with the disclosure by each party of information that will "support its claims or defenses." Rule 26(a)(1) disclosure is made by describing or categorizing potentially relevant materials so that the opposing party can make an informed decision about which documents it may wish to examine. The Rule does not require production of the actual documents, but the parties may agree to do so independently. [*See* Comas v. United Telephone Company of Kansas, 1995 WL 476691 (D. Kan. 1995)]

2. **Documents Party Does Not Plan to Use--**

Cummings v. General Motors Corp., 365 F.3d 944 (10th Cir. 2004).

Facts. The Cummings (Ps) sued General Motors Corporation (D) to recover for injuries sustained by Mrs. Cummings in an automobile accident. The jury returned a verdict in favor of D, and Ps appealed. After filing the appeal, Ps discovered videotapes of child safety seat acceleration tests conducted by D. Ps argue that the tests fall within their prior requests for production and would have demonstrated the impossibility of D's argument that Mrs. Cummings was injured in part because of the reclined position of her seat. Seven months later, Ps filed a motion for relief under Rule 60(b). The district court denied the motion as untimely and as lacking in support. Ps appeal.

Issue. Is a party required automatically to disclose documents that it does not intend to use?

Held. No.

♦ (Before the 2000 amendments, Rule 26(a)(1) required each party to provide information "relevant to disputed facts alleged with particularity in the pleadings.") Ps did not object to the magistrate's ruling that the 2000 amendments would govern this action. Under the amendments, parties need only make initial disclosures of "all documents, data compilations, and tangible things that are in the possession, custody, or control of the party and that the disclosing party may use to support its claims or defenses, unless solely for impeachment."

♦ If D did not intend to use the videotapes to support its claims or defenses, it was not required to disclose them as part of its initial disclosures.

---

3. **Disclosure of Insurance Coverage.** Under Rule 26(a)(1)(D), parties must disclose insurance agreements, even though such agreements will not be admissible at trial.

C. THE MECHANICS OF REQUESTED DISCOVERY

1. **Depositions.**

   a. **Definition of deposition.** A deposition is an out-of-court examination of either an opposing party or a potential witness. Because in many ways the taking of a deposition resembles a "miniature trial," this discovery device offers the attorney a rare opportunity to evaluate firsthand both the credibility of the deponent's story and his general demeanor. For this reason, the deposition is the most widely used and most valuable of the modern discovery devices, despite its relative expense.

      1) **Federal Rule of Civil Procedure 30(c).** "The officer before whom the deposition is to be taken shall put the witness on oath or affirmation and shall personally, or by someone acting under the officer's direction and in the officer's presence, record the testimony of the witness. . . ."

   b. **Barring or limiting scope of depositions--**

Polycast Technology Corp. v. Uniroyal, Inc., 1990 WL 138968 (S.D.N.Y. 1990).

Facts. Uniroyal, Inc. (D) sold its subsidiary, Uniroyal Plastics Company ("Plastics"), to Polycast Technology Corp. (P). P sued, alleging that it made the purchase based on misleading financial information D provided about Plastics. The parties have taken substantial discovery from Deloitte & Touche ("Deloitte"), a non-party who performed audits of both D and Plastics during the relevant time. P seeks to take the deposition of Durant, a Deloitte employee who was involved in an audit of Plastics immediately after D acquired it. Deloitte seeks a protective order barring the deposition for lack of relevance and because it would be duplicative of the deposition testimony of Bowman, Deloitte's engagement partner on the relevant audit.

Issue. Is it generally appropriate to bar a party from taking a deposition?

Held. No. Request denied, but deposition limited to one day.

- Orders barring the taking of a deposition are disfavored. While Deloitte may be entitled to greater protection as a non-party, the audit is entirely relevant to this action, and Durant, due to his presence during the audit, will be able to provide information that Bowman could not.

- We will not bar the deposition of Durant, but will limit it to one day for the purpose of filling in the gaps in Bowman's testimony and other evidence obtained about the audit.

---

c.   Videotaping depositions--

Wilson v. Olathe Bank, 184 F.R.D. 395 (D. Kan. 1999).

Facts. Two defendants seek protective orders to prohibit the plaintiffs (Ps) from videotaping their depositions, and another defendant, Community Bank, seeks to prohibit Ps from videotaping the deposition of its president.

Issue. Should a party be barred from videotaping depositions if there is no showing that the deponents will be unavailable for trial?

Held. No. Motions denied.

- Rule 30(b)(2) permits the videotaping of depositions and contains no requirement regarding the availability of the deponents at trial. Under Rule 26(c), a party may move for a protective order if the videotaping of the deposition would result in annoyance, embarrassment, oppression, and undue burden or expense.

- Movants make no showing of annoyance, embarrassment, or oppression. Movants argue that they will bear the expense of purchasing a copy of the video. Movants are not required to purchase the video, however, and such a purchase does not rise to the level of "undue expense." Movants also assert that they may face increased taxable costs as a result of the videotaping. However, the speculative possibility that a party may incur increased taxable costs is not a good reason to prevent the videotaping, as to do so would undermine the choice given to the deposing party by Rule 30. Furthermore, the court does not find that increased taxable costs necessarily equates with "undue expense."

---

2.   **Depositions upon Written Questions.** Under Rule 31, parties may take depositions upon written questions, meaning that the deponent answers written questions orally before an officer.

3.   **Interrogatories to Parties.**

      a.   **Definition of an interrogatory.** Written interrogatories are sets of written questions submitted by one party to an opposing party. The opposing party must supply written answers to the interrogatories, sworn to be true to the best of the party's knowledge and belief, within a specified period of time. In submitting and answering sets of interrogatories, each attorney has a chance to carefully consider each answer—interrogatories therefore lack the element of spontaneity that characterizes both written and oral depositions. On the other hand, answers to interrogatories must be more thorough, and in many cases much more detailed. This might require actual research by the party answering the interrogatory. Hence, there is an advantage to interrogatories as a method of establishing concrete background elements and ferreting out personal histories. [*See* Fed. R. Civ. P. 33]

      b.   **Duty to obtain information--**

***In re* Auction Houses Antitrust Litigation,** 196 F.R.D. 444 (S.D.N.Y. 2000).

Facts. In a class action alleging the existence of a price-fixing conspiracy by companies that are "in the business of providing auction services of fine and applied arts, furniture, antiques, automobiles, collectibles and other items," Christie's produced documents written by Davidge, its former chief executive officer, alleged to be evidence of the purported conspiracy. A former chairman of Sotheby's served Christie's with interrogatories seeking details about the Davidge documents. Christie's objected to most of the interrogatories on the ground that they seek information that is not in its possession, custody, or control, but is rather in the control of Davidge, whom it claims no longer to control. However, as part of an agreement entered into between Christie's and Davidge in connection with the termination of Davidge's employment, Christie's agreed to pay Davidge £5 million, of which it still owes at least £2 million, and Davidge agreed, among other things, to provide such information as the type requested here, as necessary. In another agreement, Christie's agreed to indemnify Davidge with respect to costs of litigation and liability arising from Davidge's cooperation. Sotheby's seeks an order to compel Christie's to respond to the interrogatories.

Issue. Does a company served with interrogatories have a duty to provide all responsive information not only within its control but also that is otherwise obtainable by it?

Held. Yes.

♦   A party who has been served with interrogatories must respond by "furnish[ing] such information as is available to the party."

♦   Here, Christie's has not given a persuasive reason why it cannot enforce its agreement with Davidge to compel him to provide the information sought in the interrogatories.

Christie's could withhold a great sum of money from Davidge to force him to comply with the agreement. Furthermore, the economic incentive for Davidge is sufficiently substantial to offer a real possibility that the information would be forthcoming in response to a determined effort by Christie's to obtain information from him. There is genuine ground to suspect Christie's good faith here.

---

c. **"Contention interrogatories"--**

***In re* Convergent Technologies Securities Litigation,** 108 F.R.D. 328 (N.D. Cal. 1985).

Facts. Ds filed motions to compel Ps to answer "contention interrogatories" early in the pretrial discovery period.

Issue. Should plaintiffs be compelled to answer interrogatories regarding the contentions raised by their lawsuit early in the pretrial period?

Held. Yes, under specific circumstances.

♦ "Contention interrogatories" is a phrase often used to refer to questions asking another party: (i) what it contends; (ii) whether it is making certain contentions; (iii) to state all the facts on which it bases a specified contention; (iv) to state all the evidence on which it bases a specified contention; (v) to take a position and explain or defend the position with respect to how the law applies to facts; or (vi) to state the legal basis for or theory behind a specified contention. Sometimes, a set of "contention interrogatories" includes all of these types of questions.

♦ A court can determine whether an interrogatory is proper after considering whether it is asked for an improper purpose and whether it is "unreasonable or unduly burdensome or expensive, given the needs of the case, the discovery already had in the case, the amount in controversy, and the importance of the issues at stake in the litigation."

♦ Recent authority suggests that it is wise to defer contention interrogatories until near the end of the discovery period. In some situations, however, this policy should give way to showings that important interests would be advanced if answers were provided earlier. Indeed, the benefits that can be obtained by narrowing and clarifying the issues early in the pretrial discovery period are potentially significant. On the other hand, freely allowing contention interrogatories too early could lead to discovery abuse.

♦ The court concludes that the following procedure should be used with respect to early contention interrogatories: (i) the propounding party must write specific questions that are limited in number; (ii) the responding party must examine such questions in good faith and answer those which would advance important interests as explained in this opinion; (iii) where the responding party believes a response would not advance such interests, it should communicate such objection to the propounding party; (iv) if necessary, the responding party can enter objections, placing on the propounding party the burden to file a motion to compel and the burden of justification explained in this opinion.

Conclusions of fact and law. In *Zinsky v. New York Central Railroad Co.*, 36 F.R.D. 680 (N.D. Ohio 1964), the plaintiff alleged that his duties were in furtherance of interstate commerce. The defendant denied all the allegations in the complaint. The plaintiff then sent an interrogatory asking: "Was plaintiff engaged in duties in the furtherance of interstate commerce?" The defendant objected that the interrogatory was improper because it called upon the defendant to draw conclusions of fact and law. The interrogatory was held improper, as it called for an analysis involving a conclusion upon a legal issue—interstate commerce.

----

4. **Discovery and Production of Property.**

   a. **General remarks.** At any time during discovery, a party may request that any other party produce for copying or inspection any real evidence, including documents, books, accounts, or photographs. The order may also include the right of one party to enter upon the land of another party for the purpose of inspecting the land, or undertaking other reasonable investigation in preparation for trial.

   b. **Discovery of electronic data--**

Zubulake v. UBS Warburg LLC, 217 F.R.D. 309 (S.D.N.Y. 2003).

Facts. Zubulake (P) sued UBS Warburg LLC and related defendants (Ds) for gender discrimination and retaliation. P contends that important evidence is contained in e-mails that now exist only on backup tapes or other archives. While having agreed previously to "produc[ing] responsive e-mails if retrieval is possible," Ds now contend that retrieving and reviewing those e-mails would cost more than $175,000. P filed a motion to compel production.

Issue. Under certain circumstances, is it appropriate to shift the costs of discovery onto the requesting party with regard to backup or archived electronic data?

Held. Yes.

♦ While the presumption is that the responding party bears the expense of complying with discovery requests, it may move for an order protecting it from undue burden or expense, which may include an order forcing the requesting party to bear the costs of discovery.

- ◆ Under Rule 34, electronic documents, including those residing only on backup media, are no less subject to disclosure than paper records. Thus, P is entitled to discovery of the requested e-mails so long as they are relevant to her claims, which they are. Ds have not reviewed their backup media in order to comply fully with the discovery requests.

- ◆ Deciding disputes such as these requires a three-step analysis. First, the court must understand the relevant computer system; cost-shifting should only be considered if the data is relatively inaccessible. Second, the court should fashion a way to determine what data would be found on inaccessible media; a sensible approach is requiring the responsive party to restore and produce responsive documents from a small sample of the requested media. Third, in conducting a cost-shifting analysis as to any remainder of inaccessible media, the court should consider the specificity of the order, other potential sources, the cost of production compared to the amount in controversy, the cost of production compared to each party's resources, the ability and incentive of each party to control costs, the importance of the issues, and the benefits to the parties of obtaining the information.

- ◆ Ds are ordered to produce, at their expense, all responsive e-mails that exist on five backup tapes chosen by P and to prepare an affidavit regarding the details of their search as well as time and money spent. The court will then conduct a cost-shifting analysis.

---

5. **Physical and Mental Examinations.**

a. **In general.** If, in the course of a civil action, either the physical or mental well-being of a party or a person under his control becomes an issue, upon motion and for good cause shown, the court may order that person to undergo physical or mental examinations. However, the examinations ordered must be "reasonable" in nature and in number. [*See* Fed. R. Civ. P. 35]

b. **Examination of defendants--**

Schlagenhauf v. Holder, 379 U.S. 104 (1964).

Facts. Schlagenhauf (D), driver of a cross-country bus for Greyhound Corp., was named as defendant in a negligence action filed by injured bus passengers following the collision of the bus with the rear end of a tractor-trailer. Greyhound, another defendant, cross-claimed against Contract Carriers, Inc., the tractor owner, and National Lead Co., the trailer owner, for damage to its bus, alleging that the collision was due solely to their negligence. Contract Carriers denied its negligence and asserted that the negligence of the bus driver, D, caused the bus damage. Contract Carriers and National Lead then petitioned the court for an order requiring D to submit to four separate mental and physical examinations, and presented the court with a list of nine physicians for selection. The district judge, Holder, then issued an order requiring D to submit to nine separate mental and physical examinations: two each in the specialties of internal medicine, ophthalmology, and neurology, and three separate examinations by psychiatrists. D objected, on grounds that his mental and physical well-being were not in "controversy," that the number of examinations was unreasonable and burdensome, and that no "good cause" for the examinations was ever shown. D sought a writ of mandamus against Holder to set aside the order requiring examinations. The court of appeals denied mandamus; the Supreme Court granted certiorari.

Issue. May a defendant be ordered to undergo examinations pursuant to Federal Rule 35?

Held. Yes. Judgment vacated and case remanded, however.

♦ Although to this point Rule 35 examinations have only been applied to plaintiffs, there is no basis for favoring one class of litigants over another. Therefore, defendants may be ordered to undergo physical examinations.

♦ However, the extent of examinations ordered here was excessive. Some "controversy" must center upon the physical or mental well-being of the party to be examined. At no time in the pleadings was D's physical or mental well-being ever placed in controversy. Further, an order for examination must be upon a showing of "good cause." "Good cause" in Rule 35 is more than mere relevancy—it is closer to "necessity." At no time was the necessity of an examination of D ever shown. Finally, the scope of the examinations ordered under Rule 35 must be limited and reasonable—that nine separate examinations were ordered showed neither reasonableness nor limitation.

Concurrence and dissent (Black, Clark, JJ.). The allegations of the other parties were relevant and put the question of D's health and vision in controversy.

Dissent (Douglas, J.). A rule suited to purposes of discovery against defendants must be carefully drawn in light of the great potential for blackmail.

---

6. **Requests to Admit.**

   a. **General definition and use.** At any time during discovery, a party may serve upon any other party a written request to admit the genuineness, truth, or accuracy of some document or fact. This tends to expedite preparations for trial and narrow the field of controverted issues to a minimum, since matters that are admitted are no longer issues of dispute—they are stipulated throughout the remainder of the pending proceeding.

   b.   **Effect of failure to admit or deny.** If the party upon whom is served a request to admit fails to answer sufficiently, this is often deemed an admission. Therefore, requests to admit must be answered clearly and promptly, or objected to immediately, lest the party be exposed to this sanction of implied admission.

7. **Duty to Supplement Responses.** Federal Rule 26(e) provides that a responding party must amend or supplement disclosures and discovery responses previously given to a propounding party if new information later acquired shows that the answer is incomplete or incorrect and the additional information has not been made known to the other parties. Also, when the identity of a witness is discovered after a response was given to an interrogating party, or when an expert witness is engaged subsequent to an original response, there is an obligation to disclose such information. When an expert witness has provided a report, both the report and any information provided in any deposition of the expert must be supplemented.

8. **Use of Discovery at Trial.**

   a.   **Depositions.** The Federal Rules and their state counterparts are quite liberal in allowing free use of depositions at trial either as evidence per se or in the impeachment of evidence otherwise introduced. State codes tend to be a little less liberal: as a general rule testimony taken by deposition or other discovery may be introduced at trial only to impeach offered testimony, or when live testimony of the deponent is not possible. [*See generally* Fed. R. Civ. P. 32, 36(b), and 30(e)]

   b.   **Depositions in lieu of live testimony--**

Battle v. Memorial Hospital at Gulfport, 228 F.3d 544 (5th Cir. 2000).

Facts. The Battles (Ps) sued Ds alleging negligent medical treatment that ultimately resulted in their baby son's being in a near vegetative state and requiring 24-hour-a-day care for the remainder of his life. Approximately three weeks before trial, Ps informed Ds that its expert witness Dr. Young would not be available for trial and noticed a videotape deposition of Dr. Young for approximately one week before trial. Soon after, Ps moved for a continuance of trial based on the unavailability of another expert, Dr. Whitley. Ps noticed Whitley's deposition. The court granted Ps' motion and continued the trial. Before trial, the court prohibited Ps from introducing into evidence the deposition Ds had taken of Ps' expert Dr. Lakeman, admitted Young's deposition, but prohibited Ps from calling Young as a live witness. At trial, Ds prevailed. Ps appeal, challenging each of the discovery rulings.

Issues.

(i) Did the trial court err in not admitting a videotaped deposition of a witness where the party who noticed the deposition treated it as being for discovery purposes only?

(ii) Did the trial court abuse its discretion in admitting a videotaped deposition of a witness but prohibiting the witness from testifying live?

Held. (i) Yes. (ii) No. Judgment affirmed in part, vacated in part, and case remanded.

♦ At trial, the judge held that because Ps had not demonstrated that Lakeman was unavailable and had not noticed a "trial" deposition of Lakeman, the "discovery" deposition of Lakeman was not admissible during Ps' case-in-chief. This court has held that nothing prohibits the use of a discovery deposition at trial, particularly against the party who conducted it. Here, there is no dispute that Lakeman was more than 100 miles from the place of trial. Thus, this issue turns on Rule 804's similar motive requirement.

♦ Ds argue that they did not have the similar motive to develop Lakeman's testimony during deposition as they would at trial, as required by Rule 804 of the Federal Rules of Evidence. Because similar motive does not mean identical motive, the similar motive inquiry is a factual inquiry, depending in part on the similarity of the underlying issues and on the context of the questioning. While our circuit has not addressed the issue, we agree with the Second Circuit's position that the test must turn not only on whether the questioner is on the same side of the same issue at both proceedings, but also on whether the questioner had a substantially similar interest in asserting and prevailing on the issue. Here, Ds were on the same side of the same issues at both proceedings and had the same interest in asserting and prevailing on those issues. They make no showing that Lakeman's testimony lacked reliability, and they characterize his testimony as cumulative of Whitley's testimony, which was admitted at trial. For these reasons, we find that Lakeman's deposition was admissible under Rule 804. We also find that the exclusion of the deposition was not harmless error, as his testimony was not merely cumulative but might have been determinative of an important question.

♦ Shortly before Young's deposition, when Ps moved for continuance, Ds objected to revealing their cross-examination strategy as to Young if Young was deposed and then later was allowed to testify live. Furthermore, Young lives and works more than 100 miles from the location of trial, satisfying Rule 32(a)(3)(B)'s requirement of unavailability, and a videotaped deposition, unlike a transcript, allows jurors to gauge the witness's attitude. We find that the trial court did not abuse its discretion when it attempted to balance Ds' interests in protecting their cross-examination strategy against Ps' need for Young's testimony in light of Ps' dilatory tactics during the pretrial period.

D. SPECIAL PROBLEMS REGARDING THE SCOPE OF DISCOVERY

1. **Materials Prepared in Anticipation of Trial.**

   a. **Attorney's "work product":** *Hickman v. Taylor* **rule.** After enactment of the discovery rules, which gave each party broad rights to discover his adversary's case, the Supreme Court was required to read in a limitation to protect counsel's ideas, papers, and memoranda. The Court held that a qualified privilege existed to protect an attorney's right of privacy as to her "work product," so that such materials were not subject to discovery in federal courts unless good cause were first shown.

   b. **Principal case--**

Hickman v. Taylor, 329 U.S. 495 (1947).

Facts. The tugboat "J.M. Taylor" sank; several crew members survived. Their statements were taken during an investigation into the accident. Later, in anticipation of a suit arising out of the accident, the owners of the boat privately interviewed the survivors, several witnesses, and others integrally concerned with the accident, and made transcripts of their testimony. Later, some of the survivors (Ps) filed suit against the tug owners, and by interrogatory, asked for exact copies of the testimony, which the attorney for the owners (D) obtained from them and from other witnesses during the private interviews. D responded that such "work product" information fell within the traditional lawyer-client relationship; hence, it was absolutely privileged. The district court held for Ps; the court of appeals reversed. Ps appeal.

Issue. When information sought by discovery is readily obtainable elsewhere by the party seeking discovery, will the court protect the work product of the opposing attorney?

Held. Yes. Judgment affirmed.

♦ D's work product is covered by a "conditional privilege" against discovery. Because of the extremely liberal federal discovery rules, we find it necessary to exempt from discovery any information "containing the ideas, conclusions, or personal labor of the attorney" in order not to discourage extensive investigation and preparation for trial. However, the privilege cannot be made absolute—there would exist circumstances where one counsel only would have access to testimony of a witness. Therefore, upon a showing of good cause, the work product of an attorney may be made discoverable.

♦ However, because the witnesses involved in the sinking of the "Taylor" were equally accessible to both parties, there existed no good cause why the personal interviews made by the defendant in anticipation of trial should be discoverable here.

Concurrence (Jackson, Frankfurter, JJ.). Having been supplied with names of witnesses, counsel in an adversary proceeding may interview the witnesses themselves.

---

    c.   Federal Rule 26(b)(3). Federal Rule 26(b)(3) has now gone beyond the *Hickman v. Taylor* rule. It provides that documents and things prepared in anticipation of trial by the adversary party or his "representative" (and this includes not only his attorney, but also any investigator or consultant) are discoverable if:

        1)   The party seeking discovery has "substantial need of the materials in the preparation of the party's case"; and

        2)   The discovering party is "unable without undue hardship to obtain the substantial equivalent of the materials by other means."

    d.   Rule applied. The problem, of course, is determining exactly what is and is not the attorney's work product. The trial judge, when faced with a work-product claim, must balance the need for disclosure against any harm or unfairness that disclosure might cause.

2.   Privileged Matter.

    a.   Introduction. Public policy demands that certain information be protected against disclosure. Such information is said to be "privileged." Some privileges are founded in the Constitution, some are based on common law developments, and some are statutory.

    b.   Privileged information. Each discovery device we have examined in detail is limited in scope, in that only information "not privileged" can be discovered. All privileged information falls into two categories: information absolutely privileged from discovery, and information conditionally privileged from discovery.

        1)   Absolutely privileged information. A party may not be required during discovery to divulge information that would violate any of the commonly recognized constitutional privileges (the privilege against self-incrimination, for example) or that would violate one of the quasi-constitutional privileges recognized through the rules of evidence—the privileges that exist between husband and wife, doctor and patient, or lawyer and client. Such information is absolutely privileged from discovery—no showing of good cause, or even "necessity," will cause the court to order such information to be divulged. Such an order would constitute reversible error.

        2)   Conditionally privileged information. The privileges that exist between lawyer-client or doctor-patient are limited. Only information that passes directly between the professional and his client is privileged. Information obtained from collateral sources, such as independent investigation, does not fall within the absolute privilege under discussion.

    a)   The doctor-patient privilege. Within the context of a negligence action in which the "mental or physical condition" of a party is in direct controversy, the doctor-patient privilege does not exist. Modern discovery does allow for discovery of medical information directly in issue in litigation. However, medical information not directly in controversy retains its absolutely privileged characteristic, as does generally the medical condition of parties to the action.

    b)   The attorney-client privilege.

        (1)   No common law privilege. No specific privilege existed at common law to protect the materials or papers assembled by an attorney in the preparation of his case. (Such information was not protected by the attorney-client privilege, since there was no "communication" involved with the client.) But, of course, no privilege was really needed, since at common law discovery was virtually nonexistent.

        (2)   Attorney-client privilege in corporate context--

Upjohn Co. v. United States, 449 U.S. 383 (1981).

Facts. Upjohn Co. (D), a multinational corporation, discovered that one of its foreign subsidiaries had apparently bribed foreign government officials. As part of an internal investigation, D's attorneys sent questionnaires to its foreign managers and conducted interviews with the same people and certain other employees. The IRS initiated an investigation of the tax consequences and issued a summons for production of the questionnaires and interview notes. D refused to produce the documents, claiming attorney-client privilege and work-product doctrine protection. The lower courts ordered production and D appeals.

Issue. Are disclosures made by corporate employees to corporate attorneys within the attorney-client privilege?

Held. Yes. Judgment reversed.

    ♦   The lower courts held that the attorney-client privilege applies only to communications made by employees responsible for directing D's actions in response to legal advice. This "control group" test is too restrictive, because employees at any level could, acting within the scope of their employment, cause serious legal problems for D. D's attorneys also would need to obtain information from these employees to formulate appropriate advice.

♦ To the extent that the requested documents were not communications from the client and thus privileged, the documents were attorney work-product. Documents that reveal the attorney's mental processes in evaluating the information are privileged under the work-product doctrine.

Comment. The only protections applicable in the corporate setting are the two involved in this case. In *Upjohn*, the Court broadened the application of the attorney-client privilege in the corporate context, but the work-product doctrine still provides limited protection.

---

3. **Expert Information.** The extent of discovery permitted with regard to reports or opinions of expert witnesses depends largely on whether the expert is to be called as a witness at trial. [Fed. R. Civ. P. 26(b)(4)]

a. **Attorney work product given to expert witness--**

Krisa v. Equitable Life Assurance Society, 196 F.R.D. 254 (M.D. Pa. 2000).

Facts. Krisa (P) sought to compel Equitable Life Assurance Society (D) to produce preliminary documents and documents prepared by experts in connection with D's decision to deny P's application for disability benefits. D argued that these documents are protected under Rule 26(b)(3), the work product doctrine. P argued that the documents are discoverable pursuant to Rule 26(b)(4), which authorizes discovery of testifying expert witnesses.

Issue. Are materials containing attorney work product discoverable when given to an expert witness?

Held. No. Motion to compel denied.

♦ The Rules of Civil Procedure allow discovery of the opinions expert witnesses intend to give at trial, as well as preliminary opinions that may be in conflict with the expert's final opinion. The 1993 amendments to Rule 26(a)(2) require automatic disclosure of an expert's opinions, the basis therefor, and the data or information upon which the expert relied in forming his opinion.

♦ While some courts have held that the amendments require production of all documents reviewed by an expert regardless of whether they constitute attorney work product, we believe that such a change in the scope of the Rule would require clear and unambiguous language to effectuate. We find no specific authority in the 1993 amendments to abridge the attorney work product privilege.

♦ Only one document provided to the expert by D's counsel contains attorney work product, and D will not be required to produce this document.

Comment. In *Johnson v. Gmeinder*, 191 F.R.D. 638 (D. Kan. 2000), the court found that the Advisory Committee's Notes to the 1993 amendments explicitly stated that work product protection does not apply to materials furnished to an expert witness.

E. SANCTIONS AND JUDICIAL SUPERVISION OF DISCOVERY

1. **In General.** The Federal Rules and all state codes of civil procedure prescribe certain penalties that may be inflicted upon any party who refuses or fails unjustifiably to make discovery. Generally, the battery of penalties prescribed is quite broad, and includes conviction for contempt of court, striking of pleadings, involuntary dismissal with or without prejudice, or arrest until discovery is made. However, in actual litigation the courts are reluctant to use these generally harsh penalties, and tend to restrict the use of penalties for abuse of discovery to monetary reimbursement of the opposing party for any expenses incurred as a result of the refusal to make discovery. [*See* Fed. R. Civ. P. 37]

2. **Justification for Severe Sanctions--**

Cine Forty-Second Street Theatre Corp. v. Allied Artists Pictures Corp., 602 F.2d 1062 (2d Cir. 1979).

Facts. Cine Forty-Second Street Theatre Corp. (P) sued Allied Artists Pictures Corp. (D) for antitrust violations. P secured D's consent to defer discovery on the damages issue so P could retain a certain expert. Two years later, P had still failed to retain the expert; P's answers in the meantime were clearly inadequate, and P was warned that it risked dismissal if it continued to fail to respond to the magistrate's orders compelling discovery. After another year of inadequate responses, the magistrate concluded that P's noncompliance was willful and recommended dismissal. The district judge, reluctant to impose such a severe sanction, did not dismiss, but since he was uncertain of the governing law, he certified an interlocutory appeal by D.

Issue. May grossly negligent failure to obey an order compelling discovery justify imposition of the severest disciplinary measures available?

Held. Yes. Judgment reversed.

♦ Sanctions are imposed to prevent a party from profiting from its own failures to comply, to secure compliance, as specific deterrents to such failures to comply, and, where the party is in some sense at fault, as a general deterrent that will affect both the case at hand and other litigation. The most severe sanctions, such as dismissal, generally fall in the latter category. The question is whether P's gross negligence may be considered "fault."

♦ The term "fault" includes more than merely willfulness and bad faith; it includes gross negligence like P's. The principal objective of the general deterrent policy is strict adherence to the responsibilities counsel owe to the court and to opponents. Gross professional negligence places significant and unnecessary burdens on the legal system and is a proper object of harsh sanctions. Although P may suffer, it is well recognized that a litigant chooses counsel at his peril.

XII. CASE MANAGEMENT

A. RULE 16

Rule 16 of the Federal Rules of Civil Procedure concerns pretrial conferences, scheduling, and management of cases. Two theories of the purpose of the pretrial conference between the judge and the parties to a civil dispute are currently in vogue. The first theory sees the pretrial conference as one of the procedural methods to be used to clarify issues for trial, set the bounds of the controversy at trial, and make other procedural decisions that will speed up the course of the litigation. The second theory sees the pretrial conference as a method of "coercing" settlements in suits that should not really occupy the time of the court—those suits in which the differences of opinion are minor or the amount in controversy small. A few jurisdictions have gone as far as to require attendance at pretrial "settlement conferences," in which the court pushes each party in an effort to gain concessions and to reach an equitable settlement.

1. **Mandatory vs. Discretionary Pretrial Conference.**

   a. Rule 16 does not make pretrial conferences mandatory (although it does mandate a pretrial scheduling order). However, *local* court rules in many federal districts require a pretrial in every case. In others, the conference is optional and is generally used only in more complex litigation.

   b. Some states have experimented with mandatory pretrial, but its indiscriminate use in every case has been found to lessen its effectiveness and to consume more time of court counsel than it saves.

2. **Conduct of Conference.** A pretrial conference is generally informal, often in chambers. After settlement possibilities have been explored, the court generally considers such matters as: (i) what matters can be agreed upon and what remains in dispute; (ii) whether any amendments to the pleadings are required; (iii) what additional discovery will be permitted; (iv) exchange of expert witness reports, medical information, etc.; and (v) setting of trial date.

3. **Failure to Comply with Scheduling Order--**

Velez v. Awning Windows, Inc., 375 F.3d 35 (1st Cir. 2004).

Facts. Velez (P) sued Awning Windows, Inc. and its owner (Ds) for an alleged campaign of sexual harassment leading to her discharge. After patiently granting several extensions of discovery and issuing warnings to Ds, who continually failed to comply with the deadlines imposed by the court's scheduling order, the court denied certain of their motions for noncompliance with the scheduling order, disregarded Ds' late opposition to a motion for partial summary judgment, took the proffer of P as true, and resolved the issue of liability in P's favor. The jury awarded P nearly $750,000 in damages. Ds appeal.

Issue. Did the district court err in disregarding late motions and otherwise sanctioning Ds for their repeated failure to comply with its scheduling order?

Held. No. Judgment affirmed.

♦ Ds contend that the district court should have considered their late-filed opposition to the motion for partial summary judgment. A party who requires more time to file an opposition to a motion for summary judgment must make the court aware of this need. This is typically accomplished through a Rule 56(f) motion, or its equivalent, containing a statement explaining the party's current inability to adduce essential facts, providing a plausible basis for believing that such facts can be assembled within a reasonable time, and indicating how such facts would influence the outcome of the pending summary judgment motion. Such a litigant also must have exercised "due diligence both in pursuing discovery before the summary judgment initiative surfaces and in pursuing an extension of time thereafter." Ds never invoked or substantially complied with Rule 56(f). Ds now seek to rectify some of their earlier omissions, but it is too late, and, in any event, their justifications are less than compelling. Furthermore, Ds did not exercise due diligence with regard to their prediscovery efforts. Finally, in the absence of a timely opposition, the court did its duty in granting the summary judgment motion.

♦ The district court was free to deny Ds' motions to dismiss, which did not concern non-waivable jurisdictional issues, as a sanction for their noncompliance with the scheduling order.

♦ The district court did not abuse its discretion by precluding certain hearsay testimony as a sanction for Ds' protracted delay in submitting a memorandum on the issue that the court originally gave it one month to file.

B. EXTRAJUDICIAL PERSONNEL: MASTERS AND MAGISTRATES

With the increase in caseload in the federal system, the use of masters and magistrates has been employed by the courts to handle a wide variety of judicial functions.

1. **Magistrates.** Rule 73 implements the broad authority given to federal magistrates under the 1979 amendments to the Federal Magistrates Act of 1968. These amendments permit a magistrate to sit in lieu of a district judge and to exercise civil jurisdiction over a case when the parties consent. This power extends to jury and nonjury trials as well as motions, but does not include contempt power.

2. **Masters.** Rule 53 provides for the appointment of one or more "masters" by the district court to serve as referees, auditors, examiners, commissioners, or assessors.

C. THE FINAL PRETRIAL ORDER

The order that issues out of a pretrial conference is a powerful document in the course of the ordinary lawsuit. It controls the entire future course of the litigation, unless modified at some later stage of the proceedings. It supersedes the pleadings—causes of action may be added, dropped, modified, or embellished during the pretrial conference if the court deems it in the interests of justice. It may give a direction to the entire litigation—as when the types or quantities of proof allowable are specifically described in the order—and when misused, may even determine the outcome of the litigation, as in the following case. For these reasons, skillful tacticians may often gain a substantial advantage during the pretrial conference, at the expense of the unprepared attorney, by carefully preparing for presentation a battery of suggestions and motions. The pleader is warned to never take lightly the pretrial conference.

1. **Amendment of Order Not Allowed--**

Payne v. S.S. Nabob, 302 F.2d 803 (3d Cir. 1962).

Facts. Payne (P), in this personal injury admiralty action, filed a pretrial memorandum pursuant to the court's standing order for pretrial practice, stating that he was relying upon the condition of a winch to prove his cause of action. This was noted in the judge's pretrial report. At trial, however, P argued in his opening statement that the loading had been handled improperly as an important element of his proof of unseaworthiness. S.S. Nabob (D) objected because this claim was outside the scope of the pretrial memorandum and report. The district court sustained the objection and refused to allow two of P's witnesses, not listed in his pretrial memorandum, to testify. P moved for a continuance and was denied. P appeals.

Issue. Did the district court err by refusing to allow P to amend the pretrial order?

Held. No. District court affirmed.

♦ Even though the court's local rules did not expressly designate its pretrial procedures applicable to admiralty litigation until after the trial, this admiralty action was not exempt from these procedures. Federal Rule 16, which authorizes pretrial procedure, has applied to admiralty actions since 1942. Under Rule 16, the court has tried several previous admiralty cases, and thus P's argument is without merit.

♦ Even though the court's pretrial report was not entitled an "order," it still complied with Rule 16. P's pretrial memorandum contained (i) a brief summary statement of the facts, (ii) his contentions as to D's liability, and (iii) names and addresses of all witnesses he expected to call at trial. Both parties attended the pretrial conference, and the judge's report was based on the pretrial memorandum and conference. Since the pretrial report properly reduced the action to its essentials, eliminated surplusage, named witnesses, and contained no ambiguities, it satisfied Rule 16.

♦ Notwithstanding P's contention to the contrary, the court's standing order could not be construed as a mere request to stipulate. Thus, the barring of P's unseaworthiness allegation, not mentioned in his pretrial memorandum, could not be avoided on the theory that he did not intend to stipulate and that no warning or notice was given by the standing order.

♦ Here, the court did not abuse its discretion by denying P leave to amend the pretrial order. Clearly, P made no effort during the five and one-half months after the filing of the report to change its contentions or to add additional witnesses. Thus the refusal to permit an amendment in P's opening statement and to permit the use of unlisted witnesses was reasonable.

D. CASE MANAGEMENT AND SANCTIONS

1. Rule 16(f) Sanctions--

Nick v. Morgan's Foods, Inc., 270 F.3d 590 (8th Cir. 2001).

Facts. Nick (P) sued Morgan's Foods, Inc. (D) for sexual harassment and retaliation. At the pretrial scheduling conference, the parties agreed to alternative dispute resolution ("ADR") with a court-appointed mediator, and the court issued an order referring the case to ADR. On D's request, the court agreed to postpone the first ADR conference until a later date. D then failed to file the memorandum required to be filed at least seven days before the first conference and minimally participated in the conference. The court ordered D to show cause why it should not be sanctioned for failing to participate in ADR with good faith, and, after a hearing and on P's motion, sanctioned D and D's outside counsel to pay certain sums including fines to the clerk of the district court. D filed a motion for reconsideration and vacation of the court's order. The district court denied the motion and imposed additional monetary sanctions for filing a frivolous motion. D appeals as to the fines to be paid to the clerk of court.

Issue. Does a district court have authority to impose monetary sanctions under Rule 16(f)?

Held. Yes. Order affirmed.

- Rule 16(f) expressly permits a judge to impose any other sanction he deems appropriate in addition to, or in lieu of, reasonable expenses. The judge acted well within his discretion by imposing monetary fines payable to the clerk of court.

- D's argument that any wrongful conduct on its part was the product of its trial lawyer and unknown to D is without merit. A party may be held responsible for the actions of its counsel. Litigants who are truly misled by their counsel have recourse in malpractice actions.

- The amount of the sanctions is proportionate to the abuses at issue in the present case.

Comment. Both Rule 11 and Rule 16 allow for sanctions, but the rules are different. Rule 11 deals with all motions, pleadings, and documents signed by an attorney or a party, while Rule 16 reaches aspects of pretrial management that may not have been memorialized in a writing. Also, the imposition of attorney's fees as a sanction is discretionary under Rule 11 but is mandatory under Rule 16. Furthermore, Rule 11 provides for sanctions for acts done with an improper purpose, while Rule 16 permits sanctions for certain acts regardless of purpose.

———————————————

XIII. ADJUDICATION WITHOUT TRIAL OR BY SPECIAL PROCEEDING

A. SUMMARY JUDGMENT

1. **"Speaking" Demurrer.** Under common law and early code pleading rules, a demurrer that "spoke," *i.e.,* introduced facts not contained in the pleading being demurred to, was not permitted—"outside information was not permitted to be brought to the attention of the court by demurrer." But modern pleading has recognized that often, if the challenging party is permitted to introduce extraneous material, it can be shown that "no genuine controversy of law or fact" exists and that a trial would be a waste of time. Hence, the motion for summary judgment has developed. If a pleader in challenging the truth or sufficiency of a pleading demonstrates by the use of sworn affidavits not contradicted by counteraffidavits that "no genuine controversy of law or fact exists" and demonstrates that he is deserving of judgment "as a matter of law," judgment will be awarded him upon a motion for summary judgment. Summary judgment thereafter has all the res judicata effects of a full adjudication upon the merits. [*See* Fed. R. Civ. P. 56]

2. **Motion for Summary Judgment Compared with Motion for Judgment on the Pleadings.** While a motion for summary judgment may be employed for the same purpose as a motion for judgment on the pleadings—*i.e.,* to terminate the litigation without the necessity for trial, it is radically different in approach: The motion for judgment on the pleadings attacks the legal sufficiency of the pleadings, while a motion for summary judgment attacks the basic merits of the opponent's case and is designed to *"pierce the pleadings"*—*i.e.,* to show that the opponent's case has ***no merit***, regardless of what his pleadings say.

3. **Use of Supporting Affidavits--**

Lundeen v. Cordner, 354 F.2d 401 (8th Cir. 1966).

Facts. Lundeen (P) sued an insurance company for benefits allegedly due her as beneficiary of a life insurance policy. Cordner (D) intervened in that suit and asserted that the insured had, just before his death, changed the beneficiary clause of the policy to name her as new beneficiary. The insurance company deposited the face value of the policy with the court and was dismissed as a party. D, in answer to the complaint, filed a motion for summary judgment, supported by affidavits from the insured's insurance broker, his doctor, his advisory attorney, and several employees of the insurance company, all to the effect that the insured had, days before his unexpected death, filed the necessary forms for a change of beneficiary. Only the ministerial duty of mailing out the formal notice of change of beneficiary was left to be carried out at the time of the insured's death. By state law, a change of beneficiary was effective when the insurance company received notice of a desire to change beneficiary, as it had before the death of the insured. The trial court granted summary judgment for D; P appeals.

Issue. Is summary judgment appropriate where one party's affidavits and exhibits are conclusive and uncontested by the other party?

Held. Yes. Judgment affirmed.

♦ D had shown "beyond any doubt" that she had been named as new beneficiary of the insurance policy before the death of the insured. All the affidavits introduced by her were in proper form, were admissible as evidence per se, and all tended to demonstrate clearly her right to relief. There was absolutely no evidence that the testimony of any of the affiants was to be disbelieved. P was able to submit no counteraffidavits opposing the obvious conclusions of the supporting affidavits. Summary judgment was therefore called for. P's only defense to the affidavits (that she had not had a chance to cross-examine the affiants) was not effective since P was otherwise unable to show any reason for doubting the truth of the affidavits.

Comment. *Lundeen* does not mean the credibility of an affiant may not be challenged when his affidavit supports a motion for summary judgment. Federal Rule 56 specifically provides for penalty to be imposed whenever it appears to the satisfaction of the court that an affidavit has been sworn in bad faith. But it is incumbent upon the party challenging the validity of an affidavit to present some basis for his challenge—although the type of proof necessary to cast doubt upon an affidavit has never been made clear. It is clear that a mere allegation that affiant has sworn a false affidavit, unsupported by some proof, will not cause the court to strike the affidavit. "The court does not have the right to believe the opposite of the story told by a witness upon affidavit unless there is affirmative evidence of his bad faith. Any other rule would effectively destroy the usefulness of motions for summary judgment and directed verdict." [Dyer v. MacDougall, 201 F.2d 265 (2d Cir. 1952)]

---

4.   **Existence of Factual Issues--**

Cross v. United States, 336 F.2d 431 (2d Cir. 1964).

Facts. Cross (P) was a language professor at a well-known college. In this suit he sought refund of taxes paid on income he had used in taking a trip to Europe, allegedly in order to sharpen his language skills in French and German. The Internal Revenue Code provides that income used "in the improvement of performance skills used in business . . . shall be exempt from taxation." On the basis of this section of the Code, and supported by his own personal affidavit that he had taken the trip solely to improve his language skills, P moved for summary judgment, which was granted by the trial court on grounds that "there are not triable issues of controversy" and on grounds that "defendant submitted no counteraffidavits." The United States (D) claimed a right to cross-examine P, but the trial court granted summary judgment for P. D appeals.

Issue. Is it improper to grant summary judgment based on P's explanation of his intent, which is disputed by D but not contradicted by D's evidence?

Held. Yes. Judgment reversed.

♦ Summary judgment for P was improper because the affidavit presented by P did not "preclude the possibility that there are triable controversies presented by the facts of the case." The interpretation of the Internal Revenue Code as applied to the situation at hand was by no means clear—never before had a trip to foreign lands frequented by tourists been called a "business expense" merely because of a professed desire to sharpen language skills. Therefore, reasonable persons could have differed upon the interpretation of the Code, and summary judgment was improper.

♦ Summary judgment should never have been used to decide an issue where "personal motives, intent, and feeling" were central to the proceedings. Interpretation of such motives may differ, and the chance that the moving party can ever show a right to relief as a matter of law is small.

♦ P had totally failed to show an absence of genuine issues of law or fact, for which reasons his motion should have been denied. That D failed to submit any counteraffidavits was immaterial, since P had failed to show by his own affidavits that he deserved summary judgment.

⎯⎯⎯⎯⎯⎯⎯

5. Standards Governing Burden of Production (Quantity of Evidence)--

Celotex Corp. v. Catrett, 477 U.S. 317 (1986).

Facts. Catrett (P) filed this wrongful death action against Celotex Corporation (D) and several other corporations, claiming that her husband's death resulted from exposure to asbestos manufactured or distributed by defendants. After one year of discovery, D moved for summary judgment on the ground that during discovery P failed to produce any evidence to support her allegation that the decedent had been exposed to D's product. In response, P produced documents tending to show such causation. D argued that the documents were inadmissible hearsay and thus could not be considered in opposition to the summary judgment motion. Agreeing with D, the district court granted D's motion. The appellate court reversed on the ground that D failed to meet its initial burden of production under Rule 56(c) of showing the absence of a genuine issue of material fact, because

D "made no effort to adduce *any* evidence, in the form of affidavits or otherwise, to support its motion" (emphasis in original). D appeals.

Issue. Where information derived through discovery indicates that the nonmoving party cannot prove an essential element of her cause of action at trial, must the moving party still come forward with evidence in the form of affidavits or other information to show the absence of a genuine issue of material fact within the meaning of Rule 56(c)?

Held. No. Judgment reversed.

♦   There can be no genuine issue of material fact when, after an adequate discovery period, the party opposing summary judgment fails to make a showing sufficient to establish the existence of an essential element in that party's case, and on which that party will bear the burden of proof at trial.

♦   The burden is not on the party moving for summary judgment to produce evidence showing the absence of a genuine issue of material fact with respect to an issue on which the nonmoving party bears the burden of proof. Rather, in this situation, the movant need only "show—that is, [point] out to the district court—that there is an absence of evidence to support the nonmoving party's case." And this burden may be discharged by relying on depositions, answers to interrogatories and the like, as Rule 56(c) clearly provides.

♦   The standard governing the burden of production for summary judgment "mirrors the standard for a directed verdict under Federal Rule of Civil Procedure 50(a)" in which D would not be required to support its motion with affidavits or other similar materials *negating* P's claim. The burden is on P, not D, to go forward with evidence as to P's claim.

Concurrence (White, J.). The movant must support his motion in some way other than with a conclusory assertion that the nonmovant has no evidence to prove his case.

Dissent (Brennan, J., Burger, C.J., Blackmun, J.). D failed to discharge its initial burden of production under Rule 56(c), because, having moved for summary judgment on the ground that the record contained no evidence to support an essential element of P's claim, D ignored evidence in the record that tended to support P's claim—*e.g.,* a letter from the decedent's former employer, whom P intended to call as a witness.

Comment. The principles governing the movant's burden of production under Rule 56(c) are clearly presented in Part I of Justice Brennan's dissenting opinion, and are consistent with the majority opinion. These principles indicate that the burden of persuasion at trial necessarily affects the burden of production under Rule 56(c) or (e). The burden of persuasion at trial also determines the burden of persuasion on summary judgment.

6.   Effect of Substantive Evidentiary Standard--

Anderson v. Liberty Lobby, Inc., 477 U.S. 242 (1986).

Facts. Liberty Lobby, Inc., a not-for-profit corporation, and its founder and treasurer, Willis Carto (Ps), filed a diversity libel action against certain individuals and a publishing company (Ds) for a series of articles that allegedly defamed Ps. Following discovery, Ds moved for summary judgment. Ds asserted that because Ps were public figures, Ps were required to prove their case under the *New York Times Co. v. Sullivan*, 376 U.S. 254 (1964), standard—*i.e.,* Ps had to show that Ds had acted with actual malice in publishing the alleged defamatory statements. Ds argued that summary judgment was proper because the author's affidavit, which indicates that the articles were thoroughly researched and the facts were obtained from numerous sources, established the absence of actual malice. Ps responded that an issue of fact was presented because the author had relied on sources that Ps claimed were patently unreliable and that Ds failed to verify information before publishing it. Summary judgment was granted. The court of appeals reversed as to some of the statements, holding that for purposes of summary judgment, proof of actual malice need not be made by "clear and convincing evidence," the evidentiary standard applicable to libel actions at trial. Rather, a lower burden of persuasion, one applicable to most civil actions (called the "preponderance of the evidence" standard), governs summary judgment. Ds appeal.

Issue. Must the substantive evidentiary standards that apply to the case guide a determination of whether a genuine issue of material fact exists?

Held. Yes. Judgment reversed.

♦   At the summary judgment stage, the judge's function is not to weigh the evidence and determine the truth of the matter but to determine whether the evidence presents a sufficient disagreement to require submission to a jury or whether it is so one-sided that one party must prevail as a matter of law.

♦   In this sense, the standard for summary judgment mirrors the standard for a directed verdict, which is that the trial judge must direct a verdict if, under the governing law, there can be but one reasonable conclusion as to the verdict.

♦   Since the judge must ask himself not whether he thinks the evidence unmistakably favors one side or the other but whether a fair-minded jury could return a verdict for the plaintiff on the "evidence presented," the inquiry involved in a ruling on a motion for summary judgment or for a directed verdict necessarily implicates the substantive evidentiary standard of proof that would apply at the trial on the merits.

Comment. The Court's determination of the issue of this case can also be explained by the following syllogism: (i) At the summary judgment stage, the trial judge's function is to determine whether there is a "genuine" or "triable" factual issue. (ii) A factual issue is "genuine" or "triable" if a jury could find for the nonmoving party, assuming, of course, that the moving party has discharged her initial burden under Rule 56(c). (iii) A jury could find for the nonmovant only if he has satisfied the substantive evidentiary standard of proof applicable to the merits of his case. (iv) Ergo, a summary judgment ruling necessarily implicates the substantive evidentiary standard of proof. The Court also makes a significant ruling concerning the use of summary judgment where, as in this case, the defendant's state of mind is at issue. Such a case might turn on whether the defendant's protestations of innocence are believable—*i.e.,* on the defendant's credibility or the credibility of her witnesses. In the past, the Court seemed to take the position that the defendant should seldom if ever be granted summary judgment in such a case. [*See, e.g.,* Hutchinson v. Proxmire, 443 U.S. 111, 120, n. 9 (1979)—proof of actual malice "does not readily lend itself to summary disposition"] The Court now rules that in state-of-mind cases, once the defendant has met her initial burden under Rule 56(c), the plaintiff is not "relieved of his own burden [under Rule 56(e)] of producing in turn evidence that would support a jury verdict. . . . This is true even where the evidence is likely to be within the possession of the defendant, as long as the plaintiff has had a full opportunity to conduct discovery [as Rule 56(f) allows]." Thus, not only in libel cases but also in many other cases involving state of mind (*e.g.,* employment discrimination, emotional distress, and conspiracy), credibility is no longer the exclusive province of the jury.

B. DISMISSAL OF ACTIONS

1. **Voluntary Dismissal.** A plaintiff has the option of dismissing his action voluntarily, without prejudice to himself, at any time early in the pretrial procedure. This option is usually used if an unexpected contingency develops, *e.g.,* when a key witness leaves the jurisdiction of the court, or a party is taken ill. However, because there is a chance of harassment and misuse of the tactic of voluntary dismissal, many jurisdictions provide that a party may voluntarily dismiss his action without prejudice only once—subsequent voluntary dismissals act as adjudications in favor of the defendant. [*See* Fed. R. Civ. P. 41(a)]

2. **Dismissal for Failure to Prosecute.** Once the plaintiff files his action with the court, he may not stall or dawdle—he must proceed to prosecute his action with "due diligence." Some jurisdictions define "due diligence" in terms of specific terms of years (dismissal automatic after five years), but most employ a "reasonable time" standard. Whatever standard is employed, however, dismissal for failure to prosecute, like dismissal for noncompliance with a court order, acts as an adjudication upon the merits in the defendant's favor.

C. DEFAULT JUDGMENT

1. **In General.** When a defendant in an action at law omits to plead to the complaint within the time permitted by statute, and otherwise fails to contest the

adjudication of the suit, and fails to appear at trial, she defaults, and a judgment by default may be entered against her without the formality of trial upon the merits. If the defendant thereafter within the statutorily prescribed period fails to contest the entering of a default against her, the default judgment becomes binding, and carries all the res judicata effects of a judgment upon the merits. [Fed. R. Civ. P. 55]

2. Failure to Appear at Trial--

Coulas v. Smith, 395 P.2d 527 (Ariz. 1964).

Facts. Smith (P) filed two counts on overdue notes against Coulas (D) and a cross-claimant. Both D and the cross-claimant answered, denying liability on the notes. At trial, however, D failed to appear, although the cross-claimant did appear. The trial court proceeded upon the merits against the cross-claimant, and entered judgment by default against D, both with respect to the claim running from P to D and the claim running from the cross-claimant to D. Two years later, D filed a motion to set aside both defaults. The motion was denied. D appeals.

Issue. May a default judgment be entered against a defendant who answers the charges made against him?

Held. No, but judgment affirmed on other grounds.

♦ The trial court was in error in entering a default judgment against D, since he had answered all charges against him. However, D had unreasonably delayed in challenging the default entered against him, and the judgment, whether default or not, had become finalized. Therefore, the judgment will not be set aside.

♦ Several cases hold that any attack upon jurisdiction, service, venue, or any answer upon the merits, whether or not the defendant shows up at trial, precludes entry of a default judgment. Since D answered upon the merits, the judgment entered against him should have been upon the merits rather than by default. But the relevant Arizona statute provides that no judgment may be reopened and set aside more than six months after entry. Because D waited two years to try to vacate the "default" judgment, he had waived whatever rights he may have had to reopen the default.

---

3. **Reopening a Default Judgment.** Most jurisdictions provide that judgments by default may be reopened within a certain statutory period, usually one year, for full trial upon the merits, for any "good cause" shown. Once the statutory period has run, however, default judgments become finalized, and unless a successful collateral attack is launched in another jurisdiction, the default judgment carries all the res judicata effects of a final judgment upon the merits.

4. **Default Judgment and Damages.** As a general rule, the damages prayed for in the complaint limit the damages that may be entered against the defendant upon default—at no time may a judgment by default exceed the recovery prayed for in the complaint defaulted upon. However, care must be taken to ascertain whether entry of judgment is actually by default, or whether entry is by nature a penalty for noncompliance with rules of procedure. If entry of judgment against the defendant is by nature of a penalty for disobeying a court order, the judgment is not one by default, and the damages recoverable are not limited by the prayer in the complaint. [*See, e.g.,* Trans World Airlines, Inc. v. Hughes, 32 F.R.D. 604 (S.D.N.Y. 1963)]

XIV. TRIAL

A. TRIAL BY JURY

1. Nature of the Right to Jury Trial.

a. **Sources of the right.** The right to jury trial on certain issues in American courts derives directly from the Seventh Amendment of the United States Constitution: "In suits at common law, where the value in controversy shall exceed twenty dollars, the right to trial by jury shall be preserved, and no fact tried by a jury shall be otherwise re-examined in any Court of the United States, than according to the rules of common law." As this has been interpreted in modern law, a right to jury trial exists wherever, in 1791 in English common law, a corresponding right to jury trial would have existed. Loosely, this means that in all actions at law, a right to jury trial exists today, while in all actions in equity, no jury trial right exists. Of course, since 1791 any number of new types of action have been developed. Whether a right to jury trial exists under each of these new types of actions is determined by reference to the closest similar type of action that actually did exist in 1791. More characteristically, however, the statutes that create each of these new types of actions specifically prescribe either jury trial or court trial, and this determination is rarely challenged.

b. **Effect of merger of law and equity on jury trial.** The problem of right to jury trial has become particularly troubling since law and equity have been merged in the same court system, enabling both legal and equitable issues to be presented during the same proceedings. The types of problems that are encountered are illustrated in the following cases.

1) Jury trial in the federal courts--

Beacon Theatres, Inc. v. Westover, 359 U.S. 500 (1959).

Facts. Beacon Theatres (D) was preparing a treble-damage antitrust suit against Fox West Coast Theaters, Inc. (P) when P, probably in an effort to deny D the right to jury trial that would have existed in the antitrust action, "beat Beacon to the punch" by filing a declaratory judgment action against D, asking for a judgment of nonliability and an injunction against D's bringing the antitrust suit. D then counterclaimed in P's declaratory judgment action with the antitrust suit it had been preparing to bring. The declaratory judgment statute made no provision for jury trial, and the court read the statute as "equitable in nature" requiring "court trial upon all declaratory judgment actions." Therefore, the court directed trial to the court upon all issues common to the declaratory judgment action and the antitrust suit, and in effect declared that the antitrust action was to be tried to the court rather than to a jury. D sought a mandamus writ against the district court judge in order to obtain a jury trial. The court of appeals refused the writ and D appeals.

Issue. In an action containing equitable claims by the plaintiff and legal defenses and counterclaims by the defendant, must the legal claims be tried first to a jury?

Held. Yes. Judgment of the court of appeals reversed.

♦ The Declaratory Judgment Act did not make provision for ensuring a right to trial by jury, but nevertheless the Act could not be read to deprive a litigant of a right to jury trial where it otherwise would have existed. Had D filed its antitrust action first, it would have had a right to jury trial—the issues were predominantly legal rather than equitable. But under the interpretation given the Act by the trial court, P deprived D of a jury trial right merely by filing for a declaratory judgment action of nonliability on the antitrust suit. This result was patently unjust.

♦ Therefore, the Declaratory Judgment Act should be read as a "neutral act"—where the declaratory judgment is sought upon an issue essentially legal, jury trial is proper. Where the declaratory judgment is sought upon an issue essentially equitable, court trial is proper. In the case at bar, the declaratory judgment was sought upon an issue essentially legal—antitrust—and the declaratory judgment action should have been tried to a jury, thus preserving the defendant's right to jury trial upon his antitrust claim.

Dissent (Stewart, Harlan, Whittaker, JJ.). Equity jurisdiction was properly invoked on the face of P's complaint. P's complaint, though inartistically drawn, contained allegations entitling P to equitable relief going beyond a mere defense of D's legal claims. Also, it is only by reference to D's counterclaim that one is able to determine that P has an adequate remedy at law.

---

2) **The "clean-up doctrine."** At common law, a doctrine was developed whereby, in equity courts, legal issues "incidental" to the primary equitable claim could be disposed of without a full jury trial. The legal issues were "cleaned up" as incidental to an essentially equitable action. The clean-up doctrine was retained after law and equity were merged: in the early years of the codes and the Federal Rules, legal disputes appearing in an essentially equitable claim could be disposed of by the court without jury when the legal disputes were minor or incidental. However, during the Warren court, the vitality of the right to jury trial experienced an upsurge, and the clean-up doctrine has fallen into disrepute. Today, it is a general maxim that *every* legal issue, whether or not incidental to an equitable claim, carries within itself the right to a jury trial.

3) **Doctrine overruled.** In *Dairy Queen, Inc. v. Wood*, 369 U.S. 469 (1962), the suit involved breach of contract, and injunctions were being sought to prevent Dairy Queen from buying from, selling to, or

collecting rents from other Dairy Queen sellers in the area. Dairy Queen timely requested a jury trial, which the trial court judge (Wood) refused on grounds that the dispute presented no legal as opposed to equitable issues and on grounds that if legal issues were presented, by virtue of the clean-up doctrine they could be tried to the court as incidental to the equitable issues. The Supreme Court held that since there were both legal and equitable issues presented by the complaint of the corporation, it was improper for the trial court to deny at least partial jury trial upon the legal issues. At common law, actions at law for breach of contract and damages were tried to a jury. Therefore, on the breach of contract dispute, right to jury trial existed. On the other issue, the right to injunctions, no right to jury trial existed, as these were equitable in nature. But the Court overruled the clean-up doctrine by name: "(A right to jury trial exists) whether or not the trial judge chooses to characterize the legal issues presented as 'incidental' to the equitable issues. . . Ever since *Beacon Theatres* it has been required that *any* legal issues for which a trial by jury is timely demanded be submitted to a jury. . . ." Therefore, the Court ordered a jury to attend the total trial, but ordered that the jury have the right to pass verdict only on the contract issue, the single legal issue presented by the complaint.

4) **Derivative actions.** In *Ross v. Bernhard*, 396 U.S. 531 (1970), plaintiff shareholders brought a derivative action claiming that the corporation's brokers had unlawfully large representation on its board of directors and that they had abused this control by extracting excessive fees. The suit involved both legal and equitable issues. In determining whether a jury trial was available to plaintiffs in a derivative action, the Court held that "the right to jury trial attaches to those issues in derivative actions to which the corporation, if it had been suing in its own right, would have been entitled to a jury."

c. **Civil Rights Act--**

Curtis v. Loether, 415 U.S. 189 (1974).

Facts. Curtis (P), a black woman, sued the Loethers (Ds), who are white, under the Civil Rights Act of 1968 for Ds' refusal to rent an apartment to P because of her race. The case went to trial on the issues of actual and punitive damages. Ds made a timely demand for a jury trial, which was refused. The judge awarded P $250 in punitive damages. The court of appeals reversed on the jury trial issue; P appeals.

Issue. Does the Seventh Amendment extend the right to a jury trial to actions enforcing newly created statutory rights?

Held. Yes. Judgment affirmed.

◆   Although there is little legislative history on the jury trial issue, it has long been held that the Seventh Amendment right extends beyond the common law forms of action recognized in 1791, when the amendment was adopted.

◆   *NLRB v. Jones & Laughlin Steel Corp.*, 301 U.S. 1 (1937), held that the Seventh Amendment is generally inapplicable to administrative proceedings that are not in the nature of a common law suit, recognizing congressional authority to provide for enforcement of statutory rights in administrative or other specialized proceedings. However, when Congress relies on ordinary civil actions in federal courts for enforcement of statutory rights, the Seventh Amendment will apply.

◆   Here, P's action for damages is an action to enforce "legal rights"; the statute merely defines a new legal duty, breach of which may cause the courts to compensate the injured party. Therefore, Ds were entitled to a jury trial upon demand.

---

    d.   **Two-part test.** In *Tull v. United States*, 481 U.S. 412 (1987), the Court fashioned a two-part "test" to determine whether a statutory action will go before a jury. First, a court must compare the action "to 18th-century actions brought in the courts of England prior to the merger of the courts of law and equity" and then examine the type of remedy sought to determine whether it would be categorized as an action at law or in equity. The Court held, however, that characterizing the relief sought is the more important of the two steps.

    e.   **Decisions by special tribunals.** In *Atlas Roofing Co. v. Occupational Safety & Health Review Commission*, 430 U.S. 442 (1977), the Court found that in cases where the government sues to enforce public rights created by valid statutes, the Seventh Amendment does not prohibit Congress from assigning factfinding and initial adjudication functions to an administrative forum as opposed to a jury. "[T]he Seventh Amendment was never intended to establish the jury as the exclusive mechanism for factfinding in civil cases." In *Granfinanciera, S.A. v. Nordberg*, 492 U.S. 33 (1989), the Court held that Congress lacks the power to deprive parties of a trial by jury in private matters.

    f.   **National Labor Relations Act--**

Chauffeurs, Teamsters and Helpers Local 391 v. Terry, 494 U.S. 558 (1990).

Facts. Some 27 unionized truck drivers (Ps) sued both their employer and their union (Ds) seeking back pay for alleged violation of a collective bargaining agreement and breach of the duty of fair representation. When the employer filed for bankruptcy, Ps voluntarily dismissed the collective bargaining agreement claim against it. The lower court ruled that Ps' duty of fair representation claim should be tried before a jury. The Supreme Court granted certiorari.

Issue. When members of a union seek back pay from their employer and their union for violation of the duty of fair representation, is their claim legal in nature such that they are entitled to a jury trial?

Held. Yes. Judgment affirmed.

♦   Because the National Labor Relations Act does not expressly create the duty of fair representation, resort to the statute to determine whether Congress provided for a jury trial in an action for breach of that duty is unavailing.

♦   Thus, the general prudential rule must be applied. First, we must look for an analogous cause of action that existed in the 18th century to determine whether the nature of this duty of fair representation is legal or equitable. Second, we examine the remedy sought (back pay) and determine whether it is legal or equitable in nature. The second inquiry is the more important of our analysis.

♦   As to the first inquiry, Ps' duty of fair representation claim is analogous to a claim against a trustee for breach of fiduciary duty, which is an equitable claim, but Ps' collective bargaining agreement claim is comparable to a breach of contract claim, which is a legal claim. The first part of our Seventh Amendment inquiry, then, leaves us in equipoise as to whether Ps are entitled to a jury trial.

♦   As to the second inquiry, the only remedy Ps seek is back pay. This is a legal remedy because Ps do not seek money wrongfully held by D, but wages and benefits they would have received from their employer had D processed their grievances properly. Such relief is not restitutionary. While Congress specifically characterized back pay under another statute as a form of equitable relief, Congress made no similar pronouncement regarding the duty of fair representation.

Concurrence (Brennan, J.). I would decide Seventh Amendment questions on the basis of relief sought. If the relief historically was available from courts of law, I would hold the parties have a right to trial by jury.

Concurrence (Stevens, J.). The Court has made this case unnecessarily difficult. Duty of fair representation suits are ordinary civil actions. There is no ground to exclude these actions from the right to a jury trial.

Dissent (Kennedy, O'Connor, Scalia, JJ.). We must compare the action to 18th century cases to determine the nature of rights and remedies. I disagree that whenever a cause of action contains legal issues a jury trial is required. This case involves an equitable claim. Although we have divided self-standing legal claims from equitable declaratory, accounting, and derivative procedures, we have never parsed legal elements out of equitable claims absent specific procedural justifications.

2. Province of Judge and Jury.

a. **General statement of the rule.** In a trial by jury, both the court and the jury play distinct but complementary roles. It is the province of the court to determine the applicable rules of substantive law that govern the case, while it is the province of the jury to determine the facts, on the basis of the evidence presented, that should govern the application of substantive law. Thus, in theory at least, the provinces of the jury and the court are easily separable. However, as the following case demonstrates, it is not always possible to positively state that "X issue is a determination of law rather than fact"—all too frequently, determination of facts is so integrally tied up to application of substantive law that neat division of the functions of court and jury is not possible.

b. **Interpreting contract terms--**

Markman v. Westview Instruments, Inc., 517 U.S. 370 (1996).

Facts. Markman (P) had developed and patented a system to monitor the movement of articles of clothing in a dry cleaning establishment. Westview (D) had developed a similar system. P sued D for patent infringement. The dispute centered around the meaning of the term "inventory" under the construction of P's patent. The jury determined that P's patent had been infringed. The district court disagreed and directed a verdict for D based upon its own determination of the meaning of the disputed term. P appealed, arguing that it was error for the court to substitute its own construction of the term "inventory" for the construction that the jury had presumably given it. The court of appeals affirmed and the Supreme Court granted certiorari.

Issue. Is determining the meaning of a disputed term in a patent an issue for the judge and not the jury?

Held. Yes. Judgment affirmed.

♦ P argued that the district court's action violated the Seventh Amendment guarantee that a jury will determine the meaning of any disputed term about which expert testimony is offered. While it is true that the Seventh Amendment guarantees the right to a jury's resolution of the ultimate dispute, we find that analysis of a document that determines the scope of a patentee's rights is a matter of law and therefore reserved for the courts.

♦ Patent construction is a highly technical occupation involving special training and practice. In addition, many doctrines relating to the scope and proper form of patents have developed in the courts and the Patent Office of which a jury could not be aware. A judge is better equipped and trained to interpret terms of art in such documents.

♦ Treating interpretive issues of document construction as purely legal issues promotes uniformity in the treatment of a given patent. If a jury were allowed to interpret the meaning of disputed terms in a patent, inconsistent conclusions could be reached in different cases, and a patent holder would have little real protection.

---

c. **Application of law to determined facts.** Once the court has determined the applicable substantive principles of law, and the jury has determined the operative "facts" of the case, who applies the law to the facts? This is a tricky question. In theory, the jury applies the law to the facts, under the careful direction of the court, as delivered in the instructions to the jury. But by and large, instructions to a jury tend to be long, complex, redundant, useless, and otherwise misleading. In final analysis, therefore, it is probable that it rests primarily with the jury, applying "homespun feel" for when justice is done, to apply legal principles to determined facts to reach the final verdict and relief. This is not altogether bad, of course, since the very function of jury trial is to inject this element of "popular justice" into otherwise too-legal proceedings.

1) **Facts not in dispute.** In *Dobson v. Masonite Corp.*, 359 F.2d 921 (5th Cir. 1966), the facts of the case were not in dispute. The case involved an oral contract for removal of timber. There was no dispute as to the existence of the contract or its terms. The only issue was whether the contract was for services, in which case it would be enforceable, or for the sale of the timber, in which case the oral agreement could not be enforced due to the Statute of Frauds. The jury determined that the contract was for services and rendered a verdict for the plaintiff. The Fifth Circuit Court of Appeals affirmed stating that the meaning of a contract is a question of fact that was properly presented to the jury.

3. **Demand and Waiver of Jury Trial.** Despite the inherent right to jury trial upon an issue, the right is not self-executing. It remains for a party to request a jury trial "seasonably" before it will be granted. Failure to demand a jury trial results in waiver of the right and trial to the court. Some codes of civil procedure set definite time limits within which the demand for jury trial must be made. Other codes provide simply that demand for jury trial must be made within a "reasonable time" after commencement of suit, usually not later than 20 days before commencement of trial. But whatever method of determination is provided, the limits tend to be quite strictly enforced—hence right to jury trial is a right easily waived unless relevant statutes are strictly complied with. [*See* Fed. R. Civ. P. 38(b), (c) and (d)]

4. **Selection and Composition of the Jury.**

a. **Jury size.** Although the common law jury required both 12 jurors and unanimity, the Supreme Court has permitted *six-person juries* but has not permitted *nonunanimous verdicts* in federal courts. The rationale is that the Seventh Amendment requires only jury trials, not all the incidents of common law jury trials. [*See* Colgrove v. Battin, 413 U.S. 149 (1973)] The Supreme Court has permitted both six-person juries and nonunanimous verdicts in *state courts*.

b. **Bias and prejudice.** Most codes of civil procedure provide for disqualification from the jury of any prospective juror who demonstrates "bias, prejudice, or preconceived notion" concerning either of the parties to the action, the subject matter of the action, or any other factor likely to prevent a just and impartial decision upon the merits by the jury. These biases are exposed, if ever, during voir dire examination—pretrial questioning of the prospective juror by either counsel or court. If prejudice is, or seems to be, present, a counsel may challenge the prospective juror, and if the challenge is sustained by the court, the prospective juror will be excused.

1) **Challenges for cause.** If, during voir dire examination, counsel can demonstrate that there is a reasonable doubt about the ability of a prospective juror to maintain objective neutrality about the parties or subject matter of the action, the juror may be challenged for cause. Each counsel is usually allowed unlimited challenges for cause—as many jurors may be dismissed for partiality as can be shown partial by the counsel or court during examination.

2) **Peremptory challenges.** In addition to unlimited challenges for cause, each counsel in a civil suit usually has the right to challenge a certain finite number of potential jurors without demonstrating partiality. Each counsel is allowed six such peremptory challenges in most jurisdictions, although only three are allowed in the federal courts. A juror challenged peremptorily is immediately excused—the challenge need not be for good cause, and the court may not overrule it. But since each counsel has but a few such challenges, they must be used sparingly. Indeed, skillful use of peremptory challenges is considered an art that few attorneys ever master.

c. **Composition.** Under constitutional mandate, each jury must be composed of a "representative cross-section of the community" selected "at random by a system which does not discriminate against any definable class." In some communities, names are taken from the tax rolls. In still others, names are selected by lot, or from the telephone book, or even from personal knowledge (although this method is in disfavor for obvious reasons). Whatever method is used, however, the person drawing the jury rolls is ordered, so far as is practicable, to include members of all racial, ethnic, religious, and socioeconomic groups. Needless to say, however, the method does not always work as it should; historically, racial, religious, and economic classes have been excluded from jury rolls by biased officials in many jurisdictions.

1) **Cross-section of community required.** In *Thiel v. Southern Pacific Co.*, 328 U.S. 217 (1946), the plaintiff challenged the composition of the jury in his personal injury suit. In California, jurors were paid $4 per day for service. The Supreme Court found that California's jury selection system resulted in working class groups being precluded from jury service due to economic hardship. The result was that juries were composed of mostly businessmen and their wives. The Court found that the jury in this case therefore did not represent "an impartial cross-section of the community" and mandated the state to develop a new way of calling jurors to ensure that all economic groups were represented.

2) **Establishing bias--**

Flowers v. Flowers, 397 S.W.2d 121 (Tex. Civ. App. 1965).

Facts. D and P were husband and wife, respectively, fighting over custody of their three children. During voir dire examination, one potential juror expressed extreme displeasure at the wife's (P's) occasional drinking at social gatherings, on grounds that she was opposed to all drinking. On these grounds, P's counsel challenged for cause. The court questioned the juror, and in a confusing exchange elicited a response that "just because the wife drank a little too much, and threw conniption fits at times, and just because the husband was a good church-going Methodist," the juror would not hold that against P in the custody action. The court then overruled the challenge for cause. P's motion for a new trial, based on this alleged error, was overruled. P appeals.

Issue. Where a reasonable probability of bias is shown, must the court permit disqualification for cause?

Held. Yes. Judgment reversed.

♦ P's counsel had shown that the juror was prejudiced against the wife—in fact, even the answer to the court's own question showed an under-the-surface partiality toward the husband. In cases where a reasonable probability of bias is shown by counsel, disqualification for cause is not a matter of discretion with the trial court, but is a matter of law.

♦ The court had acted as if it were within its discretion to retain or discharge a biased juror, but it was in error. The juror should have been dismissed for cause.

---

3) **Excluding jurors by race is unconstitutional--**

Edmonson v. Leesville Concrete Co., 500 U.S. 614 (1991).

Facts. Edmonson (P), who is black, sued Leesville Concrete Co. (D) in a Louisiana federal district court for negligence. During voir dire, D used two of its three peremptory challenges to strike black persons from the prospective jury. Citing *Batson v. Kentucky*, 476 U.S. 79 (1986), P requested the district court to order D to articulate a nonracial reason for striking the two jurors. Believing that *Batson* did not apply to civil cases, the district court denied the request. The impaneled jury consisted of 11 white persons and one black person. The jury returned a verdict in favor of P, assessing damages at $90,000. Finding P to be 80% at fault, however, the jury awarded P only $18,000. P appeals.

Issue. May a private litigant in a civil case use peremptory challenges to strike prospective jurors on account of their race?

Held. No. Judgment reversed and case remanded.

- If a prosecutor's race-based peremptory challenge violates the equal protection rights of the person excluded from jury service (as held in *Batson* and *Carter v. Jury Commission of Greene County*, 396 U.S. 320 (1970)), then a private attorney's race-based peremptory challenge also violates such person's equal protection rights if the private attorney's exercise of a peremptory challenge is attributable to the government: *i.e.,* if it constitutes state action.

- The private attorney's exercise of a peremptory challenge is attributable to the government because the process of determining who will serve on the jury constitutes state action. The fact that the government delegates some portion of this power to private litigants does not change the governmental character of the power exercised. When private litigants participate in the selection of jurors, they serve an important function within the government and act with its substantial assistance.

- Although a constitutional right of nonexclusion belongs to the excluded juror, any party to a civil case, regardless of race, may raise the constitutional challenge based on the well-established principle of third-party standing.

- As elaborated in *Powers v. Ohio* (a criminal case): "In the ordinary course, a litigant must assert his or her own legal rights and interests, and cannot rest a claim to relief on the legal rights or interests of third parties." We also noted, however, that this fundamental restriction on judicial authority admits of certain, limited exceptions, and that a litigant may raise a claim on behalf of a third party if the litigant can demonstrate that she has suffered a concrete, redressable injury, that she has a close relation with the third party, and that there exists some hindrance to the third party's ability to protect his own interests. All three of these requirements for third-party standing were held satisfied in the criminal context, and they are satisfied in the civil context as well.

Dissent (O'Connor, J., Rehnquist, C.J., Scalia, J.). A civil trial is essentially a private, rather than governmental, venture. The government erects the platform; it does not thereby become responsible for all that occurs upon it. Not every opprobrious and inequitable act is a constitutional violation.

Comments.

♦ Perhaps it is best to describe a civil trial not as a private venture, as Justice O'Connor does, but as a joint venture between private litigants and the government. If that description is accurate, then the state action doctrine, as developed in civil rights cases, would certainly suggest that the majority was correct in finding a government connection in the exercise of the peremptory challenge.

♦ The Supreme Court has also held that use of peremptory challenges to exclude potential jurors based solely on *gender* violates the Equal Protection Clause of the Fourteenth Amendment. [*See* J.E.B. v. Alabama *ex rel.* T.B., 511 U.S. 127 (1994)]

B. THE SCOPE AND ORDER OF TRIAL

1. **Setting the Case for Trial.** In most jurisdictions, one or the other party must make an affirmative move to place the case on an appropriate trial calendar before trial is scheduled. Cases on the trial calendar are usually tried in the order in which they are placed there—delays may range from a few weeks to several years, depending on the jurisdiction and the nature of the court. Because of these delays, the exact date and time of trial is never certain until a few days before the scheduled beginning—last minute replacement or delay is the rule rather than the exception.

2. **Trial by Judge vs. Trial by Jury.** As will be discussed later at length, in many types of cases the litigants have the right to choose either trial by jury or trial to the court alone. Whether the litigants should choose one or the other depends on several factors.

   a. **Institutional factors.** Given an equal chance of winning before a court or a jury, most litigants will choose court trial. Trial to the court alone tends to be more rapid than jury trial, tends to be much less expensive than jury trial, and tends to be less inclined toward "showmanship" than jury trial.

   b. **Psychological factors.** The same litigant does not always stand the same chance of being awarded the same relief before the court as he does before the jury. Recent studies show that, in 80% of cases, there are no differences between the award granted by a court and that granted by a jury. But in 20% of cases tried, especially where injuries to the plaintiff are particularly visible, where the actions of the defendant were particularly inexcusable, or where the defendant is a large corporation or the government, recovery before a jury tends to exceed recovery that the court would have allowed. Further, particular attorneys tend to be "jury specialists"—for these select few, jury trial verdicts tend to greatly exceed those the court would have awarded, and favorable verdicts tend to come with greater than average regularity.

3. **Selection of "Favorable Jurors."** The jurors chosen by an attorney should, by and large, identify and sympathize with the client's position or cause. Of course, it is almost impossible for an attorney to know by asking only a few questions the real sympathies of any potential juror. Therefore, private companies in a few jurisdictions maintain "jurybooks," lists of past jurors, the cases each sat on, and the award, if any, granted in each case. By examining the past history of any potential juror, an attorney can gain some insight into the personality of each member of the jury panel who has, at some previous time, served on a jury panel.

4. **Order of Trial.** Once a trial has been scheduled, discovery completed, all pretrial conferences disposed of, preparations finalized, and jurors selected (if a jury trial), the normal trial follows an almost universal format. Although the court has the inherent power, in the interests of justice, to vary the order followed at trial, as a practical matter, almost every trial follows this format:

    a. Plaintiff's opening statement (may be dispensed with in nonjury trial);

    b. Defendant's opening statement (optional, may be reserved until presentation of the defendant's case or dispensed with in nonjury trial);

    c. Plaintiff's presentation of case: calling of witnesses and introduction of evidence;

        1) Direct examination;

        2) Cross-examination;

        3) Redirect and recross examination, as needed.

    d. Defendant's presentation of case;

    e. Plaintiff's rebuttal;

    f. Defendant's rebuttal;

    g. Plaintiff's final argument (often dispensed with in nonjury trials);

    h. Defendant's final argument (often dispensed with in nonjury trials);

    i. Plaintiff's rebuttal/closing argument (often dispensed with in nonjury trials);

j.   Court's instructions to the jury (jury trial only) (may precede final arguments under the Federal Rules);

k.   Submission of the case to the jury (jury trial only);

l.   Delivery of the verdict by the jury (jury trial only);

m.   Entry of judgment (findings of law and fact by the court in nonjury trial, formal entry in jury trial).

5.   **The Burden of Proof.** The phrase "burden of proof" refers both to the burden of production and the burden of persuasion.

   a.   **The burden of production.** The burden of production holds the party going forward with the evidence responsible for producing sufficient evidence to raise a claim. In a civil action, the plaintiff typically has the burden of production with respect to her claims, while the defendant has the burden with respect to his affirmative defenses. The party with the burden must present the minimum amount of evidence necessary to prove its case. If the party fails to meet the burden, the issue or action can be disposed of on summary judgment or a motion for judgment as a matter of law.

   b.   **The burden of persuasion.** Once the burden of production is met, the party bears the burden of persuading the fact finder to rule in her favor, while the opposing party attempts to cast doubt on the reliability or credibility of the evidence and introduces additional evidence. In most civil actions, the party bearing this burden must prove her case by a preponderance of the evidence. In certain civil cases, however, including child custody proceedings, the standard is often that of clear and convincing evidence. In criminal actions, the prosecution bears the burden of proving its case beyond a reasonable doubt.

   c.   **Shifting burdens.** In certain actions, such as those for employment discrimination under Title VII of the Civil Rights Act of 1964, one party has the burden of production and, once she has met her burden, the burden shifts to the other party to persuade the jury to rule in his favor.

6.   **Tactical Considerations Regarding the Opening Statement.** In most cases, the trial begins with an opening statement by the plaintiff. In most jurisdictions today, the defendant may make an opening statement right after the plaintiff does. A carefully constructed, well thought-out statement of the case at the start of trial can sway the jury, leaving the opposing party to fight an uphill battle. An attorney must be careful not to reveal any fatal flaws in his client's case, however, as this could lead to an immediate dismissal of the case.

7.   **The Presentation of Evidence.** Because the admissibility of evidence is generally determined by rules of evidence adopted by the jurisdiction, attorneys must plan well in advance of trial to ensure that the most important of their evidence will be admitted under one rule or another. Typically, evidence is

presented through the examinations of witnesses. Sometimes, judges may question a witness in order to make a more complete record.

8. **The Closing Argument.** A closing argument is proper if it "follows from the facts of the case as supported by the evidence or inferences that properly can be drawn from the evidence." A closing argument is improper if it is based on matters that are not in evidence, if it appeals to passion or to certain prejudices, if it contains reference to financial ability or liability insurance, or if it distorts evidence to make unjustified inferences.

C. TAKING THE CASE FROM THE JURY—MOTIONS FOR JUDGMENT AS A MATTER OF LAW, DIRECTED VERDICTS, AND JUDGMENTS NOTWITHSTANDING THE VERDICT

1. **The Constitutional Issues.** In a real sense, motions for a new trial, for directed verdict before a case is submitted to the jury, and for judgment notwithstanding the verdict once a jury verdict is returned all deprive a litigant of jury trial in the purest sense of the term. However, such motions do not deprive a litigant of the type of jury trial guaranteed by the Seventh Amendment to the United States Constitution: jury trial is guaranteed only where it was guaranteed at common law. At common law, several devices existed for taking a case from the jury, including the directed verdict and the new trial (though not judgment notwithstanding the verdict). Therefore, by the very terms of the Seventh Amendment, directed verdicts and motions for a new trial are constitutional.

a. **Right to jury trial not absolute--**

Galloway v. United States, 319 U.S. 372 (1943).

Facts. In a trial based upon a claim for insurance, at the close of the evidence but before the case was submitted to the jury, the trial court granted the government's (D's) motion for a directed verdict in its favor. Judgment was entered upon the directed verdict and the jury was dismissed. Galloway (P) objected that granting any motion for a directed verdict deprived a litigant of a right to jury trial guaranteed by the Seventh Amendment.

Issue. Does a court violate the constitutional right of trial by jury when it directs a verdict, thereby preventing the evidence from going to the jury?

Held. No. Judgment affirmed.

♦ Because in 1791 at common law there existed several methods for taking a case from the jury, and because the Seventh Amendment merely perpetuates the common law right to jury trial, it is not unconstitutional for the modern federal court to take a case from the jury by directed verdict where evidence is clearly insufficient to support a right to relief.

♦ Further, it is not grounds for objection that the modern devices called directed verdict and new trial call for slightly different standards of proof and are administered in slightly different ways than they were in 1791—the Seventh Amendment does not require modern jury procedure to remain stagnant as judicial science advances. Rather, as long as a modern device is not clearly an invasion of what was a province of the jury in 1791, there is no ground for complaint.

Dissent (Black, Douglas, Murphy, JJ.). The Court's decision continues the gradual judicial erosion of the essential guarantee of the Seventh Amendment.

---

2. **Standards for Judgment as a Matter of Law (Directed Verdict and Judgment Notwithstanding the Verdict).**

   a. **The black letter rule.** The standards by which a motion for directed verdict and a motion for judgment notwithstanding the verdict (judgment n.o.v.) are measured are identical. A motion for a directed verdict may be made either at the close of the plaintiff's evidence, or at the close of all the evidence. A motion for a judgment n.o.v. may only be made after entry of a verdict by the jury. Either motion should be granted whenever, with all evidence considered most favorably toward the nonmoving party, the moving party is entitled to judgment as a matter of law—"reasonable persons could not differ that the moving party deserves judgment." [*See* Fed. R. Civ. P. 50] Rule 50 was amended in 1991. Both "directed verdict" and "judgment notwithstanding the verdict" are now called "judgment as a matter of law." This change underscored that both are to be governed by identical standards. A Rule 56 motion for summary judgment is also governed by the same standard. Rule 50(a), Rule 50(b), and Rule 56 motions differ only in the time they are made.

   b. **Failure to carry burden of proof--**

Denman v. Spain, 135 So. 2d 195 (Miss. 1961).

Facts. Denman (P) a child of seven, sued the estate of Spain (D), the driver of an automobile that collided with the car in which she was riding. In the collision everyone except P and another passenger was killed—the survivors had no personal recollection of the accident. P's only evidence was that of two witnesses, neither of whom saw the accident, and a group of photographs of the accident scene, showing wreckage of both cars shredded and thrown over a wide area. D presented no evidence. Verdict was returned in favor of P for $5,000. D moved for a judgment n.o.v. on grounds that the verdict was unjustified by the evidence presented. The court granted D's motion; P appeals.

Issue. When the burden of proof is on the plaintiff and the plaintiff fails to carry the burden by a preponderance of the evidence, is a judgment n.o.v. for the defendant in error?

Held. No. Judgment affirmed.

♦ In a negligence action, the plaintiff carries the burden of proof. Here the evidence presented by P in no way tended to prove any negligence on the part of D. It was impossible, with no eyewitnesses and given the scrambled wreckage at the accident scene, to tell who was at fault. Therefore, the verdict was unjustified by the evidence. No reasonable person applying sound principles of law could have found negligence upon the part of either P or D. The judgment n.o.v. was properly granted.

Comment. The courts will not permit judgment n.o.v. if there is any possibility that the evidence supports the jury's verdict. In *Kircher v. Atchison, Topeka, & Santa Fe Railway Co.*, 195 P.2d 427 (Cal. 1948), the court held that judgment n.o.v. was improper. The verdict was based solely on the plaintiff's own story that he tripped in a hole on a platform, stumbled, rolled, and pitched 15 feet until his head bumped into the side of a railroad car and he came to rest, with a hand outstretched, underneath a parked train on a track, where a moving train severed it.

---

c. **FELA actions--**

Rogers v. Missouri Pacific Railroad Co., 352 U.S. 500 (1957).

Facts. Rogers (P) was working on a railroad repair gang, burning weeds with a hand torch according to orders of his foreman, when he was trapped and burned by the fires he himself had set. Evidence tended to show that the flames had been fanned by the passing of a train, thus causing the sudden conflagration. P sued for negligence, on grounds that it was unreasonable to have ordered him to use such a small torch to burn the weeds, and on grounds that no trains should have been allowed to pass while the fires were burning. The Missouri Pacific Railroad (D) defended that the accident was due to the sole negligence of P personally in not keeping a sharp eye on the fires he had set. According to the Federal Employers' Liability Act ("FELA") provision under which he was suing, any negligence at all on the part of D was sufficient to allow recovery. Nevertheless, the trial court granted a motion for directed verdict on grounds that the evidence presented could not as a matter of law support a finding that D had been negligent even in the slightest degree. P appeals.

Issue. Did Congress intend, under FELA, that a jury should decide the issues of whether there was employer fault, and whether that fault played any part in the employee's injury or death?

Held. Yes. Judgment reversed.

- It is improper to grant a motion for directed verdict for insufficiency of evidence if the facts presented could reasonably support P's story, considered in the light most favorable to P. In a FELA action, the slightest negligence on the part of an employer is sufficient to support a finding of liability.

- P's story was not inherently unbelievable—indeed it even seemed reasonable. It could have supported a finding of negligence on the part of D, which would have been per se sufficient for recovery. Therefore, it could not have been said that "as a matter of law" no reasonable person could have found for the plaintiff—grant of the motion for a directed verdict was plainly error.

---

d. Defendant failed to appear at trial--

Daniel J. Hartwig Associates, Inc. v. Kanner, 913 F.2d 1213 (7th Cir. 1990).

Facts. Daniel J. Hartwig Associates (P) rendered consulting and expert witness services to Kanner (D). When D failed to pay P, claiming lack of funds, P requested D execute some promissory notes providing for interest and reasonable attorneys' fees incurred in collection. D never paid P. P brought a breach of contract suit to recover payment for services rendered and attorneys' fees incurred in collecting payment. D did not appear at trial, but claimed P misrepresented his educational background, and failed to inform D of an alleged conflict of interest. P testified at trial that he informed D of the inaccuracies in his resume and truthfully represented to D there was no conflict of interest. D presented no evidence at trial to rebut P's testimony. The district court granted a directed verdict in favor of P. D appeals.

Issue. May a court grant a directed verdict in favor of a plaintiff in a breach of contract action where the defendant claims misrepresentation but fails to present any evidence demonstrating that he relied on the alleged misrepresentations?

Held. Yes. Judgment affirmed.

- Our review is de novo. The test for a directed verdict is the law of the forum in a diversity action, and under Wisconsin law, in determining whether a directed verdict should be granted, the evidence is viewed in the light most favorable to the party against whom the motion is made. A court should direct a verdict only if there is no credible evidence to sustain a verdict in favor of the party against whom the motion was made.

- Although D presented no evidence at trial to rebut P's testimony, D contends that it is the province of the jury to determine witness credibility and that this credibility determination amounted to a material issue of fact as to whether P made misrepresentations of fact that voided the contract. We disagree.

- Even if the jury had not believed P, this alone would not have established a defense. D presented no evidence required under Wisconsin law that (i) there was a material misrepresentation, (ii) he relied on the misrepresentation, and (iii) he was injured or damaged due to his reliance.

- In this simple debt collection case, the amount sought was not in dispute, the executed promissory notes plainly evidenced the indebtedness, and P indicated at trial that D never complained about the quality of P's work or raised any issue of being damaged by P's credentials.

---

3. **Renewal of a Motion for Judgment as a Matter of Law.** A renewed motion for judgment as a matter of law (formerly judgment n.o.v.) is essentially a reserved right to make a decision on a motion for judgment as a matter of law. If a litigant in federal court desires to make a renewed motion for judgment as a matter of law, he must first make a motion for judgment as a matter of law before the jury retires. This motion is then "reserved" by the court until after the jury returns—then, if judgment as a matter of law is proper, the court so enters it. Hence, in the federal courts, a motion for judgment as a matter of law is an absolute condition precedent to proper grant of a renewed motion for judgment as a matter of law. [*See* Fed. R. Civ. P. 50(b)]

D. INSTRUCTIONS AND VERDICTS

1. **Instructions to the Jury.**

    a. **In general.** At the close of all the evidence at trial, before submission of the case to the jury, the court has the right, and in some jurisdictions the obligation, to instruct the jury on some applicable laws governing the case. Everywhere, the counsel for the various parties are permitted to submit to the court written requests for specific directions, which requests may or may not be granted by the court, according to whether they adequately summarize the existing law. Because by far the bulk of appeals taken from trial court decisions assign as error the giving or failure to give a certain instruction, much effort has been spent in developing and analyzing the various rules of instruction. Only the most important of them can be alluded to in this section.

    b. **Failure to properly instruct jury is reversible error--**

Kennedy v. Southern California Edison Co., 219 F.3d 988 (9th Cir. 2000).

Facts. The husband and children (Ps) of a woman who died from a rare form of cancer brought a wrongful death action against Southern California Edison Company (D) alleging that the cancer had been caused by exposure to nuclear radiation from nuclear rods defectively manufactured in D's plant. Applicable law in such cases required that the jury be given an instruction that stated that "plaintiff may meet the burden of proving that exposure to defendant's product was a substantial factor causing the illness by showing that 'in reasonable medical probability it was a substantial factor contributing to the . . . decedent's risk of developing cancer.'" Ps' attorney submitted a proposed instruction that erroneously stated Ps' burden of proof. The court refused to give the instruction and did not charge the jury on the issue. The jury returned a verdict for D and Ps appeal.

Issues.

(i)   When a court is presented with a proposed jury instruction that is improper but directs the court's attention to an important issue, does the court have a duty to correctly instruct the jury on that issue?

(ii)   Is failure to properly instruct the jury on the parties' respective burdens of proof reversible error?

Held. (i) Yes. (ii) Yes. Judgment reversed and case remanded.

♦   A court does not err in refusing to give incorrect or misleading instructions. However, once the issue was brought to the court's attention by Ps' submission of the erroneous instruction, the court had a duty to correctly instruct the jury on the issue.

♦   We agree with the other circuits that have stated that "[i]f the requested instruction directs the court's attention to a point upon which the jury has not been charged, but upon which instruction would be helpful, the court's error in failing to charge may not be excused by technical defects in a request to charge."

♦   The district court had a duty to frame the issue correctly and instruct the jury. An error in jury instructions relating to the parties' respective burdens of proof is not harmless error and ordinarily requires reversal.

---

c.   **Judge's comments on the evidence.** Generally, courts have held that "the right of a [d]istrict [j]udge to comment on the evidence is firmly established in the federal system." [Quercia v. United States, 289 U.S. 466 (1933)] But this right is clearly not without limits. For example, a judge must not give an opinion on an ultimate issue of fact in a case. In *Nunley v. Pettway Oil Co.,* 346 F.2d 95 (6th Cir. 1965), the ultimate fact question was whether the plaintiff was an invitee or a licensee. Upon learning that the jurors were struggling with the issue in deliberations, the district court judge urged them to keep trying to reach a verdict. In so doing, he stated that he believed that "the evidence will establish that . . . the plaintiff was a licensee and not an invitee." Although the judge went on to explain that the jury was not obligated in any way to accept his comments, and that it was the jury's responsibility to resolve the issue for themselves, the court of appeals found the comment to be tantamount to an instructed verdict for the defendant and reversed and remanded the case.

2. Verdicts.

a. Types of verdict.

1) **General verdict.** By far the most common type of verdict returned by juries is the general verdict. The general verdict consists merely of a statement by the foreman of the jury that the jury has found for one party or the other, and the relief granted, if any. It contains no other information and gives no hint as to how the actual verdict and relief were arrived at. For this reason, general verdicts are both the most easily understood and the most difficult type of verdict to appeal. Hence, their overwhelming predominance in American law.

2) **Special verdict.** The special verdict is the most rarely used type of verdict today. The special verdict consists of a series of questions asked of the jury on each facet of the case. Once the jury has answered these questions, they are returned to the court, which awards judgment and relief according to the answers. Special verdicts have several serious disadvantages. They can easily confuse the jury, as they tend to be quite legally oriented. If badly drawn, a series of questions by special verdict may direct judgment one way or another by concentrating only on one aspect of the trial. Finally, special verdicts make the activities of the jury so visible to scrutiny that elements of "homespun justice" injected by the jury are eliminated and reversals made unduly common. For all these reasons, special verdicts are disfavored by a majority of jurisdictions, save in special, compelling circumstances.

3) **General verdict plus interrogatories.** Between the general verdict and the special verdict stands the general verdict plus interrogatories. When such a verdict is desired, the court submits to the jury an instruction that they are to find liability and relief as they may, but thereafter they are to answer a set of general questions submitted to them by the court. These questions are usually an attempt to guarantee that the jury has followed the proper steps in arriving at its verdict. As generally commendable as the general verdict plus interrogatories seems, however, the practice is not without problems, as the following case demonstrates.

b. Conflict between verdict and interrogatories--

Nollenberger v. United Air Lines, Inc., 216 F. Supp. 734 (S.D. Cal. 1963).

Facts. In a wrongful death action the jury was asked to render a general verdict plus interrogatories. The interrogatories concerned generally the amount of relief to which Nollenberger (P) was entitled. The jury found for P and awarded $114,000 damages. However, according to the answers of the interrogatories, they should have awarded $172,000 damages—they had misfigured several percentages. P moved for the larger verdict to be entered, for a new trial, or for additional interrogatories to be submitted.

Issue. When the answers of the interrogatories conflict with the general verdict, may the court enter judgment based on the answers?

Held. Yes. Judgment on interrogatories entered.

♦ Federal Rule 49(b) permits three alternatives in the situation of this case: "When the answers to such interrogatories are consistent with each other but are inconsistent with the general verdict, the court may enter the judgment in accordance with the answers, notwithstanding the general verdict, may return the case to the jury for additional consideration, or may grant a new trial."

♦ P's request for additional interrogatories cannot be made in accordance with the rules. The jury cannot be reconvened for further deliberations. Before granting a new trial, the court should make calculations from the special interrogatories and enter judgment thereon.

Comment. The court of appeals later overturned the *Nollenberger* decision, reasoning that the jury could consider factors other than those included in the interrogatories in arriving at the general verdict.

---

3. **Findings and Conclusions in Nonjury Cases.**

   a. **Proposed findings of fact.** Both under the Federal Rules and under the codes, attorneys for both parties may, prior to the court's retiring to write its findings of fact and conclusions of law, submit to the court proposed findings of fact and conclusions of law. These proposed findings are intended to alert the court to the general thrust that each party's proof has attempted to take—they are in the nature of substitution for instructions to the jury in jury trial. However, use by the court of these proposed findings of fact for any reason other than as advisory opinions is error. It rests with the court, and the court alone, to write the final findings of fact and conclusions of law.

   b. **Judge ultimately responsible--**

Roberts v. Ross, 344 F.2d 747 (3d Cir. 1965).

Facts. Roberts (P) sued Ross (D) on an open account for $3,000. D denied liability generally, and specially pleaded the Statute of Frauds. The defenses appeared good, and the court, before allowing either party to submit proposed findings of fact, told the parties that judgment would go to D. The court then asked each party to submit, in final form, proposed findings of fact and conclusions of law. The court then adopted D's document verbatim and dismissed the complaint. P appeals.

Issue. May a judge adopt counsel's proposed findings and conclusions without making his own determinations?

Held. No. Judgment reversed.

♦ Federal Rule 52 requires the trial judge personally to find facts specially and write his conclusions of law thereon. The court at no point made any indication of its own personal conclusions on the case. Rather, it left its task to counsel for the defendant, and merely signed the defendant's document. For that reason, the trial court was remiss in its duty to the plaintiff, and the verdict was vacated until the trial court wrote its own findings of fact.

E. CHALLENGING ERRORS: NEW TRIAL

1. **Nature and Scope of Power to Grant a New Trial.**

    a. **In general.** Before the trial court loses jurisdiction of a case, it has the power to correct any errors or irregularities that might have influenced the outcome of the trial through the grant of a new trial. As a general rule of thumb, new trials should always be granted where error or misconduct certainly influenced the outcome of the trial, should never be granted where the error or misconduct probably did not influence the outcome of the case, and may be granted within the discretion of the court where it is not clear whether the error or misconduct influenced the outcome upon the merits.

    b. **Court must state grounds.** Some courts have held that when a court grants a motion for a new trial it must outline the specific grounds it finds for doing so. It is insufficient to simply state a general opinion, such as that the new trial was granted "in the interests of justice." [*See* Ginsberg v. Williams, 135 N.W.2d 213 (Minn. 1965)] Other courts have been more lenient in terms of the language that must be used. For example, in *Coppo v. Van Wieringen,* 217 P.2d 294 (Wash. 1950), the Washington Supreme Court upheld a trial court's grant of a new trial even though the trial judge's reason was that "substantial justice has not been done." The court found that while the statutes enumerating grounds upon which a new trial could be granted did not list this as a reason, it is the right of the trial judge to grant a new trial "when he is convinced that substantial justice has not been done, on the theory that it is an exercise of the trial court's inherent power."

c. Incoherent jury verdicts--

Magnani v. Trogi, 218 N.E.2d 21 (Ill. App. Ct. 1966).

Facts. P's complaint stated two distinct causes of action, based on two separate statutes allowing recovery for wrongful death and recovery of family expenses as a result of wrongful death. But the form of verdict that was submitted without objection to the jury contained only a single verdict, not separated by counts. A verdict was returned in favor of P for $19,000. D then objected to the trial court that the form of verdict was improper, since it was impossible to determine what amount was for wrongful death and what amount was for family expenses, and on grounds that the unified form of verdict misled the jury into believing that only a single cause of action had been sued upon. A new trial was granted. P appeals.

Issue. When the form of the verdict leaves the jury's determination of liability and damages on separate causes of action unclear, may a new trial be ordered?

Held. Yes. Judgment affirmed.

♦ The purpose of granting the trial judge the power to grant a new trial is to permit him to correct errors that he might have overlooked earlier in the proceedings. Courts of appeal usually do not disturb the decision of the trial court on the granting of a new trial unless clear abuse of the discretion is shown.

♦ By no stretch of the imagination could it be said that the trial court abused its discretion by granting a new trial where the form of the verdict may very well have misled the jury into granting relief for one cause of action only, even if the form of the verdict was not objected to by either party. Because there was no abuse of discretion, the grant of a new trial is affirmed.

Dissent. In this case, where P waived any individual interest in the verdict, D made no objection to the form of the verdict at any time before his post-trial motion, and the verdict was within the range of the evidence and the law, the trial court's grant of a new trial was erroneous.

---

d. Self-contradictory verdict--

Robb v. John C. Hickey, Inc., 20 A.2d 707 (N.J. 1941).

Facts. Robb (P) sued Hickey (D) in a negligence action. The jury instructions stated that if P had been contributorily negligent, the comparative degrees of negligence of the parties were immaterial. The jury's verdict stated that both P and D were negligent, but D more so, and P was awarded $2,000 damages. Both P and D objected; P sought to set aside the verdict and D sought to have the court mold the verdict in D's favor.

Issue. May a court mold a self-contradictory verdict into one favoring either party?

Held. No. New trial granted.

♦ Jury recommendations that go beyond the issues submitted by the court may simply be disregarded. Where a verdict is merely informal, it may be molded into a formal verdict in accordance with the jury's clear intent.

♦ Neither situation is present here, however. Both parts of the verdict respond to the issues presented, yet since they are self-contradictory, the jury's true intent cannot be ascertained. The court's only alternative is to set aside the verdict and grant a new trial.

━━━━━━━━━━━━━━

e.   **Reasons for granting a new trial.** A few of the more common reasons for which new trials have been granted are the following:

1)   Irregularity in the proceedings of the court, referee, jury, prevailing party, or other member of the court, which tends to deprive a party of a fair trial by an impartial jury;

2)   Misconduct of the jury;

3)   Accident or surprise that could not have been foreseen or prevented;

4)   Excessive or insufficient damages;

5)   Errors of law occurring during the course of the trial;

6)   Some irregularity in the verdict (*e.g.,* it is not justified by the evidence, or is contrary to law, or has been improperly obtained); and

7)   Discovery of material evidence that could not have been previously discovered through reasonable diligence.

2.   **Jury Misconduct and the Integrity of the Verdict.**

a.   **Introduction.** Strictly speaking, it is improper for the jury to decide a case on "anything but the actual merits of the action," or for it to award damages calculated on "any basis other than each juror's own personal evaluation of damage." Of course, in practice, it may be impossible for the 12 members of a jury to reach any verdict save by compromise, averaging of awards, or other give-and-take. In such cases, it is probably in favor of the judicial system that juries do not strictly adhere to the theoretical purpose of the jury—otherwise, new trials for jury misconduct would become the rule rather than the exception, and hung juries made more commonplace than now.

b. **Use of a juror's testimony to impeach verdict.** The integrity of a jury's verdict is further insured by the rule that in most cases the personal affidavit of a juror may *not* be used to impeach a verdict. Only the affidavit of someone not a member of the jury may be so used.

1) **Exceptions.**

a) **Iowa rule.** In several jurisdictions, the affidavits of a juror may be used to prove jury misconduct *only if* the misconduct complained of occurs outside the scope of the actual deliberations themselves, and is objectively provable without reference to the affidavit of the juror. It is misconduct for a jury without the consent of the court to visit the scene of an accident. Because this conduct is objectively provable by witnesses who are not jurors, and because it occurs outside the deliberations of the jurors, an affidavit of one of the jurors may be introduced to impeach the verdict in such a case. The federal courts have a similar rule. [*See* Fed. R. Evid. 606(b)]

b) **Texas rule.** In Texas and a few other states, an affidavit of a juror may be used by any party to impeach a verdict for any type of jury misconduct.

c. **Award-averaging--**

Hukle v. Kimble, 243 P.2d 225 (Kan. 1952).

Facts. In a negligence action, evidence presented by one of the jurors tended to show that, because the jury was having trouble agreeing upon a proper verdict, they added together all the damages that each member would have given and divided by 12. The resulting average was then entered as the award the jury considered proper. The defendant appeals.

Issue. Is award-averaging by a jury reversible error?

Held. Yes. Judgment reversed.

♦ Award-averaging is condemned expressly in almost every state. That the resulting award was almost exactly the relief that the plaintiff had asked for, and that, after the averaging, every member of the jury agreed that the average was a "proper award," is immaterial. Because the award had been arrived at by averaging, fair or not, it was improper. A new trial is granted.

Comment. This case was probably decided wrongly. While it is true that award-averaging is condemned in most jurisdictions, the use of the averaging to arrive at a preliminary "discussion point" is not condemned. Isn't that all that occurred in this case? Note further that upon retrial, the award again went to the plaintiff, and damages presumably figured according to the "proper system" differed from the award in the original trial by less than $50. Nothing was accomplished by way of new trial, except valuable judicial time was wasted and more costs were incurred.

---

d. **Types of jury misconduct.** Award-averaging is not the only type of misconduct for which a new trial might be awarded. Other recognized types of misconduct are: flipping a coin to arrive at a verdict; discussing the case with someone not a member of the jury; concealing personal prejudices upon voir dire examination; drinking or becoming intoxicated while deliberating; agreeing to abide by a simple majority vote; or intimidating co-members into deciding a case against their wills. In deciding whether to grant a new trial upon such types of jury misconduct, however, the court usually considers the likelihood that prejudice to either party resulted. New trials are not automatic even if minor jury misconduct is demonstrated.

1) **Inaccurate responses during voir dire.** In some cases, a new trial will be granted when a juror has provided inaccurate or incomplete information during voir dire. In such cases, the party seeking a new trial must demonstrate that a juror failed to honestly answer a material question, and that a correct response could have provided a valid basis for a challenge for cause. [*See* McDonough Power Equipment, Inc. v. Greenwood, 464 U.S. 548 (1984)] In *McDonough*, a personal injury case, the jurors were asked if they or any of their family members had ever been seriously injured. The jury foreperson had answered no, but it was later determined that his son had sustained a broken leg in a car accident. The defendant moved for a new trial citing juror misconduct. The Supreme Court reversed the grant of a new trial citing the rule above.

3. **New Trial Because Verdict Is Against Weight of the Evidence.**

a. **Concept.** Judgments as a matter of law, directed verdicts, and judgments notwithstanding the verdict, are proper only when there is no evidence supporting the nonmoving party's story, so that judgment is due the moving party "as a matter of law." Consider the case where 95% of the evidence presented is strongly favorable to the defendant, only 5% favorable to the plaintiff, but the jury returns a verdict for the plaintiff despite the overwhelming weight of the evidence for the defendant. It would be improper for the court to grant a judgment notwithstanding the verdict—the defendant is not due a judgment "as a matter of law." But the plaintiff's verdict is still tainted. The trial court therefore has the power to set aside the verdict and order a new trial because the verdict is against the weight of the evidence.

b. **Standards.** Whenever a verdict at trial is so strongly against the weight of the evidence presented at trial that reasonable persons would have to question the accuracy of the verdict, the trial court in its discretion may order a new trial. In considering the weight of the evidence, all evidence presented, including demeanor evidence, is relevant (compare with motion for a directed verdict, where only evidence favorable to the nonmoving party is relevant). Hence, within certain ill-defined bounds, the power of a court to order a new trial because the verdict is against the weight of the evidence is purely discretionary and rarely can be attacked upon appeal. It is said that "by their very natures, appeals courts are incapable of evaluating properly all the evidence presented at a trial, especially incapable of evaluating demeanor evidence. . . ."

c. **Preventing injustice--**

Aetna Casualty & Surety Co. v. Yeatts, 122 F.2d 350 (4th Cir. 1941).

Facts. During performance of an abortion, Yeatts (D), a doctor, caused injury to a patient. Aetna Casualty (P), with whom D was insured, refused to compensate the patient for the injury, alleging that D was performing a criminal abortion. D's own testimony was to the effect that the abortion was necessary to save the life of the mother and was therefore not criminal. The preponderance of the evidence tended to show that D had not obtained the permission of the state to perform the abortion, so that the abortion was at least formally criminal. But D testified that he had obtained written permission. Verdict was for D. P moved for a new trial on grounds that the verdict was against the weight of the evidence. The motion was denied. P appealed on the same grounds, and D responded that the grant of a new trial under such conditions would be unconstitutional as a deprivation of a right to jury trial.

Issue. May a federal trial judge set aside a jury's verdict and grant a new trial where the verdict is against the weight of the evidence?

Held. Yes. Judgment affirmed, however.

♦   The right of the court to grant a new trial whenever, in its sole discretion, the verdict constituted a miscarriage of justice was well recognized at common law. Therefore, grant of a new trial for a verdict against the weight of the evidence is not an unconstitutional deprivation of the limited right to jury trial reserved by the Seventh Amendment.

♦ On such a motion for a new trial, it is the duty of the trial court to set aside the verdict if it is of the opinion that the verdict is against the clear weight of the evidence, or is based on false evidence, or will result in a miscarriage of justice even if there is substantial evidence that would prevent outright direction of a verdict in favor of the moving party. But where the trial court is of the opinion that the verdict was not a miscarriage of justice, it is not error to deny such motion.

♦ The trial court in this case was of the opinion that there was ample evidence to support a finding in D's favor without working a miscarriage of justice. It was not, therefore, error to deny the motion for a new trial.

---

4. **Power to Grant Conditional and Partial New Trials: Remittitur and Additur.**

   a. **Conditional new trials.** A new trial may be granted if the verdict is excessively large or small. However, a practice has developed whereby new trials for these reasons can be avoided: a conditional new trial is granted, the condition being that a new trial will not be granted if the proper party consents to either a larger or smaller verdict than the one returned by the jury. This is the power of remittitur or additur: remittitur is the power of the court to grant a new trial unless the plaintiff accepts a reduction in an otherwise excessive verdict; additur is the power of the trial court to grant a new trial unless the defendant consents to payment of a larger verdict than was returned by the jury.

   b. **Constitutional issues.** In 1935 the United States Supreme Court, in a five-to-four decision, held that additur was unconstitutional on the grounds that it violated the right to jury trial. It distinguished additur from remittitur and upheld the constitutionality of the latter. Many states have reasoned that such a distinction is absurd. An increasing number of states have found additur constitutional. It has been suggested that there is a likelihood that the Court would overrule its 1935 decision if it were faced with this issue today.

   c. **Additur in state courts--**

Fisch v. Manger, 130 A.2d 815 (N.J. 1957).

Facts. Fisch (P) sued Manger (D) for serious injuries P suffered in an automobile accident. The jury awarded P only $3,000 damages, even though his actual medical expenditures exceeded $2,200, and his lost wages approximated $620. P moved for a new trial on the grounds that the award, at best, compensated him only for his medical bills and lost wages and not for his suffering and permanent injuries. The trial judge, believing the award grossly inadequate, wrote the parties that unless D agreed to increase the award amount to $7,500, the court would grant P a new trial limited to damages only. The trial court judge declared that P ought not have a larger sum because he had a back condition before the accident. However, the evidence presented at trial showed that P's back condition had cleared up before the accident in dispute in this case. D agreed to the damage award modification and, thereupon, the court dismissed P's motion for a new trial. P appeals.

Issue. Does the trial court judge have the discretion to deny a plaintiff's motion for a new trial upon the defendant's agreeing to an increase in the amount of damages awarded the plaintiff by the jury?

Held. Yes. Judgment reversed on the facts.

♦ The trial judge, in most state courts, has the discretion to employ the practices of remittitur and additur by which the trial judge conditions the denial of one party's motion for a new trial upon the opposing party's consent to a reduction (remittitur) or increase (additur) in the amount of damages awarded.

♦ Remittitur has been recognized almost everywhere, while some states and federal courts disallow additur. The federal law is irrelevant in considering what law applies in state court, since the Seventh Amendment does not apply to proceedings in state courts. This court does not recognize the distinction other forums draw between the two practices and, consequently, holds that neither remittitur nor additur violates the state constitution or any state statutes. If fairly invoked, these two practices serve the commendable purpose of avoiding a further trial where substantial justice may be attained on the basis of the original trial.

♦ However, in this case, the trial judge erred in his assessment of the evidence in that he stated that P should not recover a larger sum than the $7,500 proposed by the judge because of P's prior back condition. The evidence showed that P's back condition had cleared up before the accident in dispute. Therefore, allowing a second jury to determine the issue of damages will best serve the ends of justice.

Concurrence. There can be no doubt that the additur practice sanctioned here contravenes the essence of the common law right of trial by jury at the time of the adoption of the 1776 Constitution, then and ever since a basic right under the law of England; and this is the very substance of our own constitutional guaranty.

---

d. **Partial new trial.** Most codes of civil procedure provide that new trial may be granted upon "all or part" of the issues presented at trial. However, judicial precedent has limited the application of this practice somewhat: it is improper for the trial court to grant a new trial on the issue of liability in a civil action without including in the grant a new trial on the issue of damages also. Conversely, however, it is ***not*** considered improper to grant a new trial on the issue of damages alone without including in the order a grant of new trial on the issue of liability.

e. **Liability tied to damages--**

Doutre v. Niec, 138 N.W.2d 501 (Mich. Ct. App. 1965).

Facts. Doutre (P) was burned in a beauty parlor when she was treated with a bleaching agent to which she was allergic before the customary patch-test was given. The trial court excluded evidence that, contrary to common custom, the custom in Michigan was to omit the patch-test. On return of a verdict of $10,000 for P, the court granted a new trial on the issue of liability alone. P objected on grounds that no new trial should have been granted; D objected on grounds that a new trial on the issue of damages should have been included in the order. Both P and D appeal.

Issue. May the grant of a new trial be limited to consideration of negligence liability?

Held. No. New trial ordered.

♦ The standard of care used in an industry is always relevant evidence in a negligence action of the type under question. Therefore, a grant of new trial was proper. But because issues of liability are so materially influenced by, and tied up to, issues of damages, grant of a new trial on the issue of liability must be accompanied by a grant of new trial on the issue of damages also.

---

5. **Power to Set Aside a Judgment on Newly Discovered Grounds.**

   a. **Introduction.** Motions for new trials based on errors of law or irregularities in the trial usually must be made within a short period of time or the right to object is deemed waived. Policy requires that judgments be finalized as quickly as possible. But when a party discovers new evidence, or discovers fraud in the trial, or some other factor that prevented fair trial on the merits, most codes of civil procedure provide that relief from a finalized verdict may be obtained at any time within one year from the entry of the verdict. It is deemed more important that improper and fraudulent judgments be vacated than that judgments in general be finalized as quickly as possible. [*See* Fed. R. Civ. P. 60]

   b. **Mistake and excusable neglect.** Rule 60 allows a party to be relieved of a judgment against him when, through "excusable neglect or mistake," evidence relevant to the case is not presented at trial but is only thereafter discovered. But courts have refused to expand the Rule to include situations in which "pure errors of law are committed by one or the other party." [*See* Hulson v. Atchison, Topeka & Santa Fe Railway Co., 289 F.2d 726 (7th Cir.), *cert. denied,* 368 U.S. 835 (1961)] In *Hulson,* the plaintiff's attorney informed the court nine days after a verdict was returned for the defendant that he would be filing a request for a new trial. The request was not actually filed until several weeks later, long past the 10-day period set forth in Rule 59. The attorney moved to be relieved of the verdict and judgment under Rule 60 stating that he had misread the Federal Rules regarding the timeliness of filing, and that therefore he had made an error of law that the court could relieve any time within one year of the judgment. The court held that excusable neglect could not be extended to ignorance of the rules of procedure.

c. **Newly discovered evidence.** Relief from a judgment may be obtained whenever a party, after trial, discovers new and relevant evidence that was not introduced at trial. However, only evidence meeting certain tests will qualify as "newly discovered evidence" within the meaning of most statutes. First, the evidence must be such that it would probably change the results of the trial. Second, it must be admissible and relevant to the subjects tried. Third, failure to present it at trial must be excusable—evidence that could by due diligence have been uncovered before trial does not qualify. And fourth, the evidence must be positive evidence for the moving party—it is deemed insufficient to change the result of the trial if the new evidence merely impeaches the evidence of another witness. Even if such evidence is presented, it is within the further discretion of the court whether to vacate the former judgment. It is not mandatory in most jurisdictions that even the most mistaken judgment be reopened in the light of newly discovered evidence.

d. **Fraud.** A judgment obtained by fraud may be relieved by reopening of a judgment in most jurisdictions. However, in most state courts (not in federal courts), the only fraud that will be sufficient to cause reopening of a judgment is extrinsic fraud—fraud that occurs outside the scope of the trial itself. Intrinsic fraud, fraud that occurs when a witness perjures himself or evidence is faked, does not suffice to justify the reopening of trial. It is considered that the counsel against whom intrinsic fraud is perpetrated should be able to expose the fraud during trial, so that reopening of trial afterwards is rendered unnecessary. In federal courts, however, any demonstrated fraud of sufficient gravity, intrinsic or extrinsic, suffices to cause reopening of a judgment within one year after its entry.

XV. SECURING AND ENFORCING JUDGMENTS

A. IN GENERAL

Securing a judgment against a defendant is a meaningless act if the defendant is able to escape payment of the judgment against her. Because there is a natural tendency for defendants to try to escape payment of judgments, all codes of civil procedure provide a battery of judicial devices that a judgment plaintiff may use to ensure payment of the judgment-debt. Such devices are of two types: provisional remedies are devices a plaintiff contemplating lawsuit may use to ensure that the potential defendant does not flee the jurisdiction of the court with all her property, and ex post remedies are devices the judgment-plaintiff may bring to bear upon the judgment-debtor after entry of judgment. Despite the rather wide variety of such remedies, however, a judgment-debtor who earnestly desires to escape payment of a judgment debt can usually delay, stall, appeal, and flee until it no longer becomes possible for the judgment-creditor to maintain pressure to pay the debt.

B. METHODS OF SECURING JUDGMENT—PROVISIONAL REMEDIES

1. **In General.** Provisional remedies are statutory devices a plaintiff may use to ensure that the defendant does not flee the jurisdiction of the court with all her property. Characteristically, these devices may be used before any judgment on the merits of an action is rendered if there seems a chance that the defendant may run before termination of suit. But because of the potential abuse of such provisional remedies, they are usually not used except in compelling cases, and even then the plaintiff may have to put up a sizable bond to ensure the defendant against any loss due to the action of the provisional remedy, in case judgment on the merits goes for the defendant rather than the plaintiff.

2. **Attachment.** The use of attachment prior to filing of suit has been discussed earlier in connection with jurisdiction quasi in rem and in rem. But in actions in personam, when the defendant personally is within the jurisdiction of the court, attachment of the defendant's property may be used as a provisional remedy to ensure payment of any judgment debt. If the defendant flees the jurisdiction of the court without paying the judgment debt against her, the attached property may be used by the court to compensate the judgment-plaintiff.

   a. **Mechanics of attachment.** To obtain a writ of attachment, the plaintiff must show "good cause" to the trial court. If satisfied that the writ should issue, the court directs to the sheriff or other county officer a writ specifying the dollar value of property that should be attached by the officer, and specifying the time for which such attachment is valid. The sheriff then seizes the described property for public storage, thereby depriving the defendant of use and control of it for the duration of the lawsuit.

b. **Denial of attachment.** Even if all statutory requirements for attachment are met, and "good cause" is shown, the court need not issue a writ of attachment over the defendant's property—attachment is within the discretionary power of the court. Usually writs will not issue if the property to be attached exceeds greatly the value of the probable judgment, or if attachment would work some undue hardship upon the defendant. This is especially true when the property sought to be attached is wages or salary, or is business property, or is homestead, or would force the defendant to lower her standard of living during the litigation of the suit.

3. **Preliminary Injunctions and Temporary Restraining Orders.** When a defendant is acting in some manner that threatens direct and irreparable harm to a plaintiff, the plaintiff may cause the court to issue a preliminary injunction against the defendant's action without trial on the merits. Of similar nature is the temporary restraining order, which also issues against a defendant threatening harm to a plaintiff without full trial on the merits. Each of these types of proceedings threaten harm to the defendant, and in a sense deny the right to trial, because each issues without full trial on the merits. For these reasons, injunctions and restraining orders obtained in this manner are usually of short duration, and given only for "compelling good cause."

4. **Receivership.** When there is a substantial chance that property that is the subject of a pending adjudication will be lost, injured, destroyed, or removed from the jurisdiction of the court, the court upon "good cause shown" may appoint an impartial officer of the court as receiver of the goods. The basic duty of the receiver of property is to protect and preserve it, and if necessary to manage it to preserve its fullest value. Property in receivership no longer is under the control of the defendant—receivership has the same effect as attachment. If the defendant flees the jurisdiction of the court, the property in receivership may be used to satisfy any judgment against her. However, if the plaintiff causes the defendant's property to be taken into receivership, and the defendant thereafter wins on the merits of the adjudication, the plaintiff may be held liable for any loss that has been occasioned the defendant by the actions of the receiver.

5. **Civil Arrest.** The most radical of the provisional remedies that may be used against a defendant to ensure her appearance at trial is the civil arrest. Upon a motion for civil arrest made to the court, and for compelling justification only, the court may order the civil defendant imprisoned pending trial. If release of the defendant upon bail is permitted, the bail becomes security. In the event the defendant thereafter forfeits, the amount of bail, usually rather large, is then used to satisfy whatever judgment debt is owed the plaintiff by the defendant. Legislation in many jurisdictions limits the availability of this remedy.

6. **Notice of Pendency.** At common law, a prospective buyer of property had the duty to check all court records to make sure that the property she was buying

was not the subject of pending litigation. If she bought subject to such an action, the claim of the purchaser was secondary to that of the judgment-debtor. A similar concept is retained in many jurisdictions today—if the plaintiff desires to frustrate the defendant's attempts to transfer her real property in anticipation of a judgment-debt, the plaintiff may record in the public record notice of pendency of suit. This notice is deemed constructive notice to any purchasers of the defendant's property that their claim is secondary to that of the possible judgment-debtor, and generally frustrates any attempt by the defendant to quickly sell real property in order to flee the jurisdiction of the court.

C. METHODS OF COLLECTING AND ENFORCING A JUDGMENT

1. **Execution.** Once the plaintiff has obtained a judgment-debt against the defendant, he may execute upon any of the defendant's property within the jurisdiction of the court in payment of that debt, unless the plaintiff and the defendant make some other provision for payment. However, the plaintiff may only execute upon enough land to cover the value of the debt at fair market value—he may not cause all of the defendant's property to be executed to pay a debt of substantially smaller magnitude.

   a. **Limited to judgment amount--**

Griggs v. Miller, 374 S.W.2d 119 (Mo. 1963).

Facts. Brookshire had been found liable upon several judgment-debts in two separate counties. The largest single debt was $17,000, and all debts totaled $20,600. Brookshire owned a 322-acre parcel of prime land with a total estimated value of between $50,000 and $90,000. In addition, Brookshire owned almost $30,000 worth of cattle grazing on the parcel of land. Upon motion of the two judgment-debtors, one in each of two counties, execution proceedings were begun against the *entire* 322-acre parcel. At public auction in one county, the parcel worth $90,000 sold for $23,000, barely enough to pay the judgment-debt. The cattle and other property levied on in the other county, worth $30,000, sold for less than $10,000. Therefore, after the levy of land and property worth $120,000 to pay $20,000 worth of debt, Brookshire ended up with only $14,000 in cash. State law stated that only property *equal to* the value of a judgment-debt at *market value* could be executed. The sheriffs who had levied on the land and cattle were ignorant of the law when they sold the entire ranch. Miller (D), trustee for Brookshire's estate, appeals.

Issue. May a sheriff sell property in excess of the amount needed to satisfy the judgment?

Held. No. Judgment reversed.

♦   By objective calculation, the defendant lost $86,000 in excess of the judgment-debts through the process of execution of his land and cattle at the poorly advertised public auction. This was patently unfair. The purpose of a levy and execution is not punitive—it is compensatory to the limit of a judgment-debt only.

♦ The land of the defendant could quite easily have been segmented and a piece worth exactly $20,600 sold to satisfy the total debts against him. There was no need to levy and execute on the entire piece of land. Therefore, the sheriff was in error in executing the entire land and property of the defendant far in excess of the outstanding debt against him, and the execution sale is set aside on condition that the defendant within three months make available to the judgment-creditors the sum of $20,600.

───────────

b. **Exceptions from execution.** Typically, statutes making available execution or garnishment of wages to the judgment-creditor also protect the judgment-debtor by exempting from execution certain types of property. A certain proportion of monthly income is usually exempt from garnishment or execution. Homesteads are usually exempt from garnishment at least to a certain dollar value, as are certain types of business property, and personal property "necessary to maintain a reasonable standard of living." Unfortunately, the relevant debtor-statutes are often out of date, and hardship may be worked upon the judgment-debtor under many of the obsolete versions of these statutes. Modernization is woefully needed in this area of the law.

2. **Supplementary Proceedings.** Execution is not always the solution to satisfaction of a judgment-debt, especially when the debtor is concealing assets by fraudulent transfers to third parties. To augment execution, many state codes of civil procedure provide for supplemental proceedings against the debtor. These proceedings, only quasi-judicial in nature, are designed to force disclosure, under penalty of contempt, of all assets, legal or equitable, held by the judgment-debtor. Upon disclosure of hidden assets, an order may issue that the assets be liquidated and the income therefrom applied to the judgment-debt. Unfortunately, because such supplemental proceedings are often conducted in front of a minor officer of the court rather than the judge, they are often ineffective. Again, updating of the relevant statutes is called for.

3. **Contempt and Body Execution.** A few jurisdictions have supplemented their power to force payment of judgment-debts by treating failure to pay a reasonable installment, as ordered by the court, as contempt of court for which the debtor may be imprisoned. It has been argued that such statutes are tantamount to imprisonment for civil debt, and thus an unconstitutional deprivation of due process. But in truth such statutes do not call for imprisonment for civil debt per se; rather, they call for imprisonment upon willful disobedience of a court order directing reasonable payment of a lawfully entered debt.

a.   **Contempt imprisonment constitutional--**

Reeves v. Crownshield, 8 N.E.2d 283 (N.Y. 1937).

Facts. A state statute provided that a court could order a judgment-debtor to pay off a judgment in reasonable installments, given circumstances as determined by a hearing. After such a hearing, the court ordered the judgment-debtor to pay the creditor $20 a month toward a $400 debt, out of a monthly income of $230. The debtor refused and was jailed for contempt of court. The debtor did not challenge the amount of the monthly payment; rather, he challenged the constitutionality of the practice, arguing that it denied him a right to due process of law, and amounted to imprisonment for civil debt.

Issue. Does a statute unconstitutionally provide for imprisonment for debt if it permits a court to order a judgment-debtor to make payment out of income and refusal to pay after such order is punishable by contempt?

Held. No. Judgment affirmed.

♦   Imprisonment for contempt of court is a well-recognized practice, sanctioned by the Constitution. The debtor was not imprisoned for nonpayment of his debt; rather, he was imprisoned for contempt of a court order concerning the method of his repayment of a debt. This was a remedy provided for by state statute. Because the statute did not contravene the Constitution, the judgment of the trial court, including the jailing of the debtor for contempt of court, was proper.

4.   **Liens and Priorities of Liens.** Once the debt running from the debtor to the creditor has been officially recognized, as by court proceeding, the debt is secured. His debt is recognized in the form of a lien against the real property of the debtor. If the debt is not paid according to court order, the lienor may cause the liened property to be levied and sold at public auction, the proceeds of the sale going toward payment of the debt. If two or more creditors have established liens on the property of the debtor, however, and the sale of the property is not sufficient to cover all the debts, the priority of the liens becomes important—the proceeds of the sale are distributed first to the lienor with the highest priority, the remainder going to lienors of lesser priority until the proceeds are exhausted. While each specific type of lien is covered by slightly different rules governing priority, as a general rule the first lien to be perfected and recorded against the property of the debtor has priority over later liens. Therefore, the diligence of the creditor in making officially known his desire to collect the debt may play an important role in determining whether the debt is actually paid.

XVI. APPELLATE REVIEW

A. THE PRINCIPLE OF FINALITY

1. **Basic Concept.** From earliest common law, a basic maxim of appellate review of trial court decisions has been that only final decisions of the trial court are reviewable for error—interlocutory decisions, even if crucial to the litigation, were at common law unreviewable. Modern law has been characterized by a schizophrenic attitude toward this common law maxim. On the one hand, the values of the principle of finality in speeding decisions upon the merits free from burdensome interlocutory appeal is recognized. On the other hand, a desire to correct obviously erroneous decisions upon interlocutory motions made to the trial court has been felt, since such interlocutory decisions may shape the course of trial upon the merits.

   a. **Partial summary judgment--**

Liberty Mutual Insurance Co. v. Wetzel, 424 U.S. 737 (1976).

Facts. Sandra Wetzel (P), an employee of Liberty Mutual Insurance Co. (D), filed a complaint in federal district court alleging that D's employee insurance benefits and maternity leave regulations discriminated against women employees in violation of Title VII of the Civil Rights Act of 1964. P sought injunctive relief, damages, costs, and attorneys' fees. The district court granted P's motion for partial summary judgment, finding that D's insurance and maternity leave policies violated federal law. Also, the court directed that final judgment be entered for P upon this claim since it determined that there was no just reason for delay. The court of appeals held that it had jurisdiction over D's appeal based on 28 U.S.C. section 1291, which grants courts of appeals jurisdiction of appeals from all "final decisions" of federal district courts. The appeals court then affirmed the judgment of the district court. The Supreme Court granted certiorari.

Issue. Was the district court's order a final, appealable order under 28 U.S.C. section 1291 or section 1292?

Held. No. Judgment reversed.

♦ Section 1291 grants federal courts of appeals jurisdiction in all "final decisions" by the federal district courts. A federal court of appeals is obligated to question its jurisdiction even if the parties fail to raise the issue.

♦ Even assuming that the district court's order was a declaratory judgment on the issue of liability, it left unresolved the issue of P's remedies and thus was not a final, appealable order.

♦ Federal Rule 54(b) does not apply to a single claim action but is expressly limited to multiple claim actions in which one or more but less than all of the multiple claims have been finally decided. A complaint asserting only one legal right, even if seeking multiple remedies for the alleged violation of that right, states a single claim of relief. Although the district court made the recital required by Rule 54(b)—that final judgment be entered on the issue of liability and that there was no just reason for delay—the court's order was not appealable because P set forth only one claim. Rather, the district court's grant of partial summary judgment limited to the issue of P's liability was interlocutory, and because damages and other relief remained to be resolved, it was not final within the meaning of section 1291. The only possible authorization for appeal would have been section 1292.

♦ Notwithstanding, the order was not appealable pursuant to section 1292's interlocutory appeals provisions.

> The order was an interlocutory order denying an injunction to a defendant and thus section 1292(a)(1) (which only applies when a plaintiff's request for an injunction is denied) was not available.

> Since it appears that P did not apply to the court of appeals for leave to appeal within 10 days, the order was not appealable pursuant to section 1292(b) as involving a controlling question of law to which there was substantial ground for difference of opinion. Moreover, there was no assurance that the court of appeals would have exercised its discretion under section 1292(b).

Comment. The "final judgment" rule is intended to prevent the costs and delays that would occur if an appeal could be taken from every intermediate order or ruling made by the trial court.

---

2. **State Court Practice.** State courts do not abide as strictly by the principle of finality as do the federal courts. Many state codes of civil procedure allow interlocutory appeals upon certain types of nonfinal trial court decisions, especially if the decision may affect the subsequent course of the litigation. The New York Code allows appellate review as a matter of right of virtually every final or interlocutory judgment or decision, in effect nullifying the principle of finality in the practice of that state. In diversity actions in federal courts, in which state law is applied, the state courts' rules are conclusive for purposes of the *Erie* doctrine: rules governing the appellate review of interlocutory decisions are seen as outcome determinative in practice.

3. **Departures from Final Judgment Rule in Federal Court.**

a. **Amelioration of the basic concept.** The common law practice of not allowing interlocutory appeal of trial court decisions often caused hardship and prejudice: even the most obviously erroneous ruling could not be appealed. For that reason, modern law has to some extent recognized a broad exception to the principle of finality: Whenever a decision upon a case made by a trial court is "collateral" to the merits of the action, and whenever a hardship or inconvenience or prejudice will be worked upon the appealing party by not allowing appeal, the principle of finality will not be applied. Also, where individual causes of action within a complaint, or even parts of a single cause of action, are readily separable as to substantive content, appeal of interlocutory orders affecting such parts may be permitted where to do otherwise would result in hardship.

1) Nonfinal decisions having irremediable consequences--

Gillespie v. United States Steel Corp., 379 U.S. 148 (1964).

Facts. Gillespie (P) sued United States Steel Corp. (D) for the death of her son, under the Jones Maritime Negligence Act, the Ohio Wrongful Death law, and the Ohio Survivorship Compensation law. Upon motion, the trial court ruled that the Jones Act provided her sole relief, and struck all mention of the other causes of action. P appealed the ruling; D argued that the decision was not "final" and so was not appealable. The court of appeals ruled against P on the merits of the ruling. P appeals.

Issue. Does the term "final decision" in 28 U.S.C. section 1291 mean the last order that could possibly be made in a case?

Held. No. Decision of the court of appeals affirming the district court order affirmed.

♦ A "final" decision within the meaning of 28 U.S.C. section 1291 does not necessarily mean the last order possible to be made in a case. Where a decision of the trial court is "collateral" to the main litigation, as here, the question of reviewability is usually close.

♦ Allowing review in this case would not have worked a hardship upon either party. But not allowing review would have worked a possible hardship upon P. If the trial court's order to strike were reversed, an additional trial upon the issues of liability under the two Ohio statutes would have been called for. Given these circumstances it was not error for P to file for interlocutory review of the decision to strike the order of the trial court.

Dissent (Harlan, J.). This case illustrates the vice inherent in a system that permits piecemeal litigations of the issues in a lawsuit. Here, the parties are remanded to a trial on the merits, but only after needless delay and expense due to the court of appeals allowing review.

---

2) Practical finality--

Coopers & Lybrand v. Livesay, 437 U.S. 463 (1978).

Facts. Livesay and other purchasers of Punta Gorda stock (Ps) filed a class action against Coopers & Lybrand (D), Punta Gorda's accountant, in which Ps alleged that D violated federal securities laws. The district court first certified, and then, after further proceedings, decertified the class. The court of appeals accepted jurisdiction under 28 U.S.C. section 1291 pursuant to the "death knell" doctrine. This doctrine allows plaintiffs in a class action to take an immediate appeal from a district court's refusal to allow the lawsuit to proceed as a class action when, as a practical matter, the lawsuit cannot be prosecuted individually by the class members because their individual claims are too small to make suing cost-effective (*e.g.,* attorneys' fees would be greater than the anticipated recovery). The court of appeals reversed the decertification order. D appeals.

Issue. Is a determination that a lawsuit may not be maintained as a class action pursuant to Federal Rule 23 a "final decision" within the meaning of 28 U.S.C. section 1291 and therefore appealable as a matter of right?

Held. No. Judgment reversed.

♦ Application of the "death knell" doctrine would result in a waste of judicial resources. In order to apply it, the district court must take evidence concerning the merits and size of individual claims to determine whether a refusal to certify would cause plaintiffs to abandon individual lawsuits, and the court of appeals "must review that record and those findings simply to determine whether a discretionary class determination is subject to appellate review."

♦ Also, the "death knell" doctrine discriminates in favor of plaintiffs, since it does not allow defendants to seek an immediate appeal from an order certifying a class. It only comes into play when a district court refuses to certify a class. "Perhaps the principal vice of the 'death knell' doctrine is that it authorizes *discriminate* interlocutory review of decisions made by the trial judge," which circumvents the congressional design of section 1292(b) to carefully restrict appellate review of nonfinal orders. In the present case, Ps consciously avoided appellate review through section 1292(b).

♦ Finally, Congress, rather than the judiciary, is empowered to decide what type of decisions are appealable, and Congress has spoken in sections 1291 and 1292.

Comment. There is really nothing plaintiffs can do when faced with a refusal-to-certify order. If the plaintiffs fail to prosecute and the action is dismissed therefor, the only issue that could be raised on appeal is whether the plaintiffs have in fact failed to prosecute.

---

b.   Evasion of the principle of finality—mandamus.

1) **Writ of mandamus.** As a method of avoiding the consequences of the principle of finality, the writ of mandamus was developed. By such a writ, a court of appeals may, "when justice so calls," mandate a lower court to change or correct an interlocutory order before a final decision on the merits has been reached. [*See* 28 U.S.C. §1651(a)]

2) **Overseeing administration of justice--**

La Buy v. Howes Leather Co., 352 U.S. 249 (1957).

Facts. In this complex antitrust suit, the trial court ordered the entire case submitted to a master for determination. Both parties objected and, because the trial court refused to change its ruling, asked the court of appeals for a writ of mandamus to force the trial court to change its ruling. The trial court judge, La Buy (D), defended on grounds that the court of appeals had no power to issue a writ of mandamus in this instance and that even if it did, this was an inappropriate case in which to do so. The court of appeals issued the writ; D appeals.

Issue. May a district court's referral of a case to a master be reviewed through a petition for a writ of mandamus?

Held. Yes. Judgment affirmed.

♦ Masters were intended to be used only to advise a judge, not to take the judge's place. To have referred the entire antitrust suit to a master effectively deprived both the plaintiff and the defendant of a trial in a court of law. It was therefore error for the trial court to so refer the case, and error for it not to have reconsidered its own motion.

♦ Where such "unusual and compelling circumstances" as this exist, the courts of appeal may properly use a writ of mandamus to oversee the proper administration of justice without committing error—the principle of finality was never intended to allow obvious commission of gross error to go unappealed until late in the proceedings. Therefore it was not error to grant a writ of mandamus to correct the error committed by the trial court in depriving both litigants of a right to trial in the court of law.

Dissent (Brennan, Frankfurter, Burton, Harlan, JJ.). The Court's decision marks a clear departure from the settled principles governing the issuance of extraordinary writs. D did not exceed or refuse to exercise his jurisdiction. Permitting the court of appeals to act here introduces a standard of interlocutory review that will surely result in multiplication of piecemeal appeals.

Comment. Until the 1940s, the writ of mandamus was quite limited in operation and scope—it was considered to violate the principle of finality and therefore to be only rarely invoked in the most pressing circumstances. Since 1950, however, the writ of mandamus has enjoyed ever-widening use as a method of "overseeing" the fair administration of justice in lieu of the traditional notion of appeal upon merits. It is impossible at this point in time to circumscribe the limits of the use of the writ, other than to say that the "compelling circumstances" spoken of in *La Buy, supra*, seem to become less and less compelling the more widely the writ is used.

---

c. **Discretionary appeals--**

Atlantic City Electric Co. v. General Electric Co., 337 F.2d 844 (2d Cir. 1964).

Facts. D posed interrogatories to P concerning whether damages sustained by P were "passed on" to P's customers, a "novel" matter that D intended to use as a defense. The district court sustained P's objections to the interrogatories. D applied to the court of appeals for pretrial leave to appeal.

Issue. May a court deny pretrial leave to appeal over a discovery issue where to allow the appeal would delay the disposition of the case?

Held. Yes. Application denied.

◆　　　It is not appropriate to decide this question of law before final judgment. If pretrial discovery were allowed, it could easily develop into a number of full scale rate cases which could overwhelm the already extensive pretrial proceedings. If a judgment adverse to the defendant is based in whole or in part on this error, the defendant will have full opportunity to appeal. The ultimate disposition of these cases would be delayed, not advanced by granting this application.

B.　TIME TO APPEAL

1.　**General Rule.** It is considered of extreme importance that a judicial decree be finalized and insulated against any further action or modification within a fairly short time after rendition of the final judgment of the court. For this reason, the taking of an appeal from a final decision of a trial court must be timely. In some jurisdictions, specific time limits for the taking of an appeal from such a final decision are set out and rather strictly enforced. In other jurisdictions, including the federal court system, timeliness of the taking of an appeal from a court order or judgment is left to be defined by specific circumstances as determined by the appellate court. But whichever method is provided for, the time limits considered timely for the taking of an appeal from a final judgment tend to be short and conclusive.

2. **Notice of Appeal from Nonfinal Decision.** If a notice of appeal is filed after the court informs the parties of its decision but before formally entering the judgment, the notice is considered to take effect on the date the judgment is entered. The Supreme Court has cautioned that this does not permit a notice of appeal from a clearly interlocutory decision, but only from an appealable decision. [*See* Firstier Mortgage Co. v. Investors Mortgage Insurance Co., 498 U.S. 269 (1991)]

C. THE AMBIT OF APPELLATE REVIEW

1. **Issues Subject to Review.** The study of the scope of reviewability of issues is best undertaken as the study of several basic maxims and the exceptions to those maxims. The basic maxims most commonly encountered in decisions concerning the reviewability of issues are illustrated in the following material.

    a. **Harmless error doctrine.** Courts of appeal will not review a case in which any errors committed were harmless, in that the outcome of the case was not affected. Only when there is a reasonable chance that an error committed during trial was substantial enough to have caused some prejudice to either party will the courts of appeal be willing to accept rather than dismiss an appeal.

        1) **Error must affect outcome--**

J.F. White Contracting Co. v. New England Tank Industries of New Hampshire, Inc., 393 F.2d 449 (1st Cir. 1968).

Facts. New England Tank (P), the owner of oil tank dock facilities, brought this action to recover for alleged defects in a dock built by J.F. White (D). The dock consisted of four cylindrical metal cells filled with sand and gravel connected with each other and the shore by catwalks. The jury returned a verdict in P's favor in the amount of $20,000. On appeal, D argued that P was barred from recovering by a contract stipulation that provided that approval of invoices by P's engineer was "final, conclusive, and binding on all parties." D had failed to offer this argument to the district court. D further argued on appeal that the district court erred in allowing the question of one of the cells being "out of round" to go to the jury. The cell had been struck in the process of installation by a ship and knocked "out of round." There was no evidence of the extent to which it was damaged; nor was there evidence that the utility or longevity of the cell was affected. There was also a lack of evidence regarding the cost of repairing the dent. The only evidence presented on the issue of damages was a diver's underwater inspection report that estimated the cost of repairs to be $43,150.

Issue. Was it reversible error for the district court to have allowed the issue of one of the cells being "out of round" to go to the jury?

Held. No. Judgment of the district court is affirmed.

- ◆ Issues neither pleaded by a defendant as an affirmative defense nor raised, considered, or passed upon by the district court cannot be considered on appeal. Consequently, since D failed to raise the issue of the contract stipulation at the district court level, it cannot be considered on appeal.

- ◆ Even if an issue had been properly presented to the district court, a district court's error is not ground for reversal if it was mere harmless error. That is, the alleged error must have affected the outcome below. [Fed. R. Civ. P. 61]

- ◆ Here, while the court erred in submitting the "out of roundness" issue to the jury, it was mere harmless error, since there was not even a remote possibility that it affected the verdict. Even though the evidence was insufficient on the issue of damages, any alleged error was harmless in view of the fact that P's counsel did not argue the issue to the jury. Also, the district court's instructions on damages, which emphasized that only evidence of value (including evidence of cost of repairs) could be considered, are consistent with the arguments set forth by the parties in their appellate briefs. There is no reason to suspect that the jury did not follow these instructions.

---

b. **Winning party.** "A party may not appeal from a judgment in his favor for the purpose of obtaining a review of findings he deems erroneous but which are not vital or necessary to support the decree issued in his favor." This should not be taken to mean that the winning party is never afforded the right to review, for example, when the judgment in his favor is too small to suit him. But the winning party may not appeal a finding of the court in his favor on the issue of liability—if indeed a winning party would ever desire to do such a thing.

1) **Winner may appeal unfavorable findings--**

Electrical Fittings Corp. v. Thomas & Betts Co., 307 U.S. 241 (1939).

Facts. In the original complaint, Thomas & Betts Co. (P) advanced a patent infringement suit in two counts. The patent in the first count was held valid, but was held not infringed by Electrical Fittings Corp. (D). The second count was held invalid as no patent existed. P did not appeal, but D, nominally the winning party, appealed the finding of the court on count one that the patent was valid, even though not infringed. P objected that a winning party may not appeal a finding in his favor. The court of appeals dismissed the appeal, but the Supreme Court granted certiorari.

Issue. May a winning party appeal particular issues decided against it?

Held. Yes. Judgment reversed and case remanded.

- The district court adjudicated an issue not directly in controversy in the patent infringement case when it in effect issued a declaratory judgment that the patent allegedly infringed in count one was valid (even if not infringed). Therefore, on the issue of the validity of that specific patent, D lost rather than won.

- To have denied D the right to challenge this finding would have been prejudicial to D—since it was possible that the finding on the issue of the patent could have been asserted as res judicata in another related action. Without specifically overruling the maxim that only losing parties may appeal on the issues upon which they lose, we hold that D has the right to appeal the finding of the trial court in so far as it found P's patent valid.

---

c.   **Cross-appeals--**

International Ore & Fertilizer Corp. v. SGS Control Services, Inc., 38 F.3d 1279 (2d Cir. 1994).

Facts. D agreed that it would transport fertilizer for P. D's ship was not clean enough and the fertilizer was contaminated. Consequently, the buyer would not accept the shipment. P sued D for breach of contract and negligent misrepresentation. The trial court found for D on the contract claim and for P on the negligent misrepresentation claim, and awarded P damages. D appealed, and the appellate court found that the negligent misrepresentation claim should have been dismissed. The court also found that the contract claim should have been upheld, but it was argued that the court could not make such a ruling because P had not cross-appealed.

Issues.

(i)   If a party has not filed a cross-appeal, can he seek to sustain the judgment on grounds supported by the record?

(ii)   If so, may he be awarded a greater amount of damages than that awarded by the trial court?

Held. (i) Yes. (ii) No.

- Generally, where a party fails to file a cross-appeal, he cannot use the appeal of the opposing party to attack the judgment below for the purpose of enlarging his rights thereunder or lessening the rights of the opposing party. He may, however, urge in support of a decree any matter appearing in the record.

- Several of our recent decisions refer to the discretionary nature of the court's power to disregard the cross-appeal requirement. Under such cases, we have found that a party who has not filed a cross-appeal may nevertheless seek to sustain a judgment on any grounds supported by the record. We may, therefore, uphold the finding that D is liable for breach of contract. We may not, however, allow a party who has not cross-appealed to obtain a larger amount of damages. Thus, we may not award the full amount of damages to which P may be entitled under a breach of contract theory.

---

2.   **Scope of Review of Facts.**

a.   **In general.** It is not clear how far a court of appeals may go in reviewing facts and inferences from facts (as opposed to questions of law) that come to it in the record of the trial. It is clear that the courts of appeal may today exercise considerable review of factual inferences, especially where an inference drawn by a trial court is unwarranted. And it is clear that a court of appeals may constitutionally review factual determinations of a jury, and even reverse them if clearly erroneous. But because in actuality the power of courts of appeal to review factual inferences arrived at during trial is exercised with reserve, the scarcity of decisions on the subject makes a drawing of lines quite impossible.

b.   **Scope of discretion--**

Corcoran v. City of Chicago, 27 N.E.2d 451 (Ill. 1940).

Facts. Corcoran (P) sued Chicago (D) for damages on grounds that the city maintained unsafe streets. Evidence was conflicting, and the jury determined the case for P. D's motion for a new trial on grounds that the jury's inferences were against the weight of the evidence presented was denied by the trial court. But upon initial appeal, the intermediate court, reviewing the facts presented at the trial, did grant D's request for a new trial on grounds that the verdict was against the weight of the evidence. P appeals, maintaining that courts of appeal could not properly review factual inferences drawn by a jury where evidence was conflicting, without denying a right to jury trial as guaranteed by the Illinois Constitution.

Issue. Do courts of appeal retain discretion to review factual issues?

Held. Yes. Judgment affirmed.

♦   Since common law, courts of appeal have had the power to supervise every aspect of lower court trials occurring in their respective jurisdictions. At times, this has meant that courts of appeal have had to directly intervene in the factual determinations made in lower courts where such determinations were completely against the weight of the evidence presented and necessary burdens of proof were not met. Because such a practice existed at common law, review of factual determinations by courts of appeal today is not an unconstitutional infringement of the limited rights to jury trial guaranteed by the Illinois (or the United States) Constitution.

♦ The question of *when* such a review is proper is more complex. Such review is proper, in theory, only when the factual determination made by a jury is completely, or clearly, or unreasonably against the weight of the evidence presented. But a large area of discretion is allowed, both for trial courts and courts of appeal. The court of appeal determined reasonably that the evidence presented did not satisfy the plaintiff's burden of proof, and ordered a new trial. Because the issue of the propriety of such a determination vis-a-vis a contrary determination by a jury was so close in this case, we are reluctant to reverse the grant of a new trial, even though a contrary jury verdict and contrary ruling in the trial court is thereby overruled.

---

c.   **Federal Rule 52(a)--**

Pullman-Standard v. Swint, 456 U.S. 273 (1982).

Facts. Swint and others (Ps) worked for Pullman-Standard (D). D and the labor union maintained a seniority system that allowed different pay standards and working conditions depending on seniority. Section 703(h) of Title VII of the Civil Rights Act of 1964 (42 U.S.C. 2000e-2h) allows such disparate treatment under a bona fide seniority system as long as the differences are not the result of an intention to discriminate because of race. Ps brought suit, claiming that D's seniority system violated the Act. The district court found that the differences were not the result of an intention to discriminate because of race and upheld D's system. The court of appeals reversed. It held that a finding of nondiscrimination under section 703(h) was a finding of "ultimate fact," and that the reviewing court could make an independent determination of such facts. The Supreme Court granted certiorari.

Issue. May a federal court of appeals make an independent determination of allegations so as to reverse the judgment of a district court?

Held. No. Judgment reversed and case remanded.

♦ Under section 703(h), a seniority system may be valid even if it has some discriminatory consequences, as long as there was no discriminatory purpose behind the system.

♦ Federal Rule 52(a) specifies that district court findings of fact may not be set aside unless clearly erroneous. It does not create a distinction between "ultimate" and "subsidiary" facts. Rule 52(a) does not apply to legal conclusions; however, the court of appeals reversed on the basis of its own finding of fact. Discriminatory motive is neither a question of law nor a mixed question of law and fact.

♦ The court of appeals could properly reverse only if the district court's finding was clearly erroneous. Although the court concluded that the district court had failed to consider certain relevant evidence, the proper response is a remand for further proceedings, not the making of its own independent findings.

Dissent (Marshall, Blackmun, JJ.). The court of appeals merely rejected the district court's erroneous finding and then concluded that a finding of discriminatory purpose was compelled by all of the relevant evidence.

———————

d. **Errors of law.** Note that Rule 52(a) does not inhibit an appellate court's power to correct errors of law or a finding of fact that is predicated on a misunderstanding of the governing rule of law. [*See* Bose Corp. v. Consumers Union of United States, Inc., 466 U.S. 485 (1984)] In *Bose,* the appellate court had conducted a *de novo* review of the district court's decision and found that, even accepting all of the factual findings of the district court, the record did not contain clear and convincing evidence to support the existence of actual malice in the plaintiff's allegation of defamation. The Supreme Court affirmed stating that the clearly erroneous standard "does not prescribe the standard of review to be applied in a determination of actual malice" in a defamation suit. "Appellate judges in such a case must exercise independent judgment and determine whether the record establishes actual malice."

D. REVIEW BY COURTS ABOVE APPELLATE COURTS

1. **Federal System.** In the federal system, the highest court is the United States Supreme Court.

   a. **Review from courts of appeals.** Decisions of the courts of appeals may be reviewed by the Supreme Court (i) by *writ of certiorari* granted upon the petition of any party in any case before or after rendition of the judgment or decree; or (ii) by *certification* by the court of appeals at any time of any question of law as to which it desires instructions from the Supreme Court. [28 U.S.C. §1254]

   b. **Review of state court decisions.** The Supreme Court will review the final judgments of the highest state court by *writ of certiorari*, where the validity of a treaty or statute of the United States is drawn into question or where the validity of a statute of any state is drawn into question on the ground of its being repugnant to the Constitution, treaties, or laws of the United States, or where any title, right, privilege, or immunity is specially set up or claimed under the Constitution or the treaties or statutes of, or any commission held or authority exercised under, the United States. [28 U.S.C. §1257]

    c.   **Direct review.** In some circumstances, the United States Supreme Court can hear a direct appeal from a United States district court. [*See, e.g.*, 28 U.S.C. §1253]

2.   **State Court Systems.** More than three-quarters of the states have intermediate appellate courts, generally for the purpose of allowing the states' highest courts to focus on important and novel questions of law and to maintain uniformity in the law applied by the trial courts. Every state system with intermediate courts, however, like the federal system, has provisions for bypassing the appellate courts.

3.   **The Final Judgment Requirement.** The United States Supreme Court may only review "final judgments of the highest state court in which a decision could be had." [28 U.S.C. §1257]

XVII. THE BINDING EFFECT OF PRIOR DECISIONS: RES JUDICATA AND COLLATERAL ESTOPPEL

A. INTRODUCTION

The policy of finality (*i.e.,* the notion that litigation must come to an end) is a major force in civil procedure. It promotes several other procedural values—namely, judicial efficiency or economy, consistency in judicial determinations, and avoidance of harassing or vexatious litigation. These policies provide the rationale for the doctrine of res judicata and collateral estoppel. Under modern terminology favored by the Restatement (Second) of Judgments, res judicata in its narrow sense is referred to as ***claim preclusion***, and collateral estoppel is referred to as ***issue preclusion***.

B. CLAIM AND DEFENSE PRECLUSION

1. **Claim Preclusion.** Claim preclusion arises when the following three elements are present: (i) there is a final, valid judgment on the merits; (ii) the parties in the subsequent action are ***identical*** to those in the prior action (distinguish issue preclusion, *infra*); and (iii) the claim in the subsequent suit involves matters properly considered in the prior action. The objective of claim preclusion is to avoid multiple suits on identical rights or obligations between the same parties.

   a. **Effect of adjudication upon the cause of action involved: merger and bar.**

      1) **Merger.** In a legal sense, merger is the fusion of two causes of action into a single right of action. When a party acquires several causes of action arising out of the same transaction or series of transactions, he is usually required to assert all his causes of action in a single lawsuit. Failure to do so may result in the waiver of the causes of action not so joined—the unjoined causes of action are said to have been merged in the adjudication of the asserted causes of action. All of a plaintiff's related claims are merged into the single judgment he obtains. And all of a defendant's defenses are merged into the judgment in her favor—she may not relitigate defenses to a cause of action she has already won.

      2) **Bar.** Bar and merger are corollaries. If the plaintiff prevails upon his causes of action, remaining causes of action may be merged and thereby waived. Similarly, if the plaintiff loses on the merits, he may be barred from thereafter asserting in any other action the same, or

similar, causes of action. The two concepts, bar and merger, proce-durally similar, are both directed toward the achievement of one end; *i.e.,* ensuring that judicial time is not wasted by parties asserting and reasserting the same causes of action in numerous lawsuits. Under the doctrines of bar and merger, a party is given one chance to liti-gate fairly and fully his grievances, and no more than one chance.

b.   **Single action rule--**

Rush v. City of Maple Heights, 147 N.E.2d 599 (Ohio), *cert. denied,* 358 U.S. 814 (1958).

Facts. Rush (P) was injured in a fall from her motorcycle. She sued the city of Maple Heights (D) for negligent maintenance of its streets. In her first action, she sued for dam-age to her cycle, recovering a judgment of $100. In a second and separate action, she sued for her own personal injuries and recovered a judgment of $12,000. D appealed the sec-ond judgment on grounds that all of P's causes of action had been merged in her first judgment of $100, so that she could not reassert the same set of facts to recover for her personal injuries in a second separate suit. The court of appeals affirmed; D appeals.

Issue. May a plaintiff sue in two actions for damages resulting from a single accident?

Held. No. Judgment reversed.

♦   The single accident gave rise to two distinct causes of action, one for personal injuries, another for property damage. But to allow P to bring suit separately on both causes of action would have been to encourage vexatious and time-consum-ing litigation. Therefore, the majority of jurisdictions require that such "twin" causes of action as these be sued on simultaneously, in a single action. Failure to do so results in merger of the second cause of action into the first, with the result that the second may never be brought.

♦   P logically should have asserted both the personal injury and the property damage causes of action in her original suit. Because she did not do so, the second of her two causes of action was lost by merger. Therefore, she improperly brought her personal injury action. The original judgment of $100, through the doctrine of merger, was all the redress that P could obtain for both the twin causes of action.

c.   **Res judicata (claim preclusion) as bar--**

Mathews v. New York Racing Association, Inc., 193 F. Supp. 293 (S.D.N.Y. 1961).

Facts. Mathews (P) brought an action against New York Racing Association (D), alleging that he was "assaulted," "kidnapped," "falsely arrested," and "falsely imprisoned" on April 4, 1958, by D's employees. Also, he charged D with malicious prosecution of a disorderly conduct charge that he was convicted of on April 10, 1958. P requests money damages and an injunction restraining D from interfering with his future attendance at race tracks, from publication of libelous statements, and from acting as peace officers. D moved for summary judgment, arguing that a judgment in favor of its employees in a prior action was res judicata as to the present claim. In the prior action, P sued D's employees, alleging that he was assaulted by them on April 4, 1958 and that they made libelous statements about him on several occasions, including at his April 10, 1958, trial for disorderly conduct. He requested money damages and an injunction from further interference at race tracks. Judge Palmieri found that P failed to state a claim against D's employees. More specifically, he found that P physically resisted removal from the race track and that D's employees used no more force than was reasonably necessary under the circumstances.

Issue. Is P's current claim the same claim that he pressed in the prior suit for res judicata purposes?

Held. Yes. Judgment entered in favor of D.

- Res judicata operates as a bar to subsequent suits involving the same parties, and those in privity with them, when the prior suit ended in a judgment on the merits. Its purpose is to prevent needless multiplication of litigation. It is clear that D is in privity with the defendants of the prior suit.

- In determining whether a claim alleged is the same as that raised in an earlier suit for res judicata purposes, the term "claim" refers to the facts surrounding a single occurrence or transaction. That is, it is the facts surrounding an occurrence that make up a claim and not the legal theory a plaintiff relies on.

- A corporation can act only through its agents, and if they are not at fault, there is no basis for liability.

- The judgment entered against P in the prior suit bars his present suit against D. The same facts are the basis for liability in each suit. The acts complained of by P against D's employees in the prior suit form the basis of P's present suit against D. Since it has already been determined that D's agents committed no actionable wrong, D cannot be held liable here.

---

d.   Merger--

Jones v. Morris Plan Bank of Portsmouth, 191 S.E. 608 (Va. 1937).

Facts. Jones (P) purchased an automobile financed by Morris Plan Bank of Portsmouth (D). The finance agreement provided for monthly installments and contained the usual acceleration clause to the effect that, if any one payment was in arrears, the entire balance became due and payable. P missed two monthly payments. D repossessed the automobile and sued P (in another action) for the money due him from the two payments missed. In this action, P sued D for conversion of the automobile, on grounds that D's right to repossess the automobile under the acceleration clause was merged with the cause of action for the two missed monthly installments, and therefore could not be asserted. The appellate court upheld the judgments for D. P appeals.

Issue. Is an action on an overdue debt merged with a separate foreclosure action?

Held. Yes. Judgment reversed.

♦ As soon as P missed the first installment, the entire contract became due and payable. Because of this acceleration clause, the contract was not separable once P missed a payment, but contained only one large cause of action—for breach of the entire contract. But D sued P for only part of the amount due, to wit, two monthly installments. D's failure to sue P for the entire amount of the contract constituted a waiver, or merger, of the right to sue on the remainder. Therefore, D's later repossession of the automobile, and its later actions to force payment of the remainder of the contract, were not allowed.

---

2. Defense Preclusion--

Mitchell v. Federal Intermediate Credit Bank, 164 S.E. 136 (S.C. 1932).

Facts. Mitchell (P) assigned the proceeds from the sale of his potatoes ($18,000) to the Federal Intermediate Credit Bank (D) as security for two notes totaling $9,000. D sued on the notes, and P asserted the sales proceeds as a defense (offset). P now sues for the amount of the proceeds in excess of the offset earlier used. The trial court held that P's claim was merged in the earlier judgment. P appeals.

Issue. May a party split a cause of action arising out of one transaction by asserting one portion of a claim as a defense and another portion as an affirmative claim in a separate action?

Held. No. Judgment affirmed.

♦ P had the option of demanding judgment against D in the first suit by way of counterclaim. By so doing he might have recovered in the first suit, on the same allegations and proofs that he now asserts, the judgment he now seeks. Settled principles of law prevent P from splitting his action in this manner.

C. ISSUE PRECLUSION

1. **In General.** A right, question, or fact put in issue and determined by a court of competent jurisdiction as a ground for recovery cannot be disputed in a subsequent suit between the same parties or parties in privity with them. Issue preclusion differs from claim preclusion in that issue preclusion never applies to matters not argued or decided in a prior action.

2. **Issues Actually Litigated.** The principle of issue preclusion prohibits a party from relitigating in a subsequent action issues actually litigated in a prior action. In this respect it is quite different from claim preclusion and defense preclusion, which may be effective against all issues that should have been litigated at the earlier time. To have been litigated in the first action within the meaning of the principle of issue preclusion, it is necessary that the issue was actually raised in that action, that a decision was reached on the issue, and that the issue was necessarily decided in the earlier action. Hence, if the earlier action could have rested on any of several alternative grounds, or if the issue in the earlier trial was "stipulated" rather than adjudicated, there is usually no issue preclusion effect. Issue preclusion is the modern term used to encompass the doctrine of collateral estoppel.

   a. **Same subject matter--**

Cromwell v. County of Sac, 94 U.S. (4 Otto) 351 (1876).

Facts. In an earlier action, a different plaintiff had sued the same defendant, county of Sac (D), for maturation coupons attached to municipal bonds issued by D. The court in that earlier action had held that the bonds and coupons in the hands of that earlier plaintiff were void as not purchased for value. Cromwell (P in this action) thereafter obtained the same bonds and brought this action for the accrued interest due. D asserted the earlier judgment as conclusive on the general validity of the bonds by collateral estoppel, and therefore denied that any interest was due. P appeals a judgment for D.

Issue. Does the doctrine of collateral estoppel preclude further litigation regarding the same subject matter even when a different issue is raised in the second suit?

Held. No. Judgment reversed.

♦ Where two actions involve generally the same subject matter, but the causes of action litigated are different or the parties involved are different, the first action is conclusive as against the second only on issues actually and necessarily litigated in the course of the first trial. The bonds issued by D would have been valid obligations in the hands of a bona fide purchaser for value at the time of the first trial, but that issue was not litigated then.

♦ Because no evidence was presented as to whether P was a bona fide purchaser for value of the bonds, the finding of invalidity of the bonds in the first trial had no collateral estoppel effect as against P unless it were first shown that he, too, had not paid value for them. The case is remanded to determine whether P was a bona fide purchaser for value of the bonds.

---

3. **Requirement of Certainty.** If, in the first action, it is not clear whether a point later asserted as res judicata has actually been litigated and decided, there is no issue preclusion or collateral estoppel. Thus, when a holding rests upon several alternative grounds, each of which could support the plea, there is issue preclusion (collateral estoppel) on none of those issues by the general rule. It is said that none of the issues so decided had been expressly and necessarily determined in the prior case.

a. **Precise issues decided in prior case unknown--**

Russell v. Place, 94 U.S. (4 Otto) 606 (1876).

Facts. In an earlier suit, Russell (P) sued Place (D) for patent infringement upon several different counts, any one of which, if proved, would have supported a verdict in P's favor. In due course, P did recover in that action, but the court's decision gave no hint as to the specific infringement for which relief was granted. In this suit, P again sued D, and D set up defenses identical to those he had set up earlier in the first action. P moved to have all of D's defenses dismissed on grounds that they all had been litigated and disposed of in the previous action. P appeals adverse lower court actions.

Issue. Does collateral estoppel apply where the precise question raised and decided in the earlier case is not disclosed?

Held. No. Judgment affirmed.

♦ If there is any uncertainty in the record of the first trial as to whether a distinct issue was raised and litigated, or if it appears that several issues have all been litigated as a "group" rather than singly, as here, the whole subject matter will be at large and subject to relitigation. The decision of the trial court at the first patent infringement trial did not show which of D's defenses, or which of P's claims, were specifically litigated and decided. Because some doubt existed as to what actually was litigated in the former trial, the former trial will be denied any collateral estoppel effect upon the issues resubmitted at the second trial.

---

4. **Requirement of Necessity.** If, in the first action, the judicial decision on a certain point was not necessary to support the decree eventually entered—if it

was more dictum than decision—the prior decision on that point is denied issue preclusion (collateral estoppel) effect in any later trial where it might otherwise have had such effect.

a.   Gratuitous finding--

Rios v. Davis, 373 S.W.2d 386 (Tex. Ct. App. 1963).

Facts. In a prior action, the employer of Rios (P) sued Davis (D) for damage to the company truck sustained in an accident between P and D. D counterclaimed on grounds that P had been solely responsible for the accident, sued the employer for damages, and joined P as a third-party defendant. The trial court found all parties contributorily negligent and denied recovery. In this action, P in his own name filed an independent suit against D for negligence. D pleaded the prior decision in the suit between the employer and himself as res judicata on the issue of P's contributory negligence. The trial court entered judgment for D; P appeals.

Issue. May collateral estoppel effect be given to a finding that was not necessary to the result of the earlier judgment?

Held. No. Judgment reversed.

◆   Collateral estoppel works only where an issue decided in an earlier trial was necessarily decided in that trial. In the earlier trial between P's employer and D, in order to deny either party recovery upon the theory of contributory negligence, it was not necessary for the court to decide, as it did, that P personally had been negligent. A finding of negligence on the part of D and the employer was all that was necessary to that suit—the court's finding that P as well as his employer had been negligent was purely "gratuitous."

◆   Because the earlier decision on P's personal negligence was not necessary to the determination of that suit, the decision had no collateral estoppel effect on the suit at bar. Note that this rule is based on the fact that the right of appeal is from a judgment and not a finding. Since the judgment in the prior action was in P's favor, he had no right to deny negligence on appeal, no matter how erroneous such finding may have been.

---

5.   **Limits on the Scope of Issue Preclusion or Collateral Estoppel.** Statutes are drawn and administered with a certain goal in mind. As the following cases will indicate, it often happens that rigid application of the rules of issue preclusion (collateral estoppel) will work to defeat or hinder achievement of a policy goal. Therefore, as a general rule of thumb, where application of the principles of issue preclusion will work to hinder some established policy of substantive

law, whether statutory or decisional, the present trend is to defeat operation of the principle.

a. **Erroneous view or application of law.** In *United States v. Moser*, 266 U.S. 236 (1924), P, a retired naval captain, won a ruling that his service as a cadet in the Naval Academy during the Civil War was sufficient to entitle him to retire with a higher rank and pay. In two later suits for installments of his pay, the court found for P on res judicata grounds, even though the Court of Claims had changed its interpretation of the pension statutes. In a fourth action for installments, the Court of Claims reinstated its initial interpretation of the pension statutes and also found that P was entitled to judgment under the doctrine of res judicata. On appeal, the Supreme Court affirmed only on the ground of res judicata, holding that "a fact, question or right distinctly adjudged in the original action cannot be disputed in a subsequent action, even though the determination was reached upon an erroneous view or by an erroneous application of the law."

b. **Change in law between lawsuits--**

Commissioner of Internal Revenue v. Sunnen, 333 U.S. 591 (1948).

Facts. In 1928, Sunnen (D) entered into a contract whereby he was to be paid royalties for the use of a patent. The final payment under this contract, $4,800, was paid directly to his wife rather than to him. In an earlier tax suit, D was held liable for taxes on royalties paid directly to him but not for those paid directly to his wife. In 1937 he entered into new contracts, identical to the old ones, except that all royalties were to be paid directly to his wife. The Commissioner (P) sued D for taxes due on the royalties paid to his wife. D interposed the earlier decision as res judicata on the issue of his liability for income paid directly to his wife. The Tax Court held that the $4,800 payment was not taxable to D because of the principle of res judicata, but that payments under the second contract were taxable to D. The court of appeals held that D was not subject to tax on any of the payments. P appeals.

Issue. Does collateral estoppel apply where the material facts are unchanged but the legal principles underlying the first decision have changed?

Held. No. Judgment reversed.

♦ Between the original decision and the time of the second suit, the decisional law relating to interfamily assignments of income had eliminated the rule that the husband's income assigned to the wife was not taxable through the husband. Therefore, had the court applied the doctrine of collateral estoppel, it would have been forced to have ruled in favor of the taxpayer and contrary to then-accepted principles of law. To have done so would have been inequitable to other like taxpayers who would have been liable for interfamily income. Where collateral estoppel runs counter to accepted principles of law, collateral estoppel must fall. Therefore, the earlier decision on the liability of the husband for his wife's assigned income does not collaterally estop the court from reexamining the same question later because of intervening circumstances.

D. THE REQUIRED QUALITY OF JUDGMENT

1. Judgments of Judicial Tribunals--

Hanover Logansport, Inc. v. Robert C. Anderson, Inc., 512 N.E.2d 465 (Ind. 1987).

Facts. Hanover Logansport, Inc. (D) and Robert C. Anderson, Inc.(P) entered into a lease agreement whereby D agreed to lease property to P for a liquor store. P brought an action for breach of the lease when D failed to deliver the premises on the agreed upon date. Prior to trial, D offered to deliver the property and P accepted. A portion of P's acceptance of the offer of judgment between P and D states that P accepted D's offer for purposes of mitigation only, and P did not waive damages for D's breach of contract between the date the lease was signed and the date the court entered its order of settlement. D filed a motion to dismiss the earlier breach of contract action. The trial court denied the motion. D appeals.

Issue. May a plaintiff who accepts an offer of judgment that conforms to one of the affirmative prayers for relief contained in his complaint then seek additional damages arising from the same cause of action?

Held. No. Judgment reversed and case remanded.

- ♦ P's complaint seeks specific performance or, in the alternative, money damages for lost profits over the term of the lease.

- ♦ Indiana Trial Rule 68, which is similar to Federal Rule Civil Procedure 68, requires the clerk to enter judgment when the defendant has made an offer consistent with one of the alternatives (specific performance) in the plaintiff's complaint and the plaintiff has accepted the offer and taken possession.

- ♦ A consent judgment is viewed by different courts in different ways: some view it as an agreement with contractual implications and judge its preclusive effect by ascertaining the parties' intent; others focus on the entry of a consent judgment and argue that such a judgment possesses the same force with regard to res judicata and collateral estoppel as a judgment on the merits.

- ♦ We adopt the consent-judgment-as-contract theory. The intent of the parties must govern. However, both parties must have agreed to reserve a claim or issue, which must be an inherent part of the original complaint, and those claims or issues being reserved must be clearly stated in the offer of judgment itself.

◆ Here, P did not include a claim for damages for delay in tendering the real estate in its complaint, and is, therefore, precluded from reserving such a claim in the consent judgment.

---

2. Judgments of Nonjudicial Tribunals--

Holmberg v. State, Division of Risk Management, 796 P.2d 823 (Ala. 1990).

Facts. Holmberg (P), an employee of the state of Alaska, had been denied permanent total disability benefits by the Alaska Workers' Compensation Board ("AWCB"). Later, the Public Employees Retirement Board ("PERB") determined that, due to her back condition, P was not physically able to perform her duties as an employee of Risk Management (D), a state agency, and found her permanently and totally disabled. Based on the PERB decision, P was awarded disability benefits from the Public Employee Retirement System ("PERS"). P then appealed the AWCB decision, arguing that the decision should be reversed because of the preclusive effect of the later PERB decision. The trial court affirmed the AWCB's decision, and P appeals.

Issue. Is a decision rendered by one state agency or official binding on another agency or official of the same government even if there is no privity between the two?

Held. No. Judgment affirmed.

◆ Preclusion may be defeated if a court finds that there are such important differences between the functions of the different agencies involved that one does not have the authority to represent the other. In this case, the lower court noted that PERB and AWCB have different disability standards, but found no reason to relitigate the narrow factual question of whether P is physically able to perform her job.

◆ Because we find no reason not to give PERB decisions preclusive effect in AWCB proceedings, we must determine if the necessary requirements of collateral estoppel are present in this case. We find that the requirement of privity is not met.

◆ PERS is not a state agency but an independent retirement plan in which public employees are members. It is funded by contributions from both employees and participant employers. While a state agency administers PERS and represents it during appeals, the state as an employer is only one participant. The state as a participant in PERS is not in privity with PERS. Because privity is lacking, we cannot afford any preclusive effect to the PERB decision as against the state.

E. PERSONS BENEFITED AND PERSONS BOUND BY PRECLUSION

1. **The Traditional Model.** It was the traditional maxim of both res judicata and collateral estoppel that the doctrines were operative only where all parties to the second action were also parties to, or in privity with parties to, the former action. Therefore, all estoppel had to be "mutual"—the person asserting the estoppel against another party would himself have been bound by estoppel had the decision in the former action gone the other way. The requirement of "mutuality of estoppel" effectively precluded a stranger to the former action from using collateral estoppel defensively when a once-litigated cause of action was reasserted against him. However, a growing number of decisions repudiate the requirement of "mutuality of estoppel" and allow a stranger to the former action to assert collateral estoppel (issue preclusion) defensively.

2. **Mutuality--**

Bernhard v. Bank of America National Trust & Savings Association, 122 P.2d 892 (Cal. 1942).

Facts. Mrs. Sather gave Cook some money to deposit in her bank account, but Cook, after deposit, withdrew the money and used it for his own purposes. Upon the death of Mrs. Sather, Bernhard (P) and the other next of kin sued Cook for embezzlement. Judgment went for Cook on grounds that Mrs. Sather had given him the money as a gift. Thereafter, P sued the Bank of America (D) in which Mrs. Sather had had her account, asserting that the bank had illegally allowed Cook to make withdrawals out of the Sather account. D, a stranger to the first action, nonetheless asserted the judgment in the first action—the money was a gift—as collateral estoppel. The lower courts gave judgment for D; P appeals.

Issue. Is a plea of res judicata available only where there is privity and mutuality of estoppel (*i.e.*, only a party bound by a previous action may assert it as res judicata)?

Held. No. Judgment affirmed.

- ♦ Only three questions need be asked when a stranger attempts to assert defensively a decision in a prior action against a party to the former action: Was the issue decided in both cases identical? Was the adjudication of the issue final and necessary? And was the party ***against whom*** the plea is to be asserted a party to the original action? "Mutuality of estoppel," in that both parties to the second action must have been parties to the first before either could assert res judicata, is expressly overruled. It is sufficient if the party against whom the estoppel is asserted was a party.

- ♦ Because P, against whom the plea of collateral estoppel was pleaded, was a party to the former action, no reason existed for not allowing D, though a stranger to the former action, to assert the former action as conclusive. Therefore, P was bound by the earlier court's finding that the money deposited in D was a gift given to Cook, so that it was not illegal for him to withdraw it.

---

3. Offensive Use of Prior Judgment--

Parklane Hosiery Co. v. Shore, 439 U.S. 322 (1979).

Facts. Shore (P) brought a stockholder's class action against Parklane Hosiery Co. (D) for damages caused by a false and misleading proxy statement. Prior to trial, the Securities and Exchange Commission ("SEC") brought a separate action (a nonjury trial), with essentially the same allegations as P's, and won a declaratory judgment. P moved for partial summary judgment as to the issues litigated in the SEC action. The district court denied the motion on grounds that it would deprive D of its Seventh Amendment right to a jury trial. P appealed, and the court of appeals reversed. D appeals.

Issue. Does the mutuality doctrine still apply to collateral estoppel?

Held. No. Judgment affirmed.

♦ In *Blonder-Tongue Laboratories, Inc. v. University of Illinois Foundation*, 402 U.S. 313 (1971), the Court held that the mutuality doctrine should not apply to patent cases. That holding is now broadened. However, that case involved defensive use of collateral estoppel and was greatly influenced by the undesirability of forcing a defendant to relitigate issues that the plaintiff had previously lost.

♦ When collateral estoppel is used offensively, as here, it should not be allowed if the plaintiff could have joined in the earlier case, out of fairness to the defendant. But P here could not have joined in the SEC action; therefore its use by P is permissible. D is not prejudiced thereby because it had a full and fair opportunity to litigate its claims in the SEC action.

♦ D's Seventh Amendment rights to a jury trial are not violated here. Even though mutuality was required for collateral estoppel when the Bill of Rights was adopted, procedural devices may develop to assure substantial justice and not violate the Seventh Amendment.

Dissent (Rehnquist, J.). The Court has effectively ignored the Seventh Amendment. The development of "nonmutual" estoppel is not a mere change in "procedure."

---

4. Binding on Parties--

Martin v. Wilks, 490 U.S. 755 (1989).

Facts. A group of white firefighters (Ps) sued the city of Birmingham, Alabama and the Jefferson County Personnel Board (Ds) in federal court alleging that Ds were making race-conscious promotion decisions in reliance on two consent decrees that settled a prior Title VII lawsuit brought by their black co-workers and Ds, and that these decisions constituted impermissible racial discrimination against Ps under the Constitution and Title VII. Ps were not parties to the first Title VII lawsuit or signatories to the consent decrees. However, Ps had an opportunity to intervene in the prior lawsuit, but chose not to do so. Ps' union ("BFA") had been allowed to appear and file objections as amicus curiae in a hearing on the consent decrees. After the consent decrees were approved over BFA's objections, BFA and two white firefighters (also members of BFA) had moved to intervene. The motions were denied as untimely. BFA and several white firefighters then filed a complaint against Ds seeking to enjoin the consent decrees. The district court denied relief and the court of appeals affirmed on the ground that because the white firefighters could institute an independent Title VII lawsuit asserting that Ds' actions violated their rights, they had not shown the potential for irreparable harm from the operation of the consent decrees. Ps then brought the present action. A group of black firefighters (Petitioners) were allowed to intervene in Ps' lawsuit to defend the consent decrees. Ds moved to dismiss Ps' lawsuit as an impermissible collateral attack on the consent decrees. The court of appeals reversed. Petitioners appeal.

Issue. Does Ps' lawsuit constitute an impermissible collateral attack on the consent decrees, given the fact that Ps chose to pass up an opportunity to intervene in the lawsuit that produced the consent decrees? In other words, does the impermissible collateral attack doctrine—"the attribution of preclusive effect to a failure to intervene"—apply to this case?

Held. No. Judgment affirmed.

- The impermissible collateral attack doctrine is inconsistent with Rules 19 and 24 and the general principle of Anglo-American jurisprudence that one is not bound by a judgment in personam in a litigation in which he is not designated as a party or to which he has not been made a party by service of process.

- Rule 19 indicates that existing parties to a lawsuit bear the burden of adding new parties where such a step is in order. Rule 24 indicates that potential new parties have no duty to intervene. In this sense, joinder under Rule 19 is mandatory, and intervention under Rule 24 is permissive.

- The impermissible collateral attack doctrine should not be added to the class of exceptions to the mandatory joinder rule, permissive intervention rule, and general Anglo-American principle, because the system of joinder presently contemplated by Rules 19 and 20 serves the many interests involved in the run of litigated cases, including cases like the present one.

Dissent (Stevens, Brennan, Marshall, Blackmun, JJ.).

- Although the Court is quite right that Ps could not be deprived of their legal rights in the prior Title VII lawsuit because they were not parties or intervenors in that action, there is no reason why the consent decrees might not produce changes in conditions at Ps' place of employment that, as a practical matter, may have a serious effect on their opportunities for employment or promotion even though they are not bound by the decrees in a legal sense. Moreover, if, after the rendition of a judgment by a court of competent jurisdiction, and after the period has elapsed when it becomes irreversible for error, another court may in another suit inquire into the irregularities or errors in such judgment, there would be no end to litigation and no fixed established rights. In addition, such collateral attacks can lead to the extraordinary situation of a trial court reviewing a judgment entered by a court of greater authority. The impermissible collateral attack doctrine should, therefore, apply in this case.

- As to the merits of Ps' claim of intentional discrimination, the fact that an employer is acting under court compulsion may be evidence that the employer is acting in good faith and without discriminatory intent.

Comment. The 1991 Civil Rights Act reverses the holding in *Martin.* A person who had actual notice of a proposed judgment and a reasonable opportunity to present objections to such judgment, or whose interest is adequately represented in the first lawsuit, cannot collaterally attack the judgment.

F. INTERSYSTEM PRECLUSION

1. Interstate Preclusion--

Hart v. American Airlines, 304 N.Y.S.2d 810 (1969).

Facts. An American Airlines (D) plane crashed en route from New York to Kentucky killing 58 of the 62 passengers. Various lawsuits were filed as a result. An action filed in the United States District Court for the Northern District of Texas was the first to be tried. That suit resulted in a verdict for the plaintiff on the issue of D's liability for the crash. Landano and Kirchstein (Ps) filed this action in New York state court. It is undisputable that the issue of D's liability in this case is identical to that determined in the Texas action. Ps moved for summary judgment on the issue of liability arguing that under the doctrine of collateral estoppel, the determination in the Texas action is conclusive on the issue of D's liability for the plane crash in the present action. D argued that it should be able to retry the issue of liability because the issue in the Texas action was submitted to the jury under the substantive law of Kentucky, which is less favorable to D than the corresponding New York law.

Issue. Can collateral estoppel be used offensively to preclude religitation of a finding of liability that was previously decided by a court in another state?

Held. Yes. Ps' motion for summary judgment granted.

♦ For collateral estoppel to be applied in this situation, there must be (i) an identity of issue that has necessarily been decided in the prior action and is decisive of the present action, and (ii) there must have been a full and fair opportunity to contest the decision now said to be controlling.

♦ In an airplane crash such as this, the issue of the airline's liability for the crash in which the plaintiff's decedents perished is clearly identical to the issue of liability in the previous action. In this type of case, we do not have the problems with respect to "identity of issue," which might arise in other types of situations such as multiple party car accidents.

♦ It is clear that D had a full and fair opportunity to litigate the issue of its liability in the first trial, which lasted 19 days. The burden is on D to show that it did not, and there is no evidence to so indicate.

♦ D's argument that collateral estoppel cannot apply because the issue would be litigated under a different state's (New York's) law in this case is completely without merit. Clearly, the instant case, as the Texas case, would be determined under the substantive law of Kentucky, where the crash occurred.

---

2. Child Custody Laws and Preclusion--

Thompson v. Thompson, 484 U.S. 174 (1988).

Facts. The Los Angeles Superior Court awarded sole custody of a divorcing couple's son to the mother (D) pending a court investigator's submission of a report on custody. Once the report was received, the court intended to make a final custody determination. D moved with the child to Louisiana to take a job. After living in Louisiana for three months, D filed a petition in state court for enforcement of the California custody decree and a judgment of sole custody. The Louisiana court granted the petition and awarded sole custody to D. Two months later, the California court, having reviewed the investigator's report, awarded sole custody to the child's father (P). P filed suit in federal court requesting, under the Parental Kidnapping Prevention Act ("PKPA"), an order declaring the Louisiana decree invalid and the California decree valid. The district court granted D's motion to dismiss due to lack of subject matter and personal jurisdiction. The appellate court affirmed, and the Supreme Court granted certiorari.

Issue. Does the PKPA furnish an implied cause of action in federal court to determine which state's custody decision is valid?

Held. No. Judgment affirmed.

♦ We find that the context, language, and history of the PKPA mandate against inferring a cause of action in federal court to determine which of two state's custody decrees is valid. We will not find a remedy in any act that Congress did not intend to provide.

♦ Custody orders are normally subject to modification. For this reason, some courts doubted that such orders were sufficiently final to require application of full faith and credit requirements. This uncertainty created an incentive for a parent to abduct a child and initiate custody proceedings in another state. The PKPA was enacted to address this problem in the hopes of decreasing parental abductions.

♦ Congress's aim in enacting the PKPA was to furnish rules for courts to use in determining custody disputes between sister states by applying full faith and credit doctrine, and not to create an entirely new cause of action.

---

3. **State-Federal Preclusion.** Usually, a state court judgment is accorded preclusive effect in the federal court on any issues that were or should have been litigated in the state court proceeding. Thus, the doctrines of res judicata and collateral estoppel apply to state court judgments unless there is some clear indication by Congress limiting the application of these doctrines to federal causes of action.

a. **Section 1983 claim--**

Allen v. McCurry, 449 U.S. 90 (1980).

Facts. At a hearing before his criminal trial in the state court, McCurry (P) invoked the Fourth and Fourteenth Amendments to suppress evidence that had been seized by police officers. The state court denied the motion in part, and P was subsequently convicted after a jury trial. The conviction was affirmed on appeal. Because P did not assert that the state courts had denied him a "full and fair opportunity" to litigate his search and seizure claim, P is barred from seeking a writ of habeas corpus in a federal district court. Instead, P filed a 42 U.S.C. section 1983 action in the federal court against the officers against whom P alleged a violation of his constitutional rights. The district court granted summary judgment against P on the ground that collateral estoppel precluded P from relitigating the search and seizure question already decided against him in the state courts. The court of appeals reversed the judgment and directed the trial court to allow P to proceed to trial. The Supreme Court granted certiorari.

Issue. Does the unavailability of federal habeas corpus relief prevent raising a state criminal court's partial rejection of the constitutional claim as a collateral estoppel defense to a section 1983 suit for damages?

Held. No. Judgment reversed.

- The federal courts generally have accorded preclusive effect to issues decided by state courts. Thus, res judicata and collateral estoppel not only reduce unnecessary litigation but also promote comity between state and federal courts that has been recognized in *Younger v. Harris*, 401 U.S. 37 (1971), as a bulwark of the federal system.

- While section 1983 says nothing about the preclusive effect of state court judgments, the legislative history of the section does not in any clear way suggest that Congress intended to repeal or restrict the traditional doctrine of preclusion. Congress intended to afford an opportunity for legal and equitable relief in a federal court for certain types of injuries.

- It is doubtful that the drafters of section 1983 considered it a substitute for a federal writ of habeas corpus, the purpose of which is not to redress civil injury, but to release the applicant from unlawful physical confinement.

Dissent (Blackmun, Brennan, Marshall, JJ.). The Court's ruling ignores the clear import of the legislative history of the statutes and disregards the important federal policies that underlie its enforcement. Although Congress did not expressly state whether the then-existing common law doctrine of preclusion would survive enactment of section 1983, they plainly anticipated more than the creation of a federal statutory remedy to be administered indifferently by either a state or federal court. Congress deliberately opened the federal courts to individuals in response to the states' failure to provide justice in their own courts. It is inconsistent now to narrow our previous understanding of the distribution of power between state and federal courts. The criminal defendant is an involuntary litigant in the state tribunal. To force him to choose between forgoing either a potential defense or a federal forum for hearing his constitutional civil claim is fundamentally unfair.

---

4. **Federal-State Preclusion.** Generally, federal judgments are given full faith and credit in state courts even though the Full Faith and Credit Clause does not actually apply to this situation. Almost all courts agree that federal preclusion rules will apply in state court when the prior federal judgment involved a federal question. But when a case is in federal court due to diversity jurisdiction alone and involves determination of state law claims, it is unclear which rules of preclusion (federal or state) a subsequent court should apply. The Supreme Court recently indicated that the law of the forum state of the prior action should determine the preclusive effect of a prior diversity action.

    a. **Forum state's preclusion rules control--**

Semtek International Inc. v. Lockheed Martin Corp., 531 U.S. 497 (2001).

Facts. Semtek (P) brought suit in California state court against Lockheed Martin Corporation (D) alleging breach of contract and other business torts. The action was removed to federal court based on diversity of citizenship, where it was dismissed on the merits and with prejudice because it was barred by California's two-year statute of limitations. P then brought suit in Maryland state court alleging the same causes of action, which were not time barred under that state's three-year statute of limitations. D filed a motion to dismiss on the ground of res judicata, and the Maryland court granted the motion. The court of special appeals affirmed the dismissal, finding that the res judicata effect of federal diversity judgments is prescribed by federal law, under which the earlier dismissal was on the merits and claim preclusive. The Supreme Court granted certiorari.

Issue. Did the court err in finding the claim barred due to the judgment of the federal court sitting in diversity?

Held. Yes. Judgment reversed.

♦ The Maryland court appeared to base its decision in part on Federal Rule of Civil Procedure 41(b), which states that a dismissal is "upon the merits" unless the court specifies otherwise. (There are three exceptions to this rule that are not relevant here.) We find that the claim preclusive effect of the California federal diversity judgment is not governed by Rule 41(b).

♦ Originally, the phrase "on the merits" as used in Rule 41(b) indicated a judgment that had actually passed directly on the merits of the case. Over time, the meaning of the phrase has been broadened and it has come to be applied to some judgments that do not pass upon the substantive merits of the case. In such a situation, as here, the judgment is not entitled to claim preclusive effect.

♦ The general rule regarding expiration of the statute of limitations is that a dismissal on this ground merely bars the remedy and does not extinguish the substantive right, such that a dismissal on this ground does not have claim preclusive effect in other jurisdictions where the limitations period has not expired.

♦ There is no federal provision addressing the issue of the preclusive effect of a dismissal by a federal court sitting in diversity. It is up to this Court to determine the appropriate rule. We therefore adopt, as the federally prescribed rule of decision, the law that would be applied by state courts in the state in which the federal diversity court sits. Thus, California's law of claim preclusion (which we do not address) would apply to determine the issue in this case. Because the Maryland court applied a federal standard in dismissing the action and not California's law on claim preclusion, the judgment is reversed.

---

5. **Administrative Preclusion.** Many state courts are giving preclusive effect to the determinations of state administrative agencies. In *United States v. Utah Construction & Mining Co.*, 384 U.S. 394 (1966), the Court noted that res

judicata has been applied in the federal courts when the administrative body is "acting in a judicial capacity and resolves disputed issues of fact properly before it which the parties have had an adequate opportunity to litigate." The Court has since recognized a presumption of administrative preclusion unless it "would be inconsistent with Congress' intent in enacting the particular statute" at issue. [*See* Astoria Federal Savings & Loan Association v. Solimino, 501 U.S. 104 (1991)]

XVIII. ALTERNATIVE DISPUTE RESOLUTION

A. AVOIDING THE COURTS

1. **Litigation.** Litigation usually takes place only when the parties are unable to resolve their problems privately. Given the expense and time-consuming nature of litigation, a rational person may decide that it is better to suffer through relatively minor injuries, use self-help, or resort to a scaled-down method of dispute resolution (*e.g.,* arbitration, mediation, or small claims court) rather than seek full-blown judicial relief.

2. **Small Claims Courts.** Small claims courts normally are not separate courts; they represent a simplified form of procedure available in the state court of limited jurisdiction (*e.g.,* the municipal court). Jurisdiction is limited by a low amount in controversy (*e.g.,* $1,000 or $1,500). Trial is by the court and is usually without the aid of lawyers—lawyers often are unwelcome. Evidentiary rules are relaxed. Judgments, however, are not self-executing—they must be enforced by ordinary means, and the expense of collection will increase if a recalcitrant defendant attempts to hide assets. It is sometimes argued that judges in small claims courts will merely split the difference between the parties, rather than spend the amount of time needed to determine which party is entitled to full judgment.

3. **Arbitration.** Arbitration offers some distinct advantages over litigation (mainly reduced costs and time due to the informality of procedure) as well as distinct disadvantages (mainly possible lack of formal legal education of the arbitrator, the inability to obtain review of ordinary procedural errors, and the tendency to become too formal and expensive). Arbitration was not favored at common law, on the ground that it ousted the court of its jurisdiction. Today, it is now a favored form of resolving disputes. When the parties have agreed to arbitration in lieu of seeking a judicial resolution of their dispute, any judicial proceedings filed by either party before arbitration takes place can be enjoined by the courts. Also, arbitration awards are enforceable in state and federal courts. The arbitrator's award will be reviewed by a court only under limited circumstances—*e.g.,* the arbitrator has acted "irrationally" or beyond the scope of authority, or has been subjected to undue influence.

4. **ADR in the Courts--**

In re **African-American Slave Descendants' Litigation,** 272 F. Supp. 2d 755 (N.D. Ill. 2003).

Facts. Plaintiffs (Ps), identified as formerly enslaved and descendants of formerly enslaved African-Americans, seek monetary and injunctive relief against corporate defendants (Ds) for present and past wrongs in connection with the institution of slavery. Ps filed a motion to appoint a mediator or a special master.

Issue. Should the court order mediation despite Ds' strong objection?

Held. No. Motion denied.

♦ Where one party does not voluntarily submit to mediation, the court may order mandatory mediation if supported by: (i) the court's local rules; (ii) an applicable statute; (iii) the Federal Rules of Civil Procedure; or (iv) the court's inherent powers.

♦ This court's local rule does not provide for court-ordered mediation and contains provisions for voluntary mediation only for claims unrelated to Ps' claims. The Alternative Dispute Resolution Act, cited by Ps, encourages but does not require courts to order mediation if one of the parties objects. Similarly, Federal Rule 16(c), also cited by Ps, does not give the court authority to order mediation on unwilling litigants.

♦ The court does have the inherent power to order the parties to mediation. The court's inherent powers, however, must be used in a way reasonably suited to the enhancement of the court's processes, including the orderly and expeditious disposition of pending cases. Here, requiring mediation at this juncture would not facilitate an expeditious end to the litigation. Ds have moved to dismiss the claims, raising a question as to the claims' viability. Additionally, Ds have objected to mediation, which reduces the likelihood that a settlement would be reached. Arguably, the motion for the appointment of a mediator may be premature.

Comment. Mediation is the most frequently used ADR method in the federal courts.

NOTES

NOTES